1,000,000 Books
are available to read at

Forgotten Books

www.ForgottenBooks.com

Read online
Download PDF
Purchase in print

ISBN 978-1-332-60862-1
PIBN 10175611

This book is a reproduction of an important historical work. Forgotten Books uses state-of-the-art technology to digitally reconstruct the work, preserving the original format whilst repairing imperfections present in the aged copy. In rare cases, an imperfection in the original, such as a blemish or missing page, may be replicated in our edition. We do, however, repair the vast majority of imperfections successfully; any imperfections that remain are intentionally left to preserve the state of such historical works.

Forgotten Books is a registered trademark of FB &c Ltd.
Copyright © 2018 FB &c Ltd.
FB &c Ltd, Dalton House, 60 Windsor Avenue, London, SW19 2RR.
Company number 08720141. Registered in England and Wales.

For support please visit www.forgottenbooks.com

1 MONTH OF FREE READING

at
www.ForgottenBooks.com

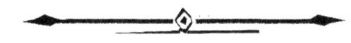

By purchasing this book you are eligible for one month membership to ForgottenBooks.com, giving you unlimited access to our entire collection of over 1,000,000 titles via our web site and mobile apps.

To claim your free month visit: www.forgottenbooks.com/free175611

* Offer is valid for 45 days from date of purchase. Terms and conditions apply.

English
Français
Deutsche
Italiano
Español
Português

www.forgottenbooks.com

Mythology Photography **Fiction**
Fishing Christianity **Art** Cooking
Essays Buddhism Freemasonry
Medicine **Biology** Music **Ancient Egypt** Evolution Carpentry Physics
Dance Geology **Mathematics** Fitness
Shakespeare **Folklore** Yoga Marketing
Confidence Immortality Biographies
Poetry **Psychology** Witchcraft
Electronics Chemistry History **Law**
Accounting **Philosophy** Anthropology
Alchemy Drama Quantum Mechanics
Atheism Sexual Health **Ancient History**
Entrepreneurship Languages Sport
Paleontology Needlework Islam
Metaphysics Investment Archaeology
Parenting Statistics Criminology
Motivational

JOHN EVELYN, ESQ. F.R.S.

AUTHOR OF THE " SYLVA," &c. &c.

COMPRISING HIS DIARY, FROM 1641 TO 1705-6,

AND A SELECTION OF HIS FAMILIAR LETTERS.

TO WHICH IS SUBJOINED,

The Private Correspondence

BETWEEN

KING CHARLES I. AND SIR EDWARD NICHOLAS;

ALSO BETWEEN

SIR EDWARD HYDE, AFTERWARDS EARL OF CLARENDON,

AND SIR RICHARD BROWNE,

AMBASSADOR TO THE COURT OF FRANCE, IN THE TIME OF KING CHARLES I. AND THE USURPATION.

EDITED FROM THE ORIGINAL MSS.

BY WILLIAM BRAY, ESQ. F.A.S.

A NEW EDITION, IN FIVE VOLUMES.

VOL. IV.

LONDON:
HENRY COLBURN, NEW BURLINGTON STREET.

1827.

PRINTED BY J. B. NICHOLS, 25, PARLIAMENT ST

EPISTOLARY CORRESPONDENCE.

EPISTOLARY CORRESPONDENCE.

The following Letters are taken from Copies kept by Mr. Evelyn, and are given as Specimens of his Epistolary Correspondence. In those on serious subjects, there appears the most ardent piety: in those of friendship, the most sincere attachment and gratitude: in those to ladies, the most polite gallantry, expressed in easy language. In one to Mr. Thurland, a Barrister, whom he consulted in his legal affairs, he shews himself able to write with humour.

To my Lady Garret.

It had not ben now that the gratefull resentiments of y[r] La[ps] favour remained so long for a faire gale on this side, if the least opportunity had presented itselfe before the returne of this noble gentleman; and howeuer Fortune (who esteemed it too greate a favour for me) has otherwise disposed of the present which you sent me, I thinke myselfe to have received it as effectually in your La[ps] designe and purpose, as if it were now glistering upon my finger. I am onely sorry, that because I missed that, I did not receiue y[r] com'ands, and that an obligation of so much vallue seems to haue ben throwne away, whilst I remaine in another country uselesse to you. I will not say, that the way to find what is lost, is to fling another after it; but if any services of your La^p perished with that jewell, there can be no danger in re-inforcing your com'ands, and repairing the greater losse, seeing there is nothing in the world which with more passion I pretend to, then to continue, Madame,

    Your Ladyships, &c.

Paris, 9th Octob. 1651.

To Mr. Thurland.

(Since Sir Edward Thurland, and Baron of the Exchequer.)

S^r,

Nemo habet tam certam manum ut non sæpe fallatur; and yet I hope my memory shall serue me for the subscribing this epistle, which is more than yours (deare lawyer) could, it seemes, doe, when you sent me y^r sum'ons for my Court at Warley, with all those sigillary formalities of a perfect instrument. But this is a trifling σφάλμα; and I easily supplied it, by taking the boldnesse to write a new warrant in ye most ill-favour'd character I could, that it might be the more like to y^r fayre hand; & so it was dispatch'd, onely the day altered to be the next before the Terme, since otherwise I could not haue appeared, and for which præsumption if you thinke fit to amerce me, I desire it may be by the delegation of Mr. Jo. Barton *pro Vicario;* since whilst I thus indulge my noble tennant, I may not neglect to reduce my vassalls, *cum ita suggerent Chartæ sicut optimè noveris,* &c. it being the advice of a greate philosopher, and part of my Litanie, *Libera te primum metu mortis (illa enim nobis primum jugum imponit), deinde paupertatis:* the first I endeavor to secure by Physick, the latter by y^r learned counsell, the effects whereoff I much more desire to resent by the favour w^{ch} (I am assured) you may do y^r servant in promoting his singular inclynations for Albury,* in case (as I am confident it will) that seate be exposed to sale. I know you are potent, and may do much herein; and I shall eternally acknowledg to have derived from you all the favour and successe, which I augure to my selfe from y^r friendship and assistance: it being now in y^r power to fix a wanderer, oblige all my relations, and by one integral cause, render me yours for ever. I suppose the place will invite many candidates, but my money is good, and it will be the sole and greatest obligation that it shall ever be in y^r power to doe for, dear lawyer,

Lond: 25: April, 1652.   Your, &c.

---

* Albury, in Surrey, a seat of Mr. Howard. Mr. Thurland was one of the Trustees appointed for the sale of it.

To Dr. (Jeremy) Taylor.

The calamitie which lately arrived you, came to me so late, and with so much incertitude during my long absence from these parts, that 'till my returne, and earnest inquisition, I could not be cured of my very greate impatience to be satisfied concerning your condition. But so it pleased God, that when I had prepared that sad newes, and deplore your restraint,* I was assured of y^r release, and delivered of much sorrow. It were imprudent, and a character of much ignorance, to inquire into the cause of any good man's suffering in these sad tymes; yet if I have learned it out, 'twas not of my curiosity, but the discourse of some with whom I have had some habitudes since my coming home. I had read ye Preface long since to y^r Golden Grove; remember, and infinitely justifie all that you haue there asserted. 'Tis true vallor to dare to be undon, and the consequent of Truth hath euer ben in danger of his teeth, and it is a blessing if men escape so in these dayes, when not the safties onely, but

---

* The cause of this imprisonment does not appear, unless it were for the sentiments contained in his " Twenty-five Sermons," published in the preceding winter—or perhaps upon political suspicion, as he actually suffered incarceration in Chepstowe Castle in 1656 (during his well-known controversy with Bishop Warner), being suspected as an instigator of the insurrection at Salisbury.

the soules of men are betrayed: whilst such as you, & such excellent assistances as they afford us, are rendred criminal and suffer. But you, S^r, who haue furnished the world with so rare præcepts, against the efforts of all secular disasters whatsoeuer, could neuer be destitute of those consolations, which you haue so charitably and so piously præscribed unto others. Yea rather, this has turned to our im'ense advantage, nor less to y^r glory, whilst men behold you living y^r own institutions, and preaching to us as effectualy in y^r chaines as in the chàire, in the prison as in the pulpit; for me thinkes, S^r, I heare you pronounce it, as indeede you act it—

> Aude aliquid brevibus gyaris et carcere dignum
> Si vis esse aliquis ――

that your example might shame such as betray any truth for feare of men, whose mission and com'ission is from God. You, S^r, know in the general, and I must justifie in particular with infinite cognition, the benefit I haue received from the truths you haue delivered. I haue perused that excellent *Unum necessarium* of yours to my very greate satisfaction and direction: and do not doubt but it shall in tyme gaine upon all those exceptions, which I know you are not ignorant appeare against it. 'Tis a great deale of courage, and a greate deale of perill, but to attempt the assault of an errour so inveterate.

Αἰ δὲ κειναὶ κρίσεις τὸν ἀπέρατον ὁδόν. false opinion knows no bottome, and reason and præscription meet in so few instances; but certainely you greately vindicate the diuine goodnesse, which the ignorance of men and popular mistakes haue so long charged with injustice. But, S^r, you must expect with patience the event, and the fruites you contend for: as it shall be my dayly devotions for your successe, who remaine,

Revd Sir, &c.

Says-Court, 9 Feb: 1654-5.

To Dr. (Jeremy) Taylor.

Revd Sir,

It was another extraordinary charity which you did me, when you lately relieved my apprehensions of your danger, by that which I just now received: and though the general persecution re-inforce; yet it is y^r particular which most concernes me in this sad catalysis and declension of piety to which we are reduced. But, S^r, what is now to be don that the starrs of our once bright hemispheare are every where pulling from their orbs? I remember where you haue sayd it was the harbinger of the greate day: and a very sober and learned person, my worthy friend, the greate Oughtred,* did the other day seriously perswade me *parare in occursum*, and will needes haue the following yeares productiue of wonderfull and universal changes. What to say of that I know not; but certaine it is, we are brought to a sad condition. I speake concerning secular yet religious persons; whose glory it will onely be to lye buried in y^r ruines, a monument too illustrious for such as I am.

For my part, I haue learned from your excellent assistances, to humble myselfe, and to adore the inscrutable pathes of the Most High. God and his truth are still the same though the foundations of the world be shaken. Julianus Redivivus can shut the schooles indeede & the temples; but he cannot hinder our private intercourses and devotions, where the breast is the chapell, and our heart is the altar. Obedience founded in the understanding will be the onely cure and retraite. God will accept what remaines, & supply what is necessary. He is not obliged to externals, the purest ages passed under the cruelest persecutions: it is sometimes necessary; & this and the fulfilling of prophecy, are all instruments of greate advantage (even whilst they presse, and are incumbent) to those who can make a sanctified use of them. But as the thoughts of

---

* William Oughtred, Rector of Albury, author of the "Clavis Mathematica," and other works, and the most illustrious geometrician of his time.

many hearts will be discovered, and multitudes scandaliz'd; so are there diuers well disposed persons who will not know how to guide themselues, unlesse some such good men as you discouer the secret, and instruct them how they may secure their greatest interest, & steere their course in this darke and uncomfortable weather. Some such discourse would be highly seasonable now that the daily sacrifice is ceasing, and that all the exercise of your functions is made criminal, that the light of Israel is quenched. Where shall we now receive the viaticum with safety? How shall we be baptiz'd? For to this passe it is come, S^r. The comfort is, the captivity had no temple, no altar no king. But did they not obserue the passover, nor circumcise? had they no priests & prophets amongst them? Many are weake in the faith, and know not how to answer, nor whither to fly: and if upon the apotheosis of that excellent person, under a malicious representation of his matyrdome, engrauen in copper, & sent me by a friend from Bruxelles, the jesuite could so bitterly sarcasme upon the embleme—

 Projicis inventum caput, Anglia (Angla?) Ecclesia!
  cæsum
 Si caput est, salvum corpus an esse potest?—

how thinke you will they now insult, ravage, and breake in upon the flock; for the shepheards are smitten, and the sheepe must of necessity be scattered, unlesse the greate Shepheard of Soules oppose, or some of his delegates reduce and direct us. Deare Sir, we are now preparing to take our last farewell (as they threaten) of God's service in this Citty, or any where else in publique. I must confesse it is a sad consideration; but it is what God sees best, & to what we must submitt. The comfort is, *Deus providebit.* S^r, I have not yet been so happy as to see those papers which Mr. Royston tells me are printing, but I greatly rejoice that you haue so happily fortified that battérie; and I doubt not but you will maintaine the seige: for you must not be discouraged for the passions of a few. Reason is reason to me where euer I find it, much more where it conduces to a designe so salutary & necessary. At least, I wonder that those who are not convinced by y^r arguments, can possibly resist y^r charity, & y^r modesty; but as you haue greatly subdued my education in that particular, and controversy; so am I confident tyme will render you many more proselytes. And if all do not come so freely in with their suffrages at first, you must with y^r accostomed patience attend the event.

S^r, I beseech God to conduct all y^r labours, those of religion to others, and of loue and affection to me, who remayne, S^r, your, &c.

Lond: 18 Mar:* 1655.

---

* Query May? It appears by his Diary that Evelyn had attended Taylor's preaching on that day. The devout laity of

From Dr. Jeremy Taylor to John Evelyn, Esq.

Honourd and Deare S^r,

Not long after my comming from my prison (Chepstow) I mett with your kind & freindly letters, of which I was very glad, not onely because they were a testimony of your kindnesse & affections to mee, but that they gave mee most welcome account of your health, and (which now adayes is a great matter) of your liberty, and of that progression in piety in which I doe really rejoyce. But there could not be given to mee a greater & more persuasive testimony of the reality of your piety & care then that you passe to greater degrees of caution & the love of God. It is the worke of your life, & I perceive you betake your selfe heartily to it. The God of heaven & earth prosper you & accept you!

I am well pleased that you haue read over my last booke; and give God thankes that I have reason to beleive that it is accepted by God, and by

---

the Episcopal Church were, therefore, not at that time deprived of the means of grace in the manner which this letter deplores. No does it seem likely that a letter of such a length, and written in such a manner, would be addressed to a person with whom the writer expected shortly to communicate personally, or with whom he had a few hours before communicated. I am, therefore, of opinion that we should not read March but May, by which time it is extremely probable that Taylor's imprisonment at Chepstow may have commenced.—Bp. Heber's Life of Jeremy Taylor.

some good men. As for the censure of unconsenting persons, I expected it, and hope that themselves will be their owne reproovers; and truth will be assisted by God, & shall prevaile, when all noises and prejudices shall be ashamed. My comfort is, that I have the honour to be the advocate for God's justice & goodnesse, and that ye consequent of my doctrine is that men may speake honour of God and meanly of themselves. But I have also this last weeke sent up some papers in which I make it appeare that the doctrine which I now haue published was taught by the fathers within the first 400 years; and haue vindicated it both from novelty & singularity. I have also prepared some other papers concerning this question, which I once had some thoughts to have published. But what I have already said, & now further explicated & justified, I hope may be sufficient to satisfy pious & prudent persons, who doe not love to goe *quà itur* but *quà eundum est*. S^r, you see what a good husband I am of my paper and inke, that I make so short returnes to your most friendly letters. I pray be confident that if there be any defect here, I will make it up in my prayers for you & my great esteeme of you, which shall ever be expressed in my readinesse to serve you with all the earnestnesse and powers of, Deare S^r,

Your most affectionate freind & servant

Novemb: 21, 1665. JER. TAYLOR.

From Dr. Jeremy Taylor.

St. Paul's Convers: [25 Jan.] 5⅚ (1656).

Deare S^r,

I perceive by your symptomes, how the spirits of pious men are affected in this sad catalysis: it is an evil time, and we ought not to hold our peace: but now the question is, who shall speake? Yet I am highly persuaded, that, to good men and wise, a persecution is nothing but changing the circumstances of religion, and the manner of the formes and appendages of divine worship. Publick or private is all one: the first hath the advantage of society, the second of love. There is a warmth and light in that: there is beate and zeale in this: and if every person that can, will but consider concerning the essentials of religion, and retaine them severely, and immure them as well as he can with the same or æquivalent ceremonies, I know no difference in the thing, but that he shall have the exercise, and consequently the reward of other graces, for which if he lives and dies in prosperous dayes, he shall never be crown'd. But the evills are, that some will be tempted to quit their present religion, and some to take a worse, and some to take none at all. It is true and a sad story; but *oportet esse hæreses*, for so they that are faithful shall be knowne: and I am sure that He who hath promised to bring good out of evil, and that all things shall co-operate to the good of them that feare God, will verify it concerning persecution. But concerning a discourse upon the present state of things in relation to soules and our present duty, I agree with you, that it is very fitt it were done, but yet, by somebody who is in London and sees the personal necessities and circumstances of pious people: yet I was so far persuaded to do it myselfe, that I had amassed together divers of my papers useful to the worke: but my Cases of Conscience call upon me so earnestly, that I found myselfe not able to beare the cries of a clamorous conference. S^r, I thank you for imparting to me that vile distich of the deere departed saint. I value it as I doe the picture of deformity or a devil: the act may be good, and the gift faire, though the thing be intolerable; but I remember, that when the Jesuites, sneering and deriding our calamity, shewed this sarcasm to my Lord Lucas, Birkenhead* being present, replied as tartly, " it is true, our Church wants a head now; but if you have charity as you pretend, you can lend us one, for your Church has had two and three at a time." S^r, I know not when I shall be able to come to London: for our being strip'd of the litle reliques of our fortune remaining after ye shipwracke, have not cordage nor sailes sufficient to beare me thither. But I hope to be able to com-

---

* Probably John Birkenhead, author of the " Mercurius Aulicus."

mit to the presse my first bookes of Conscience by Easter terme; and then if I be able to get up, I shall be glad to wayte upon you: of whose good I am not more sollicitous then I am joyful that you so carefully provide for it in your best interest.* I shall onely give you the same prayer and blessing that St. John gave to Gaius: " Beloved, I wish that you may be in health and prosper:" and your soule prospers: for so by the rules of the best rhetorick the greatest affaire is put into a parenthesis, and the biggest buisinesse into a postscript. S[r], I thanke you for the kind expressions at the latter end of your letter; you have neuer troubled mee, neither can I pretend to any other returne from you but that of your love and prayers. In all things else I doe but my duty, and I hope God and you will accept it; and that by meanes of His owne procurement, He will, some way or other (but how I know not yet) make provisions for mee. S[r], I am in all heartinesse of affection,

Your most affectionate freind and
minister in the Lord Jesus,
JER. TAYLOR.

---

* From whatever quarter he obtained the means of his journey, it is certain, however, that Dr. Taylor visited London; for on the 12th of April, 1656, as appears by the Diary, he dined with Evelyn at Sayes Court, in company with Mr. Berkeley, Mr. Rob. Boyle, and Dr. Wilkins, and occupied with them in the discussion and examination of philosophical and mechanical subjects.

From Dr. Jeremy Taylor.

Honour'd & Deare S^r,   April 16, 1656.

I hope your servant brought my apology with him, & that I already am pardon'd, or excus'd in your thoughts, that I did not returne an answer yesterday to your freindly letter. S^r, I did beleive my selfe so very much bound to you for your so kind, so freindly reception of mee in your "Tusculanum," that I had some little wonder upon mee when I saw you making excuses that it was no better. S^r, I came to see you and your lady, and am highly pleased that I did so, & found all your circumstances to be an heape & union of blessings. But I have not either so great a fancy & opinion of the prettinesse of your aboad, or so low an opinion of your prudence & piety, as to thinke you can be any wayes transported with them. I know the pleasure of them is gone off from their height before one moneths possession; & that strangers & seldome seers feel the beauty of them more then you who dwell with them. I am pleased indeed at the order & the cleanenesse of all your outward things; and look upon you not onely as a person, by way of thankfulnesse to God for His mercies & goodnesse to you, specially obliged to a greater measure of piety, but also as one who, being freed in great degrees from secular cares & impediments, can without excuse & allay wholly intend what you so passionately desire, the service of God. But now I am considering yours, & enumerating my owne pleasures, I cannot but adde that, though I could not choose but be delighted by seeing all about you, yet my delices were really in seeing you severe & unconcerned in these things, and now in finding your affections wholly a stranger to them, & to communicate with them no portion of your passion but such as is necessary to him that uses them or receives their ministeries. S^r, I long truly to converse with you; for I doe not doubt but in those liberties wee shall both goe bettered from each other. For your " Lucretius,"* I perceive you have suffer'd the importunity of your too kind friends to prevaile with you. I will not say to you that your Lucretius is as far distant from the severity of a Christian as the faire Ethiopian was from the duty of Bp. Heliodorus; for indeed it is nothing but what may become the labours of a Christian gentleman, those things onely abated which our evil age needes not; for which also I hope you either have by notes or will by preface prepare a sufficient antidote; but since you are ingag'd in it, doe not neglect to adorne it & take what

---

* Mr. Evelyn translated, or at least published, only one book of Lucretius, which was the first, printed in octavo, at London, 1656; with an engraved frontispiece, designed by his accomplished Wife, and engraved by Hollar.

care of it it can require or neede; for that neglect will be a reproofe of your owne act, & looke as if you did it with an unsatisfied mind, & then you may make that to be wholly a sin, from which onely by prudence & charity you could before be advised to abstaine. But, S^r, if you will give me leave, I will impose such a penance upon you for your publication of Lucretius as shall neither displease God nor you; &, since you are buisy in that which may minister directly to learning, & indirectly to error or the confidences of men, who of themselves are apt enough to hide their vices in irreligion, I know you will be willing & will suffer your selfe to be intreated to imploy the same pen in the glorifications of God; & the ministeries of eucharist & prayer. S^r, if you have M^{sr} Silhon " de l' Immortalité de l'Ame," I desire you to lend it mee for a weeke, and beleive that I am in great heartinesse & dearenesse of affection,

Deare S^r, your obliged & most affectionate
freind and servant,

J. Taylor.

To Dr. Jeremy Taylor.

(Since Bishop of Down and Connor in Ireland.)

Nothing but an affaire very greate and of consequence could stay me thus long from rendering you a personal acknowledgment for y^r late kind visite; and I trouble you with this because I feare I shall not be able to performe *that* 'till the latter end of the weeke ; but I shall, after this buisinesse is over (which concernes an accoumpt with a kindsman of mine), importune you with frequent visits, and, I hope, prevaile with you that I may haue the honour to see you againe at my poor villa, when my respects are lesse diverted, and that I may treat you without ceremonie or constraint. For it were fitting you did see how I live when I am by my selfe, who cannot but pronounce me guilty of many vanities, deprehending me (as you did) at a tyme when I was to gratifie so many curious persons, to whom I had ben greately obliged, and for whom I have much vallue. I suppose you thinke me very happy in these outward things ; realy, I take so little satissfaction in them, that the censure of singularity would no way affright me from embracing an hermitage, if I found that they did in the least distract my thoughts from better things; or that I did not take more pleasure and incomparable felicity in that intercourse which it pleases God to permit me, in vouchsafing so unworthy a person to prostrate himselfe before Him, and contemplate His goodnesse. These are indeede gay things, & men esteeme me happy ; *Ego autem, peccatorum sordibus inquinatus, diebus ac noctibus opperior cum timore reddere novissimum quadrantem:* Whilst that accompt is in suspence, who can truely enjoy any thing in this life *sine verme ?* *Omnia enim tuta timeo :* My condition is too well; and I do as often wonder at it, as suspect & feare it: and yet I thinke I am not to do any rash or indiscreete action, to make the world take notice of my singularity: though I do with all my heart wish for more solitude, who was euer most auerse from being neere a greate citty, designed against it, and yet it was my fortune to pitch here, more out of necessity, and for the benefit of others, then choyce, or the least inclynation of my owne. But, S^r, I will trouble you no farther with these trifles, though as to my confessor I speake them. There are yet more behind. My Essay upon Lucretius, which I told you was engaged, is now printing, and (as I understand) neere finished: my animadversions upon it will I hope prouide against all the ill consequences, and totaly acquit me either of glory or impiety. The captiue woman was in the old law to haue ben head-shauen, and her excræscencies pared off, before she was brought as a bride to the bed of her lord. I hope I haue so done with this author, as far as I have penetrated, and for the rest I shall proceede with caution, and take y^r counsell. But, S^r, I detaine you too long, though with promises to render you a better account hereafter, both of my tyme and my studies, when I shall haue beged of you to impose some taske upon me, that may be usefull to the greate designe of virtue and a holy life, who am,

S^r, y^r &c.

Says-Court, 27 Apr: 1656.

From Dr. Jeremy Taylor.

Deare Sir, July 19, 1656.

I perceive the greatnesse of y^r affections by your diligence to enquire after & to make use of any opportunity which is offered whereby you may oblige mee. Truly, Sir, I doe continue in my desires to settle about London, & am only hindered by my *Res angusta domi;* but hope in God's goodnesse that He will create to me such advantage as may make it possible: and, when I am there, I shall expect the daily issues of the Divine Providence to make all things else well: because I am much persuaded that, by my abode in ye voisinage of London, I may receive advantages of society & bookes to enable mee better to serve God & the interest of soules. I have no other designe but it; and I hope God will second it with his blessing. S^r, I desire you to present my thankes & service to Mr. Thurland:[*] his society were argument enough to make

---

[*] Mr. afterwards Sir Edward Thurland, and one of the Barons of the Exchequer, was an eminent lawyer, and author of a work on Prayer; on which Evelyn sent him a letter. See p. 39.

mee desire a dwelling thereabouts, but his other kindnesses will also make it possible. I would not be troublesome: serviceable I would faine be, useful, and desireable: and I will endeavour it if I come. S^r, I shall, besides what I have already said to you, at present make no other returne to Mr Thurland, till a little thing of mine be publicke, which is now in Royston's* hands, of Original Sin: the evills of which doctrine I have now laid especially at ye Presbyterian doore, and discours'd it accordingly, in a missive to ye Countesse Dowager of Devonshire. When that is abroad, I meane to present one to Mr. Thurland; and send a letter with it. I thanke you for your Lucretius. I wished it with mee sooner: for, in my letter to ye Countesse of Devonshire, I quote some things out of Lucretius, wch for her sake I was forc'd to English in very bad verse, because I had not your version by mee to make use of it. Royston hath not yet sent it me downe, but I have sent for it: and though it be no kindnesse to you to reade it for its owne sake, and for the worthinesse of the worke; because it deserves more; yet, when I tell

---

* Richard Royston was bookseller to three Kings, and lived at the Angel in Ivy-lane. He held a patent for printing all the works of K. Charles I. and became Master of the Stationers' Company in 1673 and 1674. He died in 1686, in the 86th year of his age, and was buried in the south aisle of Christ Church, Newgate-street.

you that I shall, besides the worth of the thing, value it for the worthy author's sake, I intend to represent to you, not onely the esteeme I have of your worthinesse, but the love also I doe and ever shall beare to y^r person. Deare S^r, I am in some little disorder by reason of the death of a little child of mine, a boy that lately made us very glad: but now he rejoyces in his little orbe, while wee thinke, & sigh, and long to be as safe as he is. S^r, when your Lucretius comes into my hands, I shall be able to give you a better account of it. In the meane time I pray for blessings to you & your deare and excellent lady: and am,

  Deare S^r,
   Your most affectionate and endeared
    friend & servant,
      Jer: Taylor.

From Dr. Jeremy Taylor.

Honour'd & Deare S^r,

In the midst of all the discouragements which I meet with all in an ignorant & obstinate age, it is a great comfort to mee, & I receive new degrees of confidence, when I find that your selfe, and such other ingenious & learned persons as your selfe, are not onely patient of truth, and love it better then prejudice & prepossession, but are so ingenuous as to

·dare to owne it in despite of the contradictory voices of error & unjust partiality. I have lately received from a learned person beyond sea, certaine extracts of the Easterne & Southern Antiquities, which very much confirme my opinion and doctrine: for the learned man was pleased to expresse great pleasure in the reasonablenesse of it, & my discourses concerning it. S^r, I could not but smile at my owne weakenesses, & very much love the great candor & sweetnesse of your nature that you were pleas'd to endure my English poetry: but I could not bee removed from my certaine knowledge of my owne greatest weaknesses in it. But if I could have had your Lucretius when I had occasion to use those extractions out of it, I should never have ask'd any man's pardon for my weake version of them: for I would have us'd none but yours: & then I had been beyond censure, & could not have needed a pardon. But, S^r, the last papers of mine have a fate like your Lucretius;—I meane so many erratas made by the printers, that, because I had not any confidence by the matter of my discourse & the well handling it, as you had by the happy reddition of your Lucretius, I have reason to beg your pardon for the imperfection of the copy: but I hope the printer will make amends in my Rule of Conscience, which I find hitherto he does with more care. But, S^r, give me leave to aske, why you will suffer your selfe to be discouraged in the finishing Lucretius: they who can receive hurt by the fourth booke, understand the Latine of it; and I hope they who will be delighted with your English, will also be secur'd by your learned & pious annotations, which I am sure you will give us along with your rich version. S^r, I humbly desire my services and great regards to be presented by you to worthy Mr. Thurland: and that you will not faile to remember me when you are upon your knees. I am very desirous to receive the *Dies iræ, Dies illa,* of your translation; and if you have not yet found it, upon notice of it from you I will transmit a copy of it. S^r, I pray God continue your health & his blessings to you & y^r deare lady & pretty babies: for which I am daily obliged to pray, and to use all opportunities by which I can signify that I am,

  Deare S^r,

   Your most affectionate & endeared servant,

         JER. TAYLOR.

9^ber 15, 1656.

[Evelyn has written on this letter in pencil: "I would be none of y^e *Ingeniosi malo publico.*"]

To my Brother G. Evelyn.*

Deare Bro: Says-Court, 15 Decemb. 1656.

I am so deeply sensible of the affliction which presses you, that I cannot forbeare to let you understand how greate a share I have in the losse, and how reciprocal it is to us. For y^r part, I consider that your sex and your knowledge do better fortifie you against the com'on calamities and vicissitudes of these sublunary things: so that precepts to you were but impertinencys: though I also find, that the physitian himselfe has some tymes neede of the physitian; and that to condole and to counsell those who want nothing to support them but their owne virtue, is to relieue them of a considerable part of their affliction: But the feare which I haue that the tendernesse of so indulgent a mother's affection (as is that of my deare lady) may insensibly transgresse its bounds, to so huge a prejudice as we should all receive by it, (if her im'oderate griefe should continue) makes me choose rather, being absent, to contribute what aydes I can towards its remedy, then, being present, to renew her sorrows by such expressions of resentiment as of course use to fall from friends, but can add little to the cure, because but compliment. Nor do I hereby exte-

---

* On the death of his son Richard.

nuate her prudence, whose virtue is able to oppose the rudest assaults of fortune; but present my arguments as an instance of my care, not of my diffidence. I confesse there is cause of sadnesse: but all who are not stoicks know by experience, that in these lugubrous encounters our affections do sometymes outrun our reason. Nature herselfe has assigned places and instruments to the passions: and it were as well impiety as stupidity to be totaly ἀστόργος and without natural affection: but we must remember withall that we grieve not as persons without hope: least, whilst we sacrifice to our passions, we be found to offend against God, and by indulging an over kind nature redouble the losse, & loose our recompence. Children are such blossomes as every trifling wind deflowres, and to be disordered at their fall, were to be fond of certaine troubles, but the most uncertaine comforts; whilst the store of the more mature which God has yet left you, invite both your resignation and y^r gratitude. So extraordinary prosperity as you have hitherto ben encircled with, was indeede to be suspected; nor may he thinke to beare all his sailes, whose vessell (like yours) has been driven by the highest gale of felicity. We give hostages to Fortune when we bring children into the world: and how unstable this is we know, & must therefore hazard the adventure. God has suffer'd this for y^r exercise: seeke then as well your consolation in his rod, as in his staff. Are you offended that it has pleased Him to snatch y^r pretty babes from the infinite contingencies of so perverse an age, in which there is so little temptation to live? At least consider, that your pledges are but gon a little before you: and that a part of you has taken possession of the inheritance which you must one day enter, if ever you will be happy. Brother, when I reflect on the losse as it concernes our family in general, I could recall my owne, and mingle my teares with you (for I have also lost some very deare to me); but when I consider the necessity of submitting to the divine arests, I am ready to dry them againe and be silent. There is nothing of us perished; but deposited: And say not they might haue come later to their destiny: *Magna est felicitas, citò esse felicem:* 'tis no small happynesse to be happy quickly. That which may fortune to all, we ought not to accuse for a few: and it is but reason to support that patiently, which cannot be prevented possibly. But I haue now don with the philosopher, and will dismisse you with the divine. "Brother, be not ignorant concerning them which are asleepe, that you sorrow not euen as others which haue no hope: for, if we belieue that Jesus died and rose againe, euen so them also which sleepe in Jesus will God bring with him." They are the words of St. Paul, and I can add nothing to them. In the meane tyme auxiliarys against this enemy cannot render it the more formidable: and though all griefe of this nature haue a just rise, yet may it end in a dangerous fall: our deare Mother is a sad instance of it: and I conjure you to use all the art, and all the interest you are able, to compose your selfe, & consolate y^r excellent lady, which (after I haue presented my particular resentiments) is what I would haue hereby assisted you in, who am,

Dear Brother, &c.

Et consolamini alij alios istis sermonibus.

From Mr. BARLOW,* a Painter, on dedicating a Plate of Titian's Venus, engraven, to Mr. Evelyn.

Worthy S^r,

I haue beene boold to present you with a small peece of my endeavours. I hope your goodnes will pardon my confidence in that I have presumed to dedicate it vnto you, conceaving no one to be

---

* He was a native of Lincolnshire, and placed under Sheppard, a portrait-painter; but his genius led him to design after nature every species of animals, which he drew with great exactness; though his colouring was not equal to his designs. There are six books of Animals engraven from his drawings, and a set of cuts for Æsop's Fables. Some cielings of birds he painted for noblemen and gentlemen in the country: and at Clandon, in Surrey, the seat of Lord Onslow, are five pieces from his pencil. He died in 1702. Walpole's Anecdotes.

more woorthy, or to whom I am more obliged for those sivill favours I have receaved from you. It may seeme strange that I owne that an others name is to, but my occasions not permitting me so much spare time to finish it, Mr. Gaywood my freind did, which [who] desyeres his name might be to it for his advantage in his practice, soe I consented to it. The drawing after the originall paynting I did, and the drawing and outlines of this plate: I finished the heads of both the figures, and the hands and feet, and likewise the doge and the landskape. As caching [etching] is not my profeshion, I hope you will not exspect much from me. S^r, if you shall be pleased to honner my weake (yet willing) endeavours with your exseptation, I shall ever rest obliged for this and former favours.

Your servant to coommand,
FRANCIS BARLOW.

From the Black-boy over agaynst St. Dunstan's,
 Fleat-street, this 22d of December, 1656.

From Mr. EVELYN to Mr. BARLOW, in reply.

S^r,

I had no opportunity by the hand which convey'd it to returne you my acknowledgments for the present you lately sent me, and the honour which you haue conferred upon me, in no respect meriting either so greate a testimony of y^r affection, or the glorious inscription, which might better haue become some greate and eminent Mæcenas to patronise, then a person so incompetent as you haue made choyce of. If I had ben acquainted with your designe, you should on my advice have nuncupated this handsome monument of your skill and dexterity to some great one, whose relation might have ben more considerable, both as to the encouragement and the honour which you deserve. From me you can onely expect a reinforcement of that vallue and good esteeme which before y^r merites had justly acquired, and would haue perpetuated: of another you had purchased a new friend; nor lesse obliged the old, because lessé exposed him to envy; since by this you ascribe so much to me, that those who know me better, will on the one side be ready to censure your judgment, and on the other you put me out of all capacity of making you requitall. But since your affection has vanquish'd y^r reason so much to my advantage, though I wish the election were to make, yet I cannot but be very sensible of the signal honour, and the obligation which you haue put upon me. I should now extoll your courage in pursuing so noble an original, executed with so much judgment and art: but I forbeare to provoke y^r modesty, and shall in the meane tyme that I can giue you personal thankes, receiue your present as an instance of your great civility, and a memorial of my no lesse obligation to you, who remaine, S^r,

Your, &c.

Says-Court, 23 Decemb. 1656.

To Mr. MADDOX.

(In behalfe of Dr. NEEDHAM, to assist him on the Charge of his com'encement at Camb.)

S^r,

I perceive by the successe of my letter, & your most civil reply, that I was not mistaken when I thought so nobly of you, and spake those little things neither in diffidence of your bounty or to instruct it, but to give you notice when it would arrive most seasonably, and because I found the modesty of the person might injure his fortune, as well as the greatnesse of your kindnesse.—You are pleased to inform me of your course, and I cannot but infinitely approve of your motions, because I find they are designed to places in order to things of greater advantage then the vanity of the eye onely, which to other travailers has usualy ben the temptation of making tours. For at Marseilles and Toulon you will informe y^r selfe of the strength and furniture of the French on the Mediterranean Seas: you will see the gallys, the slaves, and in fine, a very map of the Levant; for should you trauell as far as Constantinople it selfe, or to the bottome of the Straites, you would find but still the same thing: and the maritime townes of Italy are no other. Nismes dos so much abound with antiquities, that the difference 'twixt it and Rome is, that I thinke the latter has very few things more worth the visiting: and therefore it may as well present you with an idea of that greate citty, as if you were an ocular spectator of it: for it is a perfect epitome of it. Montpelier is the next in order, where I suppose you will make some longer stay; because there are schollars and students, and many rarities about it. There is one Peter Borell, a physitian, who hath lately published " Centuries Historical and Medico-Physical." Montpelier was wont to be a place of rare opportùnitie for the learning the many excellent receipts to make perfumes, sweete pouders, pomanders, antidots, and divers such curiosities, which I know you will not omitt; for though they are indeede but trifles in comparison of more solid things, yet, if ever you should affect to live a retired life hereafter, you will take more pleasure in those recreations then you can now imagine. And realy gentlemen despising those vulgar things, deprive themselves of many advantages to improve their tyme, and do service to the desiderats of philosophy, which is the onely part of learning best illustrated by experiments, and, after the study of religion, certainly the most noble and virtuous. Every body hath book-learning, which verily is of much ostentation, but of small fruit unlesse this also be super-added to it. I therefore conjure you that you do not lett passe what ever offers itselfe to you in this nature, from whomsoeuer they come. Com'only indeede persons of meane condition possesse them, because their necessity renders them industrious: but if men of qualitie made it their delight also, arts could not but receive infinite advantages, because they haue both meanes and leisure to improue & cultiuate them: and, as I sayd before, there is nothing by which a good man may more sweetely passe his tyme. Such a person I look upon as a breathing treasure, a blessing to his friends, and an incomparable ornament to his country.—This is to you the true seede-tyme, and wherein the foundations of all noble things must be layed. Make it not the field of repentance: for what can be more glorious then to be ignorant of nothing but of vice, which indeede has no solid existence, and therefore is nothing? Seeke therefore after nature, and contemplate that greate volume of the creatures whilst you have no other distractions: procure to see experiments, furnish your selfe with receipts, models, and things which are rare. In fine, neglect nothing, that at your returne, you may bring home other things then talke, feather, & ribbon, the ordinary traffiq of vaine and fantastiq persons.—I must belieue that when you are in those parts of France you will not passe Beaugensier* without a visit; for certainely, though the curiosities may be much dispersed since the tyme of the most noble Peireskius, yet the very genius of that place cannot but infuse admirable thoughts into you. But I suppose you carry the Life of that illustrious & incomparable virtuoso always about you in your motions; not onely because it is so portable, but for that it is written in such excellent language by the pen of the greate Gassendus, and will be a fit Itinerary with you. When you returne to Paris againe, it will be good to refresh your gymnastiq exercises, to frequent the Court, the Barr, and the Schooles sometymes; but aboue all, procure acquaintances and settle a correspondence with learned men, by whom there are so many advantages to be made & experiments gotten. And I beseeche you forget not to inform yourselfe as diligently as may be, in things that belong to gardening, for that will serue both your selfe and your friends for an infinite diversion: and so will you haue nothing to add to your accomplishment when you come home, but to looke over the municipal lawes of your owne country, which your interest and your necessities will

---

* Belgenser, or Beaugensier, a town near Toulon, the birthplace of the celebrated Nicolaus Claudius Fabricius, Lord of Peiresk, Senator of the Parliament at Aix.

prompt you to: and then you may sweetely passe the rest of your dayes in reaping the harvest of all your paines, either by seruing your country in some public employment (if the integrity of the tymes invite you), or by securing y^r own felicity, and indeede the greatest upon earth, in a private unenvied condition, with those advantages which you will bring it of piety and knowledge. Oh the delice and reward of thus employing our youth! What a beauty and satisfaction to haue spent ones youth innocently and virtuously! What a calme & serenity to the mind! What a glory to y^r country, to y^r friends, and contentment to your instructors: in sum'e, how greate a recompence & advantage to all your concernements! And all this, Sir, I foresee and augure of Mr. Maddox, of whom may this be the least portion of his panegyriq; whilst it serues me onely to testifie how greate a part I take in all your prosperity, and how greate an honour I shall euer esteeme it to be accounted,

Sir, your, &c.

Says-Court, 10 Jan. 1657.

To the Lieutenant of the Tower.*

S^r;

I should begin with the greater apologie for this addresse, did not the consideration of the nature of y^r greate employment and my feares to importune them carry with them an excuse which I haue hope to belieue you will easily admitt. But, as it is an errour to be troublesome to greate persons upon trifling affaires, so were it no lesse a crime to be silent in an occasion wherein I may do an act of charity, and reconcile a person to your good opinion, who has deserved so well, and I thinke is so innocent. Sir, I speake in behalfe of Dr. Taylor, of whom I understand you have conceived some displeasure for the mistake of his printer; † and the readiest way that I can thinke of to do him honour & bring him into esteeme with you, is, to beg of you, that you will please to giue him leaue to waite upon you, that you may learne from his owne mouth, as well as the world has done from his writings, how averse he is from any thing that he may be charged withall

---

* " This was written for another gentleman, an acquaintance with the *villain* who was now Lieut. of ye Tower, Baxter by name, for I never had the least knowledg of him."

† Dr. Jeremy Taylor had been committed prisoner to the Tower, for setting the picture of Christ praying before his collection of Offices, contrary to a new Act concerning scandalous pictures as they called them.

to his prejudice, and how greate an adversary he has euer bin in particular to the Popish religion, against which he has employed his pen so signally, and with such successe. And when by this favour you shall haue don justice to all interests, I am not without faire hopes, that I shall have mutually obliged you both, by doing my endeavour to serve my worthy and pious friend, and by bringing so innocent and deserving a person into your protection; who am, S^r, &c.

From Greenwich, 14 Jan. 1656-7.

To Mr. E. THURLAND, afterwards Sir EDWARD THURLAND, one of the Barons of the Exchequer, and an eminent Lawyer.

Sir,

I have read y^r learned Diatriba concerning Prayer, & do exceedingly prayse your method, nor lesse admire y^r learning and reason, which by so rare an artifice has made notions that are very difficult & abstracted in themselves, so apt and perspicuous: besides, y^r arguments are drawne from the most irresistible and convincing topicks, and the designe not onely full of learning, but usefull also to a good life, which is indeede the right application of it. S^r, I am so much taken with your piece, and thinke it so excellent a homily against that abounding ingredient now in the world, that I presume you shall not neede my perswasions to induce you to make it publique; being a thing which may so greately contribute to the cure of that epidemical madnesse, and the vindication of God's glory: since w[t] Trismegistus so long tyme sayd is most true in our age, Ἡ μεγάλη νόσος τῆς ψυχῆς ἡ ἀθεότης, and Silius Italieus has interpreted with a complaint:

"Heu primæ scelerum caussæ mortalibus ægris,
Naturam nescire Deum!"———

But because you have not onely don me the honour to com'unicate so freely y[r] thoughts to me: but have also lay'd y[r] com'ands that I should returne you my opinion of it; truely, I should both greately injure the intrinsiq value of the worke, as well as my greate esteeme of the author, if I should say lesse then I have don: so that, if I am bold or impertinent in what followes, it will serve onely to make you the more admire y[r] owne, when y[u] shall find how little can be added to it. And you must onely blame the liberty you have given me, if my silence would have become more acceptable.

First then y[r] distribution is most methodical and logical; the minor produced to assert the thesis very closely and skillfully handled; but, because your conclusion comes in so long after, whither it may not a little πλεοναζειν, considering that your argument is prayer, I would therefore at the end of some of those chapters, (before you arrive at the maine assumption,) upon enumeration of the former syllogismes, mention something of it (by way of enumeration) that so the thoughts of your reader might not stray from the subject, which is to enforce the necessity of prayer: or else alter the title, and make it comprehensive of both the parts, as of God, and of prayer, or something equivalent. I doe greately approve the reasons you have given for that long digression, to convince those who doubted, Democritus, Leucippus, Diogenes, Epicurus, and the late Pseudo-politicks, with those who faintly assented, as Pythagoras, Anaxagoras, Plato, the Stoicks, Politicians, and Legislators: but I suppose that, since Sextus Empiricus was but a diligent collector of the placits and opinions of other philosophers, you shall do more honour to your book by omitting the so frequent citing of him: it will sufficiently gratifie the reader to see his scruples satisfied, and their errors convinced, without so particular an account whether you deduced the opinions from the fountaine or from the streame. And therefore you shall better cite Diogenes Laertius or Cicero then Campanella, for that passage concerning the qualities of atomes: and it is more proper to alledge Basil de legendis Ethnicorum scriptis, Augustin de Doctrinâ Christianâ, or Socrates Scholasticus, to prove the lawfullnesse and benefit of asserting your opinions by examples out of heathen poets, &c. then Sr W. Raleigh's History of the World, who was but of yesterday. Neither would I mention Selden, where you might cite Lactantius, Clemens, Josephus, or Eusebius: because they are authors which every man will judge you might reade. And rather Fonseca, or indeede Molin, then Pinellus, who brought that opinion from them.—And here, by the way, touching what you affirme concerning the fallen angels' intuitive knowledg, there be that will replye that Lucifer was never *in patriâ* but *in viâ* onely: for so St. August. in those excellent treatises De Corruptione et Gratiâ and De Dono Perseverantiæ; that the fallen angels never saw God as *Authorem gratiæ*, but as *cultorem naturæ*, enigmatically and not intuitively, being then in probation onely, as was man, and had the same use of their will: God onely at that moment confirming Michael and his fellòws who refused to come into the rebellious party, what tyme as he condemned the dragon, and the rest of those lapsed spirits.

Touching the eternity of the world, I suppose you meane *de eternitate absolutâ*: for it were else hard to say which was first, the sun, or the light which it projects; since they are not onely inseparable but *simul tempore*. God created the world in his mind from eternity say they: or, as others, *Deus fecit æternitatem, æternitas fecit mundum*. So Mereurius in Pimander.

In that passage where you prove the existence of a Deity from the wonderfull structure of the microcosme, Lactantius his booke De opificio Dei would extreamely delight and furnish you: and so, in all that *Scala visibilium ad invisibilia*, Dr Charleton's " Darknesse of Atheisme," c. 4. 1. 5. p. 130, which I therefore mention to you, because one would not say much of that which has already ben sayd in English: would it not do also well to speake something of natural conscience?—I suppose where you speake of the pismire, and other insects, you meane they have not an intellectual memory: for a sensitive doubtlesse they have; and here you might appositely have sayd something concerning that *Animalis Religio*, of which St Ambrose speakes, distinguishing it from Aquinas' *Religio rationalis*.

Concerning the lenity of God, upon which you have most rationally dilated, the 10th chapt. of the 1 booke of Proclus would extreamely delight you. Touching the knowledge of God, you must by all meanes consult that admirable little treatise of M. Felix his Octavius; and St Aug: de Concubitu Angelorum, about our prayers to them, in which you have so imitated the divine St Hierom, by your constant assertion of the Paradise deduced from Scripture, that more cannot be wished: yet something which St Paul has sayd 2 chapt. Epist. ad Coloss. and in the 9th of Ecclesiast: may be applyed.

They affirme that the devill may be an aërial body, and by that meanes enter into mens bodys without our perception: but I will not importune you further with these trifles: onely I will mind you of one passage of Jamblicus, speaking of the natural sense of God in Man. *Ante omnem* (saith he) *usum rationis inest naturaliter insita Deorum notio: imò tactus quidem divinitatis melior quàm notitia:* and to that purpose Cicero de Nat. Deor: Seneca de Providentiâ, the Golden Verses of Pythagoras, and more expressely Lactantius, l. 3. c. 9, where he proves *cultum Dei* to be naturally in man, making it a formal part of its definition, *Animal Rationale Religiosum.* To conclude, Augustine, Clemens, Lactantius, Cyrill, Arnobius, Justin Martyr, of old,—of the neoteriq, Aquinas, Plæssis Morney, Dr Andrews, Grotius, Dr Hammond, in a particular *opusculum*, I. L. Vives, Bradwardine de Causa Dei, Valesius de Sacrâ Philosophiâ, Campanella, and our most ingenious Mr. Moore in his Antidote against Atheisme, have all treated on this subject, but in so different a manner, and with so much confusion and prolixity, some few of them excepted, that it will greately add to the worth and lustre of your piece, who have comprehended so much in so little and to so excellent purpose. I wish you had as perfectly made good y^r promise in what remaines, as in what you have begun, I meane, touching the forme, matter, posture, place, and other circumstances of prayer, in which you would do wonders upon second thoughts.—Sir, I have ben bold to note places with my black-leade where y^r amanuensis has com'itted some sphalmatas, and peradventure some expressions may be advantageously altered at your leasure. But there is nothing in all this by which you will more assert your owne judgment, then in leaving out the eulogie which you are pleased to honour me withall, in citing me as an author of any vallue. By this, S^r, you see how bold I am, both to trouble you with my follys, and then to beg pardon for them; but, as I sayd at first, you must blame your selfe, partly for enjoyning me, and partly for allowing me no more tyme. But he that has the perusal of any of your discourses, cannot but emerge with the greatest advantages. It was the saying of the greate Salmasius, and shall be myne, *Nihil moror libros, et combustos omnes velim, si doctiores tantum, non etiam meliores, qui dant illis operam, reddere idonei sunt.* But such, S^r, is your excellent booke, & such is your conversation, from which I do alwayes returne both more learned and better, who am,

S^r, y^r &c.

Says-Court, 20 Jan: 1656-7.

From Dr. Jeremy Taylor.*

Dear S^r,

I know you will either excuse or acquit, or at least pardon mee that I have so long seemingly neglected to make a return to your so kind and freindly letter: when I shall tell you that I have passed through a great cloud which hath wetted mee deeper than the skin. It hath pleased God to send the small poxe and feavers among my children: and I have, since I received your last, buried two sweet, hopeful boyes; and have now but one sonne left, whom I intend, if it please God, to bring up to London before Easter, and then I hope to waite upon you, and by your sweet conversation and other divertisements, if not to alleviate my sorrow, yet, at least, to entertaine myselfe and keepe me from too intense and actual thinkings of my trouble. Deare S^r, will you doe so much for me, as to beg my pardon of Mr. Thurland, that I have yet made no returne to him for his so freindly letter and expressions. S^r, you see there is too much matter to make excuse; my sorrow will, at least,

---

* Printed from a Letter in the British Museum, which, although it has no superscription, from the internal evidence which it displays of intimacy between the parties, no less than the mention of Mr. Thurland's, which occurs in it, the late Bp. Heber considered as addressed to Evelyn, and has inserted it as such in his very interesting Life of Bishop Taylor.

render me an object of every good man's pity and commiseration. But, for myself, I bless God, I have observed and felt so much mercy in this angry dispensation of God, that I am almost transported, I am sure highly pleased, with thinking how infinitely sweet his mercies are when his judgments are so gracious. S^r, there are many particulars in your letter which I would faine have answered; but still my little sadnesses intervene, and will yet suffer mee to write nothing else: but that I beg your prayers, and that you will still own me to be,
  Dear and honoured Sir,
   Your very affectionate friend and
    hearty servant,
      JER: TAYLOR.
Feb. 22, 1656-7.

 To Mr BOYLE, Son of the Earle of CORKE.
 S^r,
 I should infinitely blush at the slownesse of this addresse, if a greate indisposition of body, which obliged me to a course of physick, and since, an unexpected journey (from both which I am but lately delivered), had not im'ediately intervened, since you were pleased to command these trifles of me. I have omitted those of brasse, &c. because they properly belong to Etching and Ingraving:

which treatise, together with five others (viz. Paynting in Oyle, in Miniature, Anealing in Glasse, Enamiling, and Marble Paper,) I was once minded to publish (as a specimen of what might be further done in the rest) for the benefit of the ingenious: but I have since ben put off from that designe, not knowing whether I should do well to gratifie so barbarous an age (as I feare is approaching) with curiosities of that nature, delivered with so much integrity as I intended them: and least by it I should also disoblige some, who made those professions their living: or, at least, debase much of their esteeme by prostituting them to the vulgar. Rather, I conceived that a true and ingenious discovery of these and the like arts, would, to better purpose, be compiled for the use of that Mathematico-Chymico-Mechanical Schoole designed by our noble friend Dr Wilkinson, where they might (not without an oath of secresy) be taught to those that either affected or desired any of them: and from thence, as from another Solomons house, so much of them onely made publique, as should from tyme to tyme be judged convenient by the superintendent of that Schoole, for the reputation of learning and benefit of the nation. And upon this score, there would be a most willing contribution of what ingenious persons know of this kind, & to which I should most freely dedicate what I have. In the meane tyme, Sir, I transmitt you this vernish, and shall esteeme my selfe extreamely honoured, that you will farther com'and whatsoever else of this, or any other kinde I possesse, who am, S^r, y^r, &c.

I beseech you, Sir, to make my most humble service acceptable to Dr. Wilkinson: and that you be pleased to communicate to me what successe you have in the processe of this receipt (myselfe not having had time to examine it), that in case of any difficulty, I may have recourse to the person from whom I received it.

Says-Court, 9 May 1657.

To Dr. Jeremy Taylor.

Sir,

Amongst the rest that are tributaries to your worth, I make bold to present you with this small toaken: and though it beares no proportion either with my obligation or your merit; yet I hope you will accept it, as the product of what I haue employed for this purpose: and which you shall yearely receive so long as God makes me able, and that it may be usefull to you. What I can handsomely doe for you by other friends, as occasions present themselves, may, I hope, in tyme supplie that which I would my selfe do. In order to which, I have already made one of my Brothers sensible of this opportunity to do God and his country an acceptable seruice: I thinke I shall prevaile as much on the other: the effects whereoff will shew themselues, and care shall be taken that you have an accoumpt of all this in due tyme, and as you shall your selfe desire it. I will not add, that by bringing you acquainted with persons of so much virtue (though I speake it of my nearest relatiues) I do at all reinforce the kindnesse: since by it I oblige you mutualy (for so *beneficium dare socialis res est*), and because it is infinitely short of his respects who (with Philemon) owes you euen him selfe, and which, if I haue not sooner payed, I appeale to philosophy, and the sentences of that wise man who, as some affirme, held intercourse with the Apostle him selfe: *Qui festinat utique reddere, non habet animum grati hominis, sed debitoris: et qui nimis cito cupit solvere, invitus debet: qui invitus debet, ingratus est:* and, S[r], you haue too far obliged me to be euer guilty of that crime who am,

Revd Sir, &c.

Says-Court, 9 May, 1657.

From Dr. Jeremy Taylor.

Honour'd & Deare S[r],

A stranger came two nights since from you with a letter & a token; full of humanity & sweetnesse that was, and this, of charity. I know it is more blessed to give then to receive; and yet as I no wayes repine at that Providence that forces me to receive, so neither can I envy that felicity of yours, not onely that you can, but that you doe give; and as I rejoice in that mercy which daily makes decrees in heaven for my support & comfort, so I doe most thankfully adore the goodnesse of God to you, whom He consignes to greater glories by the ministeries of these graces. But, S^r, what am I, or what can I doe, or what have I done that you can thinke I have or can oblige you? S^r, you are too kind to mee, and oblige mee not onely beyond my merit, but beyond my modesty. I onely can love you, & honour you, & pray for you; and in all this I can not say but that I am behind hand with you, for I have found so great effluxes of all your worthinesses and charities, that I am a debtor for your prayers, for the comfort of your letters, for the charity of your hand, and the affections of your heart. S^r, though you are beyond the reach of my returnes, & my services are very short of touching you; yet if it were possible for mee so receive any commands, the obeying of which might signify my great regards of you, I could with some more confidence converse with a person so obliging; but I am oblig'd and asham'd, and unable to say so much as I should doe to represent my selfe to be,

Honour'd & deare S^r,
    Your most affectionate & most obliged
            friend & servant,
May 15, 1657.   JER. TAYLOR.

To Dr. (Jeremy) Taylor,
(to come and Christen my Son George).
Sir,

I heartily acknowledg the Divine mercys to me, both in this, and many other instances of his goodnesse to me; but for no earthly concernement more then for what He has conveyed me by your charity and ministration towards my eternal and better interest ; and for which I wish that any new gradations of duty to God, or acknowledgments to you from me, may in the least proportion second my greate obligations, and which you continue to reinforce by new and indelible favours and friendships, which I know my selfe to be so much the more unworthy off, as I am infinitely short of the least perfection that you ascribe to me. And because you best know how sad a truth this is, I haue no reason to looke on that part of your letter but as upon your owne emanations, which like the beames of the sunn upon darke and opake bodys make them shine indeede faintly and by reflection. Every one knows from whence they are derived, and where their native fountaine is : and since this is all the tribute which such dim lights repay, τὰ σὰ ἐκ τῶν σῶν σοὶ προσφερουμεν, I must never hope to oblige you, or repay the least of your kindnesse ; but what I am able, that I will doe, and that is to be ever mindfull of them, and for ever to love you for them. Sir, I had forgotten to tell you, and indeede it did extreamely trouble me, that you are to expect my coach to waite on you presently after dinner, that you are not to expose your selfe to the casualty of the tydes, in repairing to doe soe Christian an office for, Sir,

Y^r, &c.

Says-Court, 9 June, 1657.

From Dr. Jeremy Taylor.

Honour'd & deare S^r

Your messinger prevented mine but an houre. But I am much pleased at the repetition of the Divine favour to you in the like instances; that God hath given you another testimony of his love to your person, & care of your family; it is an engagement to you of new degrees of duty, which you cannot but superadde to the former, because the principle is genuine & prolific; and all the emanations of grace are univocal & alike. S^r, your kind letter hath so abundantly rewarded and crown'd my innocent indeavours in my descriptions of freindship, that I perceive there is a freindship beyond what I have fancied, and a real, material worthinesse beyond the heights of the most perfect ideas: and I know now where to make my booke perfect, and by an appendix to outdoe the first essay; for when any thing shall be observ'd to be wanting in my character, I can tell them where to see the substance, much more beauteous then the picture, and by sending the readers of my booke to be spectators of your life and worthinesse, they shall see what I would faine have taught them, by what you really are. S^r, I know it is usual amongst civil persons to say kind things when they haue receiv'd kind expressions: but I now goe upon another account: you have forc'd me to say, what I have long thought, and spoken to others, even so much as to your modesty may seeme excessive, but that which to the merit of your person and freindship is very much too little. S^r, I shall by the grace of God waite upon you to-morrow, and doe the office you require; and shall hope that your little one may receive blessings according to the heartinesse of the prayers which I shall then & after, make for him: that then also I shall wayte upon your worthy Brothers, I see it is a designe both of your kindnesse, & of the Divine Providence.

  S^r, I am
 Your most affectionate & most faithfull friend
    and servant,
        JER. TAYLOR.

June 9, 1657.

From Dr. Jeremy Taylor.

Sir, Aug. 29, 1657.

I am very glad that your good nature hath overcome your modesty, and that you have suffered yourself to be persuaded to benefit the world rather than humour your own retirednesse. I have many reasons to incourage you, and the onely one objection, which is the leaven of your author,* *de providentiâ*, you have so well answered, that I am confident, in imitation of your great Master, you will bring good out of evil: and, like those wise physicians, who, giving αλεξικακα, doe not onely expell the poyson, but strengthen the stomach, I doubt not but you will take all opportunities, and give all advantages, to the reputation and great name of God; and will be glad and rejoyce to imploy your pen for him who gave you fingers to write, and will to dictate.

But, Sir, that which you check at is the immortality of the soule: that is, its being in the interval before the day of judgment; which you conceive is not agreeable to the Apostle's creed, or current of Scriptures, assigning (as you suppose) the felicity of Christians to the resurrection. Before I speake to the thing I must note this, that the parts which you oppose to each other may both be true. For the soule may be immortal, and yet not beatified

---

* Alluding to his translation of Lucretius.

till the resurrection. For to be, and to be happy or miserable, are not immediate or necessary consequents to each other. For the soule may be alive, and yet not feele; as it may be alive and not understand; so our soule, when we are fast asleepe, and so Nebuchadnezzar's soule, when he had his lycanthropy. And the Socinians, that say the soule sleepes, doe not suppose that she is mortal; but for want of her instrument cannot do any acts of life. The soule returnes to God; and that, in no sense is death. And I thinke the death of the soule cannot be defined; and there is no death to spirits but annihilation. I am sure there is none that we know of or can understand. For, if ceasing from its operations be death, then it dies sooner than the body: for oftentimes it does not worke any of its nobler operations. In our sleepe we neither feele nor understand. If you answer, & say it animates the body, and that is a sufficient indication of life: I reply, that if one act alone is sufficient to shew the soule to be alive, then the soule cannot die; for in philosophy it is affirmed, that the soule desires to be re-united; & that which is dead desires not: besides, that the soule can understand without the body is so certaine (if there be any certainty in mystic theology), & so evident in actions which are reflected upon themselves; as a desire to desire, a will to will, a remembering that I did remember; that, if one act be enough to prove the soule to be alive, the state of separation cannot be a state of death to the soule: because she then can desire to be re-united, and she can understand: for nothing can hinder from doing those actions which depend not upon the body, and in which the operations of the soule are not organical.

But to the thing. That the felicity of Christians is not till the day of judgment, I doe believe next to an article of my creed; and so far I consent with you: but then I cannot allow your consequent; that the soule is mortal. That the soule is a complete substance I am willing enough to allow in disputation; though, indeed, I believe the contrary; and I am sure no philosophy and no divinity can prove its being to be wholly relative & incomplete. But, suppose it: it will not follow that, therefore, it cannot live in separation. For the flame of a candle, which is your owne similitude, will give light enough to this enquiry. The flame of a candle can consist or subsist, though the matter be extinct. I will not instance Licetus his lampes, whose flame had stood still 1500 years, viz. in Tullie's wife's vault. For, if it had spent any matter, the matter would have been exhaust long before that: if it spends none, it is all one as if it had none; for what need is there of it if there be no use for it, & what use if no feeding the flame, & how can it feed but by spending itselfe? But the reason why the flame goes out when the matter is exhaust, is because that little particle of fire is soone overcome by the circumflant aire & scattered, when it wants matter to keepe it in unison and closenesse : but then as the flame continues not in the relation of a candle's flame when the matter is exhaust, yet fire can abide without matter to feed it: for it self is matter; it is a substance. And so is the soule : & as the element of fire, & the celestial globes of fire, eat nothing, but live of themselves ; so can the soule when it is divested of its relative ; & so would the candle's flame, if it could get to the regions of fire, as the soule does to the region of spirits.

The places of Scripture you are pleased to urge, I shall reserve for our meeting or another letter ; for they require particular pointing. But one thing only, because the answer is short, I shall reply to ; why the Apostle, preaching Jesus and the resurrection, said nothing of the immortality of the soule? I answer, because the resurrection of the body included and supposed that. 2. And if it had not, yet what need he preach that to them which in Athens was believed by almost all their schooles of learning? For besides that the immortality of the soule was believed by the Gymnosophists in India, by Trismegist in Egypt, by Job in Chaldea, by his friends in the East, it was also confessed by Pythagoras, Socrates, Plato, Thules Milesius, & by Aristotle, as I am sure I can prove. I say nothing of Cicero, & all the Latins ; and nothing of all the Christian schooles of philosophy that ever were.

But when you see it in Scripture, I know you will no way refuse it. To this purpose are those words of St. Paul, speaking of his rapture into heaven. He purposely and by design twice says, " whether in the body or out of the body I know not :" by which he plainly says, that it was no ways unlikely that his rapture was out of the body; &, therefore, it is very agreeable to the nature of the soule to operate in separation from the body.

Sir, for your other question, how it appears that God made all things out of nothing? I answer, it is demonstratively certain; or else there is no God. For if there be a God, he is the one principle: but, if he did not make the first thing, then there is something besides him that was never made; and then there are two eternals. Now if God made the first thing, he made it of nothing. But, Sir, if I may have the honour to see your annotations before you publish them, I will give all the faithful and most friendly assistances that are in the power of,

Deare Sir,
Your most obliged and affectionate servant,
JER. TAYLOR.

To Sir RICHARD BROWNE.

S^r,

By the reverse of this medall, you will perceive how much reason I had to be affraid of my felicity, and how greatly it did import to me to do all that I could to prevent what I have apprehended, what I deserved, and what now I feele. God has taken from us that deare childe, y^r grandson, your godsonn, and with him all the joy and satisfaction that could be derived from the greatest hopes. A losse, so much the more to be deplored, as our contentments were extraordinary, and the indications of his future perfections as faire & legible as, yet, I ever saw, or read of in one so very young: you have, Sir, heard so much of this, that I may say it with the lesse crime & suspicion. And indeede his whole life was from the beginning so greate a miracle, that it were hard to exceede in the description of it, and which I should here yet attempt, by sum'ing up all the prodigies of it, and what a child at 5 yeares old (for he was little more) is capable of, had I not given you so many minute and particular accounts of it, by several expresses, when I then mentioned those things with the greatest joy, which now I write with as much sorrow and amasement. But so it is, that has pleased God to dispose of him, and that blossome (fruit, rather I may say) is fallen; a six days quotidian having deprived us of him; an accident that has made so greate a breache in all my contentments, as I do never hope to see repaired: because we are not in this life to be fed with wonders: and that I know you will hardly be able to support the affliction & the losse, who beare so greate a part in every thing that concernes me.

But thus we must be reduced when God sees good, and I submitt; since I had, therefore, this blessing for a punishment, & that I might feele the effects of my great unworthynesse. But I have begged of God that I might pay the fine heare, and if to such belonged the kingdome of heaven, I have one depositum there. *Dominus dedit, Dominus abstulit:* blessed be his name: since without that consideration it were impossible to support it: for the stroke is so severe, that I find nothing in all philosophy capable to allay the impression of it, beyond that of cutting the channell and dividing with our friends, who really sigh on our behalfe, and mingle with our greater sorrows in accents of piety and compassion, which is all that can yet any ways alleviate the sadness of, Deare Sir, Y[r] &c.

Says-Court, 14 Feb: 1657-8.

From Dr. Jeremy Taylor.

Deare S[r],

If dividing & sharing greifes were like the cutting of rivers, I dare say to you, you would find your streame much abated; for I account my selfe to have a great cause of sorrow not onely in the diminution of the numbers of your joyes & hopes, but in the losse of that pretty person, your strangely hopeful boy. I cannot tell all my owne sorrowes without adding to yours; & the causes of my real sadnesse in your losse are so just and so reasonable, that I can no otherwise comfort you but by telling you, that you have very great cause to mourne: So certaine it is, that greife does propagate as fire does. You have enkindled my funeral torch, & by joyning mine to yours, I doe but encrease the flame. *Hoc me malè urit,* is the best signification of my apprehension of your sad story. But, S^r, I cannot choose but I must hold another & a brighter flame to you—it is already burning in your breast; & if I can but remoove the dark side of the lanthorne, you haue enough within you to warme your selfe, & to shine to others. Remember, S^r, your two boyes are two bright starres, & their innocence is secur'd, & you shall never heare evil of them agayne. Their state is safe, & heaven is given to them upon very easy termes; nothing but to be borne and die. It will cost you more trouble to get where they are; and amongst other things one of the hardnesses will be, that you must overcome even this just and reasonable greife; and indeed, though the greife hath but too reasonable a cause, yet it is much more reasonable that you master it. For besides that they are no loosers, but you are the person that complaines, doe but consider what you would have suffer'd for their interest; you haue suffer'd them to goe from you, to be great Princes in a strange country; and if you can be content to suffer your owne inconvenience for their interest, you command your worthiest love, the question of mourning is at an end. But you have said and done well, when you looke upon it as a rod of God; and He that so smites here, will spare hereafter; & if you by patience & submission imprint the discipline upon your owne flesh, you kill the cause, & make the effect very tolerable; because it is in some sense chosen, & therefore in no sense unsufferable. S^r, if you doe not looke to it, time will snatch your honour from you, & reproach you for not effecting that by Christian philosophy which time will doe alone. And if you consider that of the bravest men in the world we find the seldomest stories of their children, & the Apostles had none, & thousands of the worthiest persons that sound most in story died childlesse; you will find that is a rare act of Providence so to impose upon worthy men a necessity of perpetuating their names by worthy actions & discourses, gouernments, & reasonings.—If the breach be neuer repair'd, it is because God does not see it fitt to be; and if you will be of his mind, it will be much the better. But, S^r, if you will pardon my zeale & passion for your comfort, I will readily confesse that you have no need of any discourse from me to comfort you. S^r, now you have an opportunity of serving God by passive graces; strive to be an example & a comfort to your lady, & by your wise counsel & comfort stand in the breaches of your owne family, and make it appeare that you are more to her than ten sons. S^r, by the assistance of Almighty God I purpose to wait on you some time next weeke, that I may be a witnesse of your Christian courage and bravery; & that I may see, that God neuer displeases you, as long as the maine stake is preserv'd, I meane your hopes & confidences of heaven. S^r, I shal pray for all that you can want, that is, some degrees of comfort & a present mind; and shal alwayes doe you honour, & faine also would doe you seruice, if it were in the power, as it is in the affections & desires of,

Deare S^r,
Your most affectionate & obliged
freind & servant:
JER. TAYLOR.

Feb. 17, 1657-8.

From Dr. JEREMY TAYLOR.

Honour'd Sir,   May 12, 1658.

I returne you many thankes for your care of my temporal affaires: I wish I may be able to give you as good account of my watchfulnesse for your service, as you have of your diligence to doe me benefit. But concerning the thing it selfe, I am to give you this account. I like not the condition of being a lecturer under the dispose of another, nor to serve in my semicircle, where a Presbyterian & myself shall be like Castor and Pollux, the one up and the other downe, which methinkes is like worshipping the sun, and making him the deity, that we may be religous halfe the yeare, and every night serve another interest. Sir, the stipend is so inconsiderable, it will not pay the charge & trouble of remooving myselfe & family. It is wholly arbitrary; for the triers may overthrow it; or the vicar may forbid it; or the subscribers may die, or grow weary, or poore, or be absent. I beseech you, Sir, pay my thankes to your friend, who had so much kindnesse for me as to intend my benefitt. I thinke myselfe no lesse obliged to him & you, than if I had accepted it.

Sir, I am well pleased with the pious meditations & the extracts of a religious spirit which I read in your excellent letter. I can say nothing at present but this, that I hope in a short progression you will be wholly immerged in the delices & joyes of religion; & as I perceive your relish and gust of the things of the world goes off continually, so you will be invested with new capacities, and entertained with new appetites, for in religion every new degree of love is a new appetite, as in the schooles we say, every single angel does make a species, & differs more than numerically from an angel of the same order.

Your question concerning interest hath in it no difficulty as you have prudently stated it. For in the case, you have onely made yourselfe a merchant with them; onely you take lesse, that you be secured, as you pay a fine to the Assurance Office. I am onely to adde this; you are neither directly nor collaterally to engage the debtor to pay more than is allowed by law. It is necessary that you imploy your money some way for the advantage of your family. You may lawfully buy land, or traffique, or exchange it to your profit. You may doe this by yourselfe or by another, & you may as well get something as he get more, & that as well by money as by land or goods, for one is as valuable in estimation of merchants, and of all the world as any thing can be; & mee thinkes no man should deny mony to be valuable, that remembers, every man parts with what he hath for mony: & as lands are of a price, then (when) they are sold for ever, & when they are parted with for a yeare, so is money: since the imployment of it is as apt to minister to gaine as lands are to rent. Mony & lands are equally the matter of increase; to both of them our industry must (be) applied, or else the profit will cease; now as a tenant of lands may plough for mee, so a tenant of money may goe to sea & traffique for mee. . . . .

To Edward Thurland, Esq.

Sir,

I understand that my L^d of Northumberland has some thoughts of sending his son, my Ld Percy, abroad to travaile, and withall to allow him an appoyntment so noble and considerable, as dos become his greatnesse, and the accomplishment of his education to the best improvement. My many yeares conversation abroad and relations there to persons of merite and qualitie, having afforded me severall opportunities to consider of effects of this nature by the successes, when gentlemen of qualitie have been sent beyond the seas, resigned and concredited to the conduct of such as they call Governours, being for the greatest ingredient a pedantique sort of scholars, infinitely uninstructed for such an employment: my ambition to serve you by contributing to the designes of a person so illustrious, and worthy of the honour which I find you alwayes beare towards his Lo'p, hath created in me the confidence to request your advice and returne upon these particulars. Whether my Lord persist still in his resolution? What equipage and *honorarium* my L^d dos allow? and whether he has not yet pitched upon any man to accompanye my young Lord, &c.? Because I would, through your mediation, recom'end to his Lo'p a person of honour, addresse in Court, rare erudition, languages and credite: who, I thinke, would upon my representing of the proposition, be ready to serve my Lord in an affaire of this importance. I shall add no more of the person, *quum habeat in se, quæ quum tibi nota fuerint* συστατικώτερα πάσης ἐπιστολῆς *esse judicaberis:* and because, in truth, all that I can say will be infinitely inferior to his merite; being a person of integrity, great experience and discretion; in a word, without reproach, and such as becomes my Lord to seek out, that he may render his sonne those honourable and decent advantages of the most refined conversations, things not to be encountered in a pension with a pedant —the education of most of our nobility abroad, which makes them returne (I pronounce it with a blushe) insolent and ignorant, debauched, and without the least tincture of those advantages to be hoped for through the prudent conduct of some brave man of parts, sober, active, and of universall addresse—in fine, such as the person I would recom'end, and the greatest Prince in Europe might emulate upon the like occasion: and therefore such a one, as I cannot presume would descend to my proposition for any persone of our nation excepting my Lord of Northumberland alone, whose education of his sonne, I heare, has ben of another streine and alloy, then that we have mentioned: and such as will giue countenance and honour to a person of his merite, character, and abilities. It is not enough that persons of my L. Percy's qualitie be taught to daunce, and to ride, to speake languages and weare his cloathes with a good grace (which are the verie shells of travail), but, besides all these, that he know men, customes, courts, and disciplines, and whatsoever superior excellencys the places afford, befitting a person of birth and noble impressions. This is, S^r, the fruite of travail: thus our incomparable Sidney was bred; and this, *tanquam Minerva Phidiæ*, setts the crowne upon his perfections when a gallant man shall returne with religion and courage, knowledge and modestie, without pedantry, without affectation, materiall and serious, to the contentment of his relations, the glory of his family, the star and ornament of his age. This is truely to give a citizen to his country. Youth is theseede-tyme in which the foundation of all noble things is to layd; but it is made the field of repentance. For what can become more glorious then to be ignorant of nothing but of vice, which indeede has no solid existency, and therefore is nothing? and unlesse thus we cultivate our youth, and noblemen make wiser provisions for their educations abroad, above the vanity of talke, feather, and ribbon, the ordinary com'erce and import of their wild pererrations, I despayre of ever living to see a man truely noble indeede: they may be called " My Lord;" titles and sounds and inferior trifles; but when virtue and blood are coincidents, they both add lustre and mutual excellencys. This is what my Lord takes care to secure to his sonne, what I foresee and augure of my noble Lord Percy, and of whom (though to me no otherwise known then by fame) may this be the least portion of his panegyrick, whilst it concernes me onely to testifie, without designe, my zeale for one whom I know you so highly vallue; *quanto enim mihi carior est amicitia tua, tanto antiquior mihi esse debet cura, illam omnibus officiis testandi;* which, Sir, is the product of this impertinency, and sole ambition of, Sir, y^r, &c.

Says-Court, 8 Nov: 1658.

To my Co: GEO. TUKE, of Cressing Temple, in Essex.

Jan. 1658-9.

Speaking of his brother having been made a proselyte to the Church of Rome:—" For the rest, we must com'itt to Providence the successe of tymes & mitigation of proselytical fervours; having for my owne p'ticular a very greate charity for all who sincerely adore the blessed Jesus, our com'on & deare Saviour, as being full of hope that God (however the p^{e}sent zeale of some & the scandals taken by others at the instant afflictions of the Church of England may transport them) will at last compassionate our infirmities, clarifie our judgments, and make abatement for our ignorances, superstructures, passions & errours of corrupt tymes & interests, of wch the Romish persuasion can no way acquit herself, whatever the present prosperity & secular polity may pretend. But God will make all things manifest in his owne tyme; onely let us possess ourselves in patience & charity; this will cover a multitude of imperfections."*

From Dr. JEREMY TAYLOR.

Honoured Sir, Lisnagarvy, April 9, 1659.

I feare I am so unfortunate as that I forgot to leave with you a direction how you might, if you pleased to honour me with a letter, refresh my solitude with notice of your health & that of your relatives, that I may rejoyce & give God thankes for the blessing & prosperity of my dearest & most

---

* See Mrs. Evelyn's character of him in a letter to Lady Tuke on his death, dated Jan. 28, 1672. Sir Samuel Tuke, of Cressing Temple in Essex, Bart. was a Colonel in the King's service during the civil war, and afterwards being one of those that attempted to form a body in Essex for King Charles, he narrowly escaped with his life. He married Mary Sheldon, one of Queen Catharine's dressers, and died at Somerset House, Jan. 26, 1673. Dodd's Church History, III. 251. His accomplished son followed the fortune of King James, and was killed at the battle of the Boyne.

honoured friends. I have kept close all the winter, that I might, without interruption, attend to the finishing of the imployment I was engaged in: which now will have no longer delay than what it meetes in the printer's hands. But, Sir, I hope that by this time you have finished what you have so prosperously begun,—your owne Lucretius. I desire to receive notice of it from yourselfe, & what other designes you are upon in order to the promoting or adorning learning: for I am confident you will be as useful and profitable as you can be, that, by the worthiest testimonies, it may by posterity be remembered that you did live. But, Sir, I pray say to me something concerning the state of learning; how is any art or science likely to improve? what good bookes are lately publike? what learned men, abroad or at home, begin anew to fill the mouth of fame, in the places of the dead Salmasius, Vossius, Mocelin, Simond, Rigaltius, Des Cartes, Galileo, Peiresk, Petavius, & the excellent persons of yesterday? I perceive here that there is a new sect rising in England, the Perfectionists; for three men that wrote an Examen of the Confession of Faith of the Assembly, whereof one was D[r] Drayton, & is now dead, did starte some very odde things; but especially one, in pursuance of the doctrine of Castellio, that it is possible to give unto God perfect unsinning obedience, & to have perfection of degrees in this life. The doctrine was opposed by an obscure person, one John Tendring; but learnedly enough & wittily maintained by another of the triumvirate, Wm Parker, who indeed was the first of the three; but he takes his hint from a sermon of Dr Drayton, which, since his death, Parker hath published, & endeavours to justify. I am informed by a worthy person, that there are many of them who pretend to great sanctity & great revelations & skill in all Scriptures, which they expound almost wholly to spiritual & mysterious purposes. I knew nothing, or but extremely little, of them when I was in England; but further off I heare most newes. If you can informe yourselfe concerning them, I would faine be instructed concerning their designe, & the circumstances of their life & doctrine. For they live strictly, & in many things speak rationally, & in some things very confidently. They excell the Socinians in the strictnesse of their doctrine; but, in my opinion, fall extremely short of them in their expositions of the practical Scripture. If you inquire after the men of Dr. Gell's church, possibly you may learn much: & if I mistake not, the thing is worth inquiry. Their bookes are printed by Thos: Newcomb in London, but where is not set downe. The Examen of the Assemblie's Confession is highly worth perusing, both for the strangenesse of some things in it, & the learning of many of them.

Sir, You see how I am glad to make an occasion to talke with you: though I can never want a just opportunity & title to write to you, as long as I have the memory of those many actions of loving kindnesse by which you have obliged,

   Honoured Sir,
  Your most affectionate & endeared friend
    & humble servant,
      Jer. Taylor.

  To the Hon[ble] Robert Boyle.

Sir,   Says-Court, April 13, 1659.

Having the last year drawn a good quantity of the essence of roses, by the common way of fermentation; & remembering how soon it went away, amongst the ladies, after they had once scented it; the season of flowers now approaching, makes me call to mind, to have known it sold by some chemists (& in particular by one Longsire at Chichester) mixed with a substance not unlike it; which retained the odor of it wonderful exactly; but in such a proportion, that for seven or eight shillings a sister of mine was used to purchase more than any man living can extract out of three or four hundred weight of roses, by the vulgar, or Glauber's preparation: by which means that precious essence may be made to serve for many ordinary uses, without much detriment. Sir, I am bold to request of you, that if you know what it is (for if you know it not, I despair of encountering it) you will be pleased to instruct me; &, in lieu thereof, to command me some service by which I may testify my great ambition to obey you, & how profoundly sensible I remain of my many obligations to you, which I should not have been thus long in expressing, had not I apprehended how importune letters are to studious persons, where the commerce is so jejune; & that I can return you nothing in exchange for civilities I have already received. Sir, I have reason to be confident that you are upon some very glorious design, & that you need no subsidiaries, & therein you are happy; make us so, likewise, with a confirmation of it; that such as cannot hope to cantribute any thing of value to the adornment of it, may yet be permitted to augur you all the success which your worthy & noble attempts do merit; in the mean time, that some domestick afflictions of mine have rendered me thus long useless, both to my friends & to myself; which I wish may be thought a just apology for,

Noble Sir,

Your most humble & most obedient servant,

J. EVELYN.

Sir, I know the imposters multiply their essence of roses with *ol. lig. Rhodii,* others with that of *Ben;* but it can be neither; for the oil of rosewood will vanquish it exceedingly, neither is it so fluid; & the other grows rancid. Some have told me it was spermaceti, which I have not essayed.

Your commands will at any time find me, directed to the Hawk & Pheasant upon Ludgate-hill, at one Mr. Saunders's, a woollen-draper.

From Dr. Jeremy Taylor.

Honoured Sir, Portmore, June 4, 1659.

I have reason to take a great pleasure that you are pleased so perfectly to retaine me in your memory & affections as if I were still neere you, a partner of your converse, or could possibly oblige you. But I shall attribute this so wholly to your goodnesse, your piety & candour, that I am sure nothing on my part can incite or continue the least part of those civilities & endearments by which you have often, and still continue to oblige me. Sir, I received your two little bookes, & am very much pleased with the golden booke of St. Chrysostom, on which your epistle hath put a black enamel, & made a pretty monument for your dearest, strangest miracle of a boy; & when I read it, I could not choose but observe St. Paul's rule, *flebam cum flentibus.* I paid a teare at the hearse of that sweet child. Your other little Enchiridion is an emanation of an ingenuous spirit; & there are in it observations, the like of which are seldom made by young travellers; & though by the publication of these you have been civil & courteous to the commonwealth of learning, yet I hope you will proceed to oblige us in some greater instances of your owne. I am much pleased with your waye of translation; & if you would proceed in the same method, & give us in English some devout pieces of the fathers, & your own annotations upon them, you would do profit & pleasure to the publicke. But, Sir, I cannot easily consent that you should lay aside your Lucretius, & having beene requited yourselfe by your labour, I cannot perceive why you should not give us the same recreation, since it will be greater to us than it could be to you, to whom it was allayed by your great labour: especially you have given us so large an essay of your ability to doe it; & the world having given you an essay of their acceptation of it.

Sir, that Pallavicini whom you mention is the author of the late history of the Council of Trent, in two volumes in folio, in Italian. I have seene it, but had not leisure to peruse it so much as to give any judgment of the man by it. Besides this, he hath published two little manuals in 12mo, *Assertionum Theologicarum;* but these speake but very little of the man. His history, indeed, is a great undertaking, & his family (for he is of the Jesuit order), used to sell the booke by crying up the man: but I think I saw enough of it to suspect the expectation is much bigger then the thing. It is no wonder that Baxter undervalues the gentry of England. You know what spirit he is of, but I suppose he hath met with his match, for Mr. Peirs hath attacked him, & they are joyned in the lists. I have not seene Mr. Thorndike's booke. You make me desirous of it, because you call it elaborate: but I like not the title nor the subject, & the man is indeed a very good & a learned man, but I have not seen much prosperity in his writings: but if he have so well chosen the questions, there is no peradventure but he hath tumbled into his heape many choice materials. I am much pleas'd that you promise to inquire into the way of the Pefectionists; but I think L. Pembroke & Mrs. Joy, & the Lady Wildgoose, are none of that number. I assure you, some very learned & very sober persons have given up their names to it. Castellio is their great patriarch; & his dialogue *An per Spir. S. homo possit perfectè obedire legi Dei*, is their first essay. Parker hath written something lately of it, & in Dr. Gell's last booke in folio, there is much of it. Indeed you say right that they take in Jacob Behmen, but that is upon another account, & they understand him as nurses doe their children's imperfect language; something by use, & much by fancy. I hope, Sir, in your next to me (for I flatter myselfe to have the happinesse of receiving a letter from you sometimes), you will account to me of some hopes concerning some settlement, or some peace to religion. I feare my peace in Ireland is likely to be short, for a Presbyterian & a madman have informed against me as a dangerous man to their religion; & for using the signe of the crosse in baptisme. The worst event of the information which I feare, is my returne into England; which, although I am not desirous it should be upon these termes, yet if it be without much violence, I shall not be much troubled.

Sir, I doe account myselfe extremely obliged to your kindnesse & charity, in your continued care of me, & bounty to me; it is so much the more, because I have almost from all men but yourselfe, suffered some diminution of their kindnesse, by reason of my absence; for, as the Spaniard says, "The dead & the absent have but few friends." But, Sir, I account myselfe infinitely obliged to you, much for your pension, but exceedingly much more for your affection, which you have so signally expressed. I pray, Sir, be pleased to present my humble service to your two honoured Brothers: I shall be ashamed to make any addresse, or pay my thankes in words to them, till my rule of conscience be publicke, & that is all the way I have to pay my debts; that & my prayers that God would. Sir, Mr. Martin, bookseller, at the Bell, in St. Paul's Churchyard, is my correspondent in London, &

whatsoever he receives, he transmits it to me carefully; & so will Mr. Royston, though I doe not often imploy him now. Sir, I feare I have tired you with an impertinent letter, but I have felt your charity to be so great as to doe much more than to pardon the excesse of my affections. Sir, I hope that you & I remember one another when we are upon our knees. I doe not thinke of coming to London till the latter end of summer, or the spring, if I can enjoy my quietnesse here; but then I doe if God permit: but beg to be in this interval refreshed by a letter from you at your leisure, for, indeed, in it will be a great pleasure & endearment to,

Honoured Sir,
Your very obliged, most affectionate,
& humble servant,
JER. TAYLOR.

To the Honble ROBERT BOYLE.

Honoured Sir, Says-Court, Aug. 9, 1659.

I am perfectly ashamed at the remissness of this recognition for your late favours from *Oxon:* where (though had you resided) it should have interrupted you before this time. It was by our common & good friend Mr. Hartlib, that I come now to know you are retired from thence, but not from the muses, & the pursuit of your worthy designs, the result whereof we thirst after with all impatience; & how fortunate should I esteem myself, if it were in my power to contribute in the least to that, which I augur of so great & universal a benefit! But, so it is, that my late inactivity has made so small a progress, that, in the History of Trades, I am not advanced a step; finding (to my infinite grief) my great imperfections for the attempt, & the many subjections, which I cannot support, of conversing with mechanical capricious persons, & several other discouragements; so that, giving over a design of that magnitude, I am ready to acknowledge my fault, if from any expression of mine there was any room to hope for such a production, farther than by a short collection of some heads & materials, & a continual propensity of endeavouring in some particular, to encourage so noble a work, as far as I am able, a specimen whereof I have transmitted to Mr. Hartlib, concerning the ornaments of gardens, which I have requested him to communicate to you, as one from whom I hope to receive my best & most considerable furniture; which favour, I do again & again humbly supplicate; & especially, touching the first chapter of the third book, the eleventh & twelfth of the first; & indeed, on every particular of the whole. Sir, I thank you for your receipts: there is no danger I should prostitute them, having encountered in books what will sufficiently (I hope) gratify the curiosity of most, when

in my third I speak of the elaboratory. But I remit you to what I have written to Mr. Hartlib, & begging pardon for this presumption, crave leave to remain,
Sir,
Your most humble, & obedient servant,
J. EVELYN.

Sir, do you know whether Campanella has said any thing concerning altering the shape of fruits, &c., & how I may obtain the perusal of *Benedicti Curtii Hortorum Lib. 30. Lugd.* 1560. *fol.?*

To the Honble ROBERT BOYLE.

Noble Sir,   Says-Court, Sept. 3, 1659.

Together with these testimonies of my chearful obedience to your commands, & a faithful promise of transmitting the rest, if yet there remain any thing worthy your acceptance amongst my unpolished & scattered collections, I do here make bold to trouble you with a more minute discovery of the design, which I casually mentioned to you, concerning my great inclination to redeem the remainder of my time, considering, *quam parum mihi supersit ad metas;* so as may best improve it to the glory of God Almighty, & the benefit of others. And, since it has proved impossible for me to attain to it hitherto (though in this my private & mean station) by reason of that fond morigeration to the mistaken customs of the age, which not only rob men of their time, but extremely of their virtue & best advantages; I have established with myself, that it is not to be hoped for, without some resolutions of quitting these incumbrances, & instituting such a manner of life, for the future, as may best conduce to a design so much breathed after, &, I think, so advantageous. In order to this, I propound, that since we are not to hope for a mathematical college, much less, a Solomon's house, hardly a friend in this sad *Catalysis*, & *inter hos armorum strepitus*, a period so uncharitable & perverse; why might not some gentlemen, whose geniuses are greatly suitable, & who desire nothing more than to give a good example, preserve science, & cultivate themselves, join together in society, & resolve upon some orders & œconomy, to be mutually observed, such as shall best become the end of their union, if, I cannot say, without a kind of singularity, because the thing is new; yet such, at least, as shall be free from pedantry, and all affectation? The possibility, Sir, of this is so obvious, that I profess, were I not an aggregate person, & so obliged, as well by my own nature as the laws of decency, & their merits, to provide for my dependents, I would chearfully devote my small fortune towards a design, by which I might hope to assemble some small number together who would resign themselves to live profitably and sweetly together. But since I am unworthy so great a happiness, & that it is not now in my power, I propose that if any one worthy person, & *queis meliore luto*, so qualified as Mr. Boyle, will join in the design (for not with every one, rich & learned, there are very few disposed, and it is the greatest difficulty to find the man) we would not doubt, in a short time (by God's assistance), to be possessed of the most blessed life that virtuous persons could wish or aspire to in this miserable & uncertain pilgrimage, whether considered as to the present revolutions, or what may happen for the future in all human probability. Now, Sir, in what instances, & how far this is practicable, permit me to give you an account of, by the calculations which I have deduced for our little foundation.

I propose the purchasing of thirty or forty acres of land, in some healthy place, not above twenty-five miles from London; of which a good part should be tall wood, & the rest upland pastures or downs, sweetly irrigated. If there were not already an house which might be converted, &c. we would erect upon the most convenient site of this, near the wood, our building, viz. one handsome pavilion, containing a refectory, library, withdrawing-room, & a closet; this the first story; for we suppose the kitchen, larders, cellars & offices to be contrived in the half story under ground. In the second should be a fair lodging chamber, a pallet-room, gallery,

& a closet; all which should be well & very nobly furnished, for any worthy person that might desire to stay any time, and for the reputation of the college. The half story above for servants, wardrobes, & like conveniences. To the entry fore front of this a court, & at the other back front a plot walled in of a competent square, for the common seraglio, disposed into a garden; or it might be only carpet, kept curiously, & to serve for bowls, walking, or other recreations, &c. if the company please. Opposite to the house, towards the wood, should be erected a pretty chapel; & at equal distances (even with the flanking walls of the square) six apartments or cells, for the members of the Society, & not contiguous to the pavilion, each whereof should contain a small bedchamber, an outward room, a closet, and a private garden, somewhat after the manner of the Carthusians. There should likewise be one laboratory, with a repository for rarities & things of nature; aviary, dovehouse, physick garden, kitchen garden, & a plantation of orchard fruit, &c. all uniform buildings, but of single stories, or a little elevated. At convenient distance towards the olitory garden should be a stable for two or three horses, & a lodging for a servant or two. Lastly, a garden house & conservatory for tender plants.

The estimate amounts thus. The pavilion £400, chapel £150, apartments, walls, & out-housing

£600; the purchase of the fee for 30 acres, at £15 per acre, eighteen years purchase, £400; the total £1550, £1600 will be the utmost. Three of the cells or apartments, that is, one moiety, with the appertenances, shall be at the disposal of one of the founders, and the other half at the other's.

If I & my wife take up two apartments (for we are to be decently asunder, however I stipulate, & her inclination will greatly suit with it, that shall be no impediment to the Society, but a considerable advantage to the œconomick part) a third shall be for some worthy person; and to facilitate the rest, I offer to furnish the whole pavilion compleatly, to the value of £500 in goods and moveables, if need be, for seven years, till there be a publick stock, &c.

There shall be maintained at the public charge, only a chaplain, well qualified, an ancient woman to dress the meat, wash, and do all such offices, a man to buy provisions, keep the garden, horses, &c. a boy to assist him, and serve within.

At one meal a day, of two dishes only (unless some little extraordinary upon particular days or occasions, then never exceeding three) of plain & wholesome meat; a small refection at night: wine, beer, sugar, spice, bread, fish, fowl, candle, soap, oats, hay, fuel, &c. at £4 per week, £200 per annum; wages £15: keeping the gardens £20, the chaplain £20 per ann. Laid up in the treasury yearly £145, to be employed for books, instruments, drugs, trials, &c. The total £400 a year, comprehending the keeping of two horses for the chariot or the saddle, & two kine: so that £200 per ann. will be the utmost that the founders shall be at to maintain the whole Society, consisting of nine persons (the servants included) though there should no others join capable to alleviate the expence; but if any of those who desire to be of the Society be so qualified as to support their own particulars, & allow for their own proportion, it will yet much diminish the charge; and of such there cannot want some at all times, as the apartments are empty.

If either of the founders think expedient to alter his condition, or that any thing do *humanitus contingere*, he may resign to another, or sell to his colleague, and dispose of it as he pleases, yet so as it still continue the institution.

ORDERS.

At six in summer prayers in the chapel. To study till half an hour after eleven. Dinner in the refectory till one. Retire till four. Then called to conversation (if the weather invite) abroad, else in the refectory; this never omitted but in case of sickness. Prayers at seven. To bed at nine. In the winter the same, with some abatements for the hours, because the nights are tedious, and the evenings conversation more agreeable; this in the refectory. All play interdicted, *sans* bowls, chess, &c. Every one to cultivate his own garden. One month in spring a course in the elaboratory on vegetables, &c. In the winter a month on other experiments. Every man to have a key of the elaboratory, pavilion, library, repository, &c. Weekly fast. Communion once every fortnight, or month at least. No stranger easily admitted to visit any of the Society, but upon certain days weekly, and that only after dinner. Any of the Society may have his commons to his apartment, if he will not meet in the refectory, so it be not above twice a week. Every Thursday shall be a musick meeting at conversation hours. Every person of the Society shall render some publick account of his studies weekly, if thought fit, and especially shall be recommended the promotion of experimental knowledge, as the principal end of the institution. There shall be a decent habit and uniform used in the college. One month in the year may be spent in London, or any of the Universities, or in a perambulation for the publick benefit, &c. with what other orders shall be thought convenient, &c.

Thus, Sir, I have in haste (but to your loss not in a laconic style) presumed to communicate to you (& truly, in my life, never to any but yourself) that project which for some time has traversed my thoughts; and therefore far from being the effect either of an impertinent or trifling spirit, but the result of mature and frequent reasonings. And, Sir, is not this the same that many noble personages did at the confusion of the empire by the barbarous Goths, when St Hierome, Eustochium, & others, retired from the impertinences of the world to the sweet recesses and societies in the East, till it came to be burthened with the vows & superstitions, which can give no scandal to our design, that provides against all such snares?

Now to assure you, Sir, how pure & unmixed the design is from any other than the publick interest propounded by me, & to redeem the time to the noblest purposes, I am thankfully to acknowledge that, as to the common forms of living in the world I have little reason to be displeased at my present condition, in which, I bless God, I want nothing conducing either to health or honest diversion, extremely beyond my merit; & therefore would I be somewhat choice & scrupulous in my colleague, because he is to be the most dear person to me in the world. But oh! how I should think it designed from heaven, *& tanquam numen* διοπετές, did such a person as Mr. Boyle, who is alone a society of all that were desirable to a consummate felicity, esteem it a design worthy his embracing! Upon such an occasion how would I prostitute all my other concerments! how would I exult! &, as

I am, continue upon infinite accumulations & regards,

Sir,

His most humble, & most obedient servant,

J. EVELYN.

If my health permits me the honour to pay my respects to you before you leave the Town, I will bring you a rude plot of the building, which will better fix the idea, and shew what symmetry it holds with this description.

To the Honourable ROBERT BOYLE.

Sir,   Says-Court, Sept. 29, 1659.

I send you this enclosed, the product of your commands, but the least instance of my ambition to serve you: & when I shall add, that if an oblation of whatever else I possess can verify the expression of my greater esteem of your incomparable book, which is indicted with a pen snatched from the wing of a seraphim, exalts your divine incentives to that height, that being sometimes ravished with your description of that transcendant state of angelical amours, I was almost reconciled to the passion of Cleombrotus, who threw himself into the water upon the reading of Plato, & (as despairing to enjoy it) ready to cry out with St. Paul, *cupio dissolvi*, & to be in the embraces of this seraphick love, which you have described to that perfection, as if in the company of some celestial harbinger you had taken flight, and been ravished into the third heaven, where you have heard words unutterable, & from whence you bring us such affections & divine inclinations, as are only competent to angels & to yourself: for so powerful is your eloquence, so metaphysical your discourse, & sublime your subject. And though by all this, & your rare example, you civilly declaim against the mistakes we married persons usually make; yet I cannot think it a paralogism or insidious reasoning, which you manage with so much ingenuity, & pursue with so great judgment. But certainly it was an extraordinary grace, that at so early years, & amidst the ardours of youth, you should be able to discern so maturely, & determine so happily: avoid the Syren, & escape the tempest: but thus, when the curiosity of Psyche had lighted the taper, & was resolved to see what so ardently embraced her, she discovered an impertinent child, the weakness & folly of the passion. You, Sir, found its imperfections betimes; & that men then ceased to be wise when they began to be in love, unless with you, they could turn nature into grace, & at once place their affections on the right object. But, Sir, though you seem tender of the consequence all this while, the conclusion will speak as well as your example; that though you have said nothing of marriage, which is the result of love, yet you suppose that it were hard to become a servant without folly; & that there are ten thousand inquietudes espoused with a mistress. That the fruits of children are tears & weakness, whilst the productions of the spirit put their parents neither to charge nor trouble; that all these heroes, of whom we read, esteemed most precious of the celibate. Alexander had no child, & Hercules left no heir: Pallas was born of the brain of Jupiter; & the Venus Urania of the Platonists made love only to the soul, which she united to the essence of God (according to their divinity), & had no lower commerce than what you so worthily celebrate in your book, & cultivate in your life. But though these were all true, & all that you have added, since I find the passion of Lindamore rather to be pitied than criminal, because Hermione's was not reciprocal; though she were cruel, the sex is tender, & amiable, pious, & useful, & will never want champions to defend their virtues & assert their dues, & that is our love & our service. For if it be virtuous, it is the nearest to the seraphical; & whatever can be objected against it, proceeds from the vices of the person's defect, or extremes of the passion. But you instance in the jealousies, diseases, follies, & inconstancies of love: the sensual truly is obnoxious to all these; but who have been the martyrs, where the design was not plainly brutish, indifferent to the education, or blinded with avarice? And if you have example of their hatred, & perfidy, I can produce a thousand of their affection & integrity. What think you, Sir, of Alceste, that ran into the funeral pile of her husband? The goodness of Emilia, the chastity of Lucretia, the faith of Furia, of Portia, & infinite others who knew nothing that the Christian institution has superadded? And the Scriptures are full of worthy examples, since it was from the effects of conjugal love that the Saviour of the world, & that great object of seraphick love, derived his incarnation, who was the son of David. Take away this love, & the whole earth is but a dessert; & though there were nothing more worthy eulogies than virginity, it is yet but the result of love, since those, that shall people paradise, & fill heaven with saints, are such as have been subject to this passion, & were the products of it. In sum, it is by that the church has consecrated to God both virgins & martyrs, & confessors, these five thousand years; & he that said it was not good for man to be alone, placed the celibate amongst the inferior states of perfection, whatsoever some affirm; seeing that of St. Paul is not general, & he confesses he had no command from the Lord. It was the best advice in a time of persecution, the present distress, & for an itinerant apostle; & truly it is what I so recommend to all of that function, that, for many regards I could wish them all as seraphims, who do neither marry nor are given in marriage. But I cannot consent that such a person as Mr. Boyle be so indifferent, decline a virtuous love, or imagine that the best ideas are represented only in romances, where love begins, proceeds, & expires in the pretty tale, but leaves us no worthy impressions of its effects. We have nobler examples: & the wives of philosophers, pious & studious persons, shall furnish our instances: for such was Pudentilla, that held the lamp to her husband's lucubrations: such a companion had the learned Budæus; & the late adventure of Madam Grotius, celebrated by her Hugo, who has not heard of? We need not go abroad; the committee chambers, & the parliament lobby, are sad, but evident testimonies of the patience, & the address, the love, & the constancy of these gentle creatures. In fine, they bear us out of love, & they give us such; they divert us when we are well, & tend us when we are sick; they grieve over us when we die, & some, I have known, that would not be comforted & survive. But, Sir, Ludov. Vives has written a volume on this subject, & taken all his histories from the love of Christian women. Jacobus de Voragine gives us twelve motives to acknowledge the good we receive by them, & I could add a thousand more, were not that of Pliny *instar omnium,* who writing to his mother-in-law Hispulla, that brought his lady up, gives her this character: " Summum est acumen, summa frugalitas: amat me, quod castitatis indicium est. Accedit his studium literarum, quod ex mei charitate concepit. Meos libellos habet, lectitat, ediscit etiam. Qua illa solicitudine, cum videor acturus; quanto, cum egi, gaudio afficitur;" & a little after, "Versus quidem meos cantat etiam, formatque cithara, non artifice aliquo docente, sed amore, qui magister est optimus:" whence he well foresees, " perpetuam nobis majoremque indies futuram esse concordiam:" discoursing in that which follows, of the nobleness & purity of her affection, with this elegant and civil acknowledgement, " certatim ergo tibi gratias agimus: ego, quod illam mihi: illa, quod me sibi dederis, quasi invicem deligeris." And what if Mr. Boyle himself did love such a lady, " gratâ aliqua compede adstrictus," would it hinder him from the seraphick, or the pursuit of his worthy enquiries? There is no danger, that he should be taught philosophy as Socrates was, who already commands his passions, & has divinity sufficient to render even Zantippe a saint; & whose arguments for the seraphick love would make all men to envy his condition, & suspect their own, if it could once be admitted that those who are given to be *auxilia commoda,* should hinder them in the love of God, whereof marriage is a figure: for so the apostle makes the parallel, when he speaks of the spouse, Ephes. v. & devotion is so generally conspicuous in the female sex, that they furnish the greater part of many litanies, & whom, if we may not pray to, we ought certainly to praise God for; not so much because they were virgins, as that they were the mothers & the daughters of the greatest saints, & lights of the church, who propagated the seraphick love with their examples, & sealed it with their blood. But, dear Sir, mistake me not all this while, for I make not this recital as finding the least period in your most excellent discourse prejudicial to the conjugal state; or that I have the vanity to imagine my forces capable to render you a proselyte of Hymen's, who have already made the worthiest choice; much less to magnify my own condition, & lay little snares for those obvious replies, which return in compliments, & odious flatteries. I have never encountered any thing extraordinary, or dare lay claim to the least of the virtues I have celebrated: but if I have the conversation capable of exalting & improving our affections, even to the highest of objects, & to contribute very much to human felicity; I cannot pronounce the love of the sex to be at all misapplied, or to the prejudice of the most seraphical. And if to have the fruition & the knowledge of our friends in heaven, will be so considerable an augmentation of our felicity; how great is that of the married like to prove, since there is not on earth a friendship comparable to it? Or if paradise & the ark be the most adequate resemblances of those happy mansions, you may remember there were none but couples there, & that every creature was in love.

But why do I torment your eyes with these impertinencies? which would never have end, did I not consider, I am but writing a letter, & how much better you are wont to place your precious hours. But, Sir, I have now but a word to add, & it is to tell you, that, if after all this, we acknowledge your victory, & find all our arguments too weak to contest with your seraphical object, pronounce you wise, & infinitely happy; yet, as if envying that any else should be so, you have too long concealed the discourses, which should have gained you disciples, & are yet not afraid to make apologies for employing that talent, which you cannot justify the wrapping up all this while in a napkin. We therefore, that are entangled in our mistakes, & acknowledge our imperfections, must needs declare against it, as the least effects of a seraphick lover, which were to render all men like himself. And since there is now no other remedy, make the best use we can of, as St. Paul advises, " ut qui habent uxores, sint tanquam non habentes," &c. & for the rest, to serve & to love God as well as we may in the condition we are assigned; which if it may not approach to the perfection of seraphim, & that of Mr. Boyle, let it be as near as it can, & we shall not account ourselves amongst the most unhappy, for having made some virtuous addresses to that fair sex.

Dearest Sir, permit me to tell you, that I extremely loved you before; but my heart is infinitely knit to you now: for what are we not to expect from so timely a consecration of your excellent abilities? The *Primitiæ* sanctified the whole harvest, & you have at once, by this incomparable piece, taken off the reproach which lay upon piety, & the enquiries into nature; that the one was too early for younger persons, & the other the ready way to atheism, than which, as nothing has been more impiously spoken, so, nor has any thing been more fully refuted. But, Sir, I have finished; pardon this great excess; it is love that constrains me, & the effects of your discourses, from which I have learned so many excellent things that they are not to be numbered & merited with less than I have said, & than I profess, which is to continue all my life long,

  Sir,
 Your most humble, obliged,
  & most affectionate servant,
    J. EVELYN.

From Dr. Jeremy Taylor.

Honoured & deare Sir,

Yours, dated July 23d, I received not till All Saints day: it seemes it was stopped by the intervening troubles in England: but it was lodged in a good hand, & came safely & unbroken to me. I must needes beg the favour of you that I may receive from you an account of your health & present conditions, & of your family; for I feare concerning all my friends, but especially for those few very choice ones I have, lest the present troubles may have done them any violence in their affaires or content. It is now long since that cloud passed; & though I suppose the sky is yet full of meteors & evil prognostics, yet you all have time to consider concerning your peace and your securityes. That was not God's time to relieve his church, & I cannot understand from what quarter that wind blew, & whether it was for or against us. But God disposes all things wisely; & religion can receive no detriment or diminution but by our owne fault. I long, Sir, to come to converse with you; for I promise to myselfe that I may receive from you an excellent account of your progression in religion, & that you are entred into the experimental & secret way of it, which is that state of excellency whither good persons use to arrive after a state of repentance & caution. My retirement in this solitary place hath been, I hope, of some advantage to me as to this state of religion, in which I am yet but a novice; but by the goodnesse of God I see fine things before me whither I am contending. It is a great but a good worke, & I beg of you to assist me with your prayers, & to obtaine of God for me that I may arrive to that height of love & union with God, which is given to all those soules who are very deare to God. Sir, if it please God, I purpose to be in London in April next, where I hope for the comfort of conversing with you. In the meane time, be pleased to accept my thankes for your great kindnesse in taking care of me in that token you were pleased to leave with Mr. Martin. I am sorry the evil circumstances of the times made it any way afflictive or inconvenient. I had rather you should not have been burdened than that I should have received kindnesse on hard conditions to you. Sir, I shall not trouble your studies now, for I suppose you are very buisy there: but I shall desire the favour that I may know what you are now doing, for you cannot separate your affaires from being of concerne to,

Deare Sir,
Your very affectionate friend,
& humble servant,
JER. TAYLOR.

Portmore, Nov. 3, 1659.

From Dr. Jeremy Taylor.

Portmore, Feb. 10, 1659-60.

Honoured & deare Sir,

I received yours of Dee^r 2, in very good time; but although it came to me before Christmas, yet it pleased God, about that time, to lay his gentle hand upon me; for I had beene, in the worst of our winter weather, sent for to Dublin by our late Anabaptist commissioners, & found the evil of it so great, that in my going I began to be ill: but in my return, had my ill redoubled & fixed: but it hath pleased God to restore my health, I hope *ad majorem Dei gloriam;* & now that I can easily write, I return you my very hearty thanks for your very obliging letter, & particularly for the inclosed. Sir, the Apology* you were pleased to send me, I read both privately & heard read publikely with no little pleasure & satisfaction. The materials are worthy, & the dress is clean, & orderly, & beauteous; & I wish that all men in the nation were obliged to read it twice: it is impossible but it must doe good to those guilty persons to whom it is not impossible to repent. Your Character† hath a great part of a worthy reward, that it is translated into a language in which it is likely to be read by very many *beaux esprits.* But that which I pro-

---

* Apology for the Royal Party. See Evelyn's " Miscellaneous Writings," 1825, 4to. p. 169.

† Character of England. See " Miscellaneous Writings," p. 141.

mise to myselfe as an excellent entertainment, is your ". Elysium Britanicum." But, Sir, seeing you intend it to the purposes of piety as well as pleasure, why doe you not rather call it Paradisus than Elysium; since the word is used by the Hellenish Jewes to signify any place of spiritual & immaterial pleasure, & excludes not the material & secular. Sir, I know you are such a *curieux*, & withal so diligent & inquisitive, that not many things of the delicacy of learning, relating to your subject, can escape you; & therefore it would be great imprudence in me to offer my little mite to your already digested heape. I hope, ere long, to have the honour to waite on you, & to see some parts & steps of your progression: & then if I see I can bring any thing to your building, though but hair & stickes, I shall not be wanting in expressing my readinesse to serve & to honour you, & to promote such a worke, than which I thinke, in the world, you could not have chosen a more apt & a more ingenious.

Sir, I do really beare a share in your feares & your sorrowes for your deare boy. I doe and shall pray to God for him; but I know not what to say in such things. If God intends, by these clouds, to convey him & you to brighter graces & more illustrious glories respectively, I dare not, with too much passion, speake against the so great good of a person that is so deare to me, & a child that is so deare to you. But I hope that God will do what is best : & I humbly beg of him to choose what is that best for you both. As soon as the weather & season of the spring gives leave, I intend, by God's permission, to returne to England : & when I come to London with the first to waite on you, for whom I have so great regard, & from whom I have received so many testimonies of a worthy friendship, & in whom I know so much worthinesse is deposited.

I am, most faithfully & cordially,
Your very affectionate & obliged servant,
JER. TAYLOR.

To Dr. WILKINS,
President of our Society at Gressham Coll:
(afterwards Dean of Ripon and Bishop of Chester.)
S^r,

Though I suppose it might be a mistake that there was a meeting appoynted to-morrow (being a day of publique sollemnity and devotion), yet because I am uncertaine, and would not disobey y^r com'ands, I here send you my trifling observations concerning the anatomy of trees, and their vegetative motion. It is certaine, as Dr. Goddard has shewed,* that a section of any tree made parallel to

---

* In his " Observations concerning the nature and similar parts of a Tree," which were afterwards published in folio, 1664. Dr. Jonathan Goddard was an eminent Physician, Botanist, and promoter of the Royal Society. He was born at Greenwich about 1617, and died in 1674.

the horizon, will by the closenesse of the circles point to the North, and so consequently, if a perpendicular be drawne through them for the meridian, the rest of the cardinals, &c. found out; but this is not so universall, but that where strong reflections are made, as from walls, the warme fumes of dunghills, & especially if the southern side be shaded, &c. those ellipticall and hyperbolicall circles are sometimes very irregular; and I doubt not but by some art might be made to have their circles as orderly as those which we find in Brasile, Ebene, &c. which within a very little concenter by reason of the uniforme course of the Sun about them; which is doubtlesse the cause of their greater dilatation on the south part onely with us, when the pores are more open, and lesse constipated. The consideration whereof (though no where mention'd that I know) made the poet, giving advice concerning transplantations, to caution thus,

> Quin etiam Cœli regionem in cortice signant,
> Ut quo quæque modo steterit, qua parte calores
> Austrinos tulerit, quæ terga obverterit axi,
> Restituant: adeo in teneris consuescere multum est.

And though Pliny neglect it as an unnecessary curiosity, I can by much experience confirme it, that not one tree in 100 would miscarry were it duly observed; for in some I have made triall of it even at Midsommer. But what I would add is touching the graine of many woods, and the reason of it which I take to be the descent, as well as the ascent of moysture; for what else becomes of that water which is frequently found in the cavities where many branches spread themselves at the topps of greate trees, especially pollards, unlesse (according to its naturall appetite) it sinke into the very body of the stem through the pores? For example: in the Wallnut, you shall find when 'tis old, that the wood is rarely figur'd and marbled as it were, & therefore much more esteemed by joyners, &c. then the young, which is whiter & without any grains: for the raine distilling along the branches, where many of them come out in clusters together from the stem, sinkes in, and is the cause of these markes; for it is exceedingly full of pores. Do but plane a thin chipp off from one of these old trees, and interpose it 'twixt y^r eye and the light, and you shall perceive it full of innumerable holes. But above all conspicuous for these workes and damaskings, is the Maple (a finer sort whereof the Germans call Air, and therefore much sought after by the instrument-makers): 'tis notorious that this tree is full of branches from the very roote to the su'mite, by reason it bears no considerable fruite. These branches being frequently cutt, the head is the more surcharged with them, which, spreading like so many raies from a center, forme that cavity at the top of the stem whence they shoote, as contains a good quantity of water every time it raines: this sinking into the pores, as we hinted before, is compelled to diverte its course as it passes through the body of the tree, wherever it finds the knott of any of these branches which were cut off from the stem of the tree; because their rootes not onely deeply penetrate towards the heart, but are likewise of themselves very hard and impervious: and the frequent obliquity of this course of the subsiding waters, by reason of these obstacles, is the cause of those curious and rare undulations & workes which we find remarkable in this and other woods, whose branches grow thick from the stem.

S^r, I know not whether I have well explain'd my conception, but such as it is I offer it, and it was y^r com'ands I should do so, together with that Treatise or History of Chalcography, as part of the taske you have impos'd; but with this hope & humble request, that, knowing upon what other subject I was engaged before I had the honour to be elected one of this august Society, I may obtain its indulgence, not to expect many other things from me 'till it be accomplish'd; rather that you will take all occasions which may contribute to my designe. It is there, S^r, that I have at large discours'd of the vegetation of plants, and upon that argument which Sr K. Digby and the rest so long discours'd at our last encounter, but it shall not be so in this paper, which is now at an end, &c.

Y^r &c.

Says-Court, 17 Feb. 1660.

To the Honourable ROBERT BOYLE.

Sir,   Says-Court, Sept. 13, 1661.

I send you the receipt of the varnish, and believe it to be very exact, because it is so particular; and that I received it from the hand of a curious person, who, having made trial of it himself, affirms it to have succeeded. I send you also another trifle, which has a nearer relation to me, and you will easily pardon my indignation, however you pity the rest of my errors, to which there is superadded so great a presumption: not that I believe what I have written should produce the desired effects, but to indulge my passion, and in hopes of obtaining a partial reformation; if, at least, his Majesty pursue the resentment which he lately expressed against this nuisance, since this pamphlet was prepared. Sir, I am your creditor for Schotti, and shall faithfully render it whenever your summons calls; my leisure has not yet permitted me to transcribe some things out of it, which concerns me on another subject; but if the detaining it longer be no prejudice to you, it is in a safe depositum. Sir, I have not bought two of your last books, & yet possibly I could render you some account of them. My thirst & impatience is too great to shew the least indifferency, when any thing of your's is to be had; this does not absolve you from making him a present who, it may be, takes no greater felicity in the world than to see his small library enriched with your illustrious works, & they to come to me *ex dono authoris.* Dearest Sir, pardon this innocent stratagem, and the presumption of,

Sir,

Your most faithful, & most obedient servant,

J. Evelyn.

Sir, I must take this opportunity to give you thanks for your great civilities to my cousin Baily, & to supplicate the continuance of your favour to him, as by which you will infinitely oblige an industrious end deserving gentleman.

From Dr. Jeremy Taylor.

Dear Sir,Dublin, November 16, 1661.

Your owne worthinesse & the obligations you have so often pass'd upon me have imprinted in me so great a value & kindnesse to your person, that I think myselfe not a little concerned in yourselfe & all your relations, & all the great accidents of your life. Doe not therefore thinke me either impertinent or otherwise without employment, if I doe with some care & earnestnesse inquire into your health & the present condition of your affaires. Sir, when shal we expect your Terrestrial Paradise; your excellent observations and discourses of gardens, of which I had a little posy presented to me by your owne hand, & makes me long for more. Sir, I & all that understand excellent fancy, language, & deepest loyalty, are bound to value your excellent Panegyric, which I saw & read with pleasure. I am pleased to read your excellent mind in so excellent an idea, for, as a father, in his son's face, so is a man's soule imprinted in all the pieces that he labours. Sir, I am so full of publicke concernes & the troubles of businesse in my diocese, that I cannot yet have leisure to thinke of much of my old delightful employment. But I hope I have brought my affaires almost to a consistence, & then I may returne againe. Royston, the bookseller, hath two sermons, and a little collection of rules for my clergy, which had beene presented to you if I had thought them fit for notice, or to send to my dearest friends.

Dear Sir, I pray let me hear from you as often as you can, for you will very much oblige me if you will continue to love me still. I pray give my love & deare regards to worthy Mr. Thurland: let me heare of him & his good lady, & how his son does. God blesse you & yours, him & his. I am,
Dear Sir,
Your most affectionate friend,
JEREM. DUNENSIS.

To Tho. Chiffing,* Esq. Page of the back stairs to his Majesty and Keeper of his closet.

In answer to the laudable design of his Ma^{t}y for fit repositories of those precious Treasures & Curiosities com'itted to y^r charge, I conceive you may compleately martial them in a Catalogue (as there set forth). This were in truth a noble way to preserve his treasure intire; so as upon occasion to permit a sight of it to greate princes & curious strangers; for it is great pity it should not be made as famous as the Cabinet of the Duke of Florence & other foraign princes, which are only celebrated for [by] being more universally known, & not because his Maties collection is not altogether as worthy, his Matie being likewise himself so exquisite a judge, as well as possessor, of so many rare things as might render not onely Whitehall, but the whole nation, famous for it abroad.

If it be his Ma^{tys} pleasure, I shall, whenever you

---

* Thomas Chiffinch, of Northfleet, Esq. Keeper of the Jewels to King Charles II. Keeper of the King's Closet, and Comptroller of the Excise. He was born at Salisbury in 1600, and was brought to the Court of King Charles I. by Bishop Duppa. After the King's death, he, with his wife, went abroad to King Charles II. and continued with him till the Restoration. He died in 1666, and was buried in Westminster Abbey, where there is a monument erected to his memory. Hasted's Hist. of Kent, vol. I. p. 442.

call upon me, & that it may least importune his privacy, make the inventory of particulars.

To this I would have added, in another Register, the names & portraitures of all the exotic & rare beasts & fowls which have at any time been presented to his Ma^{t}y, & which are daily sent to his Paradise at St. James's Parke.

To my Lady Cotton.*

Madame,

It was by a visite which was made us this afternoon, that we heard how it had pleased God to dispose of ye little sweete babe; and, withall, how much the losse of it dos yet afflict you. Whatsoever concernes you in this kind is, Madame, a com'on diminution to the familie, and touches every particular of it; but so as our resentiments hold proportion to the cause, and that the losse of one dos not take away the comfort and the contentment which we ought to have in those who are left; since we must pretend to nothing here, but upon the conditions of mortalitie and ten thousand other accidents; and that we may learne to place our felicities in our obedience to the will of God, which is allways ye best, and to sacrifice our affections upon that altar, which can consecrate our very losses, and

---

* Wife to his Brother Geo. Evelyn, of Wotton.

turne them to our greatest advantage. Madame, I have heard with infinite satisfaction how graciously God had restor'd you y^r health: why should you now impaire it againe by an excesse of griefe, which can recalle nothing that God has taken to himselfe in exchange without a kind of ingratitude? There be some may haply sooth y^r Ladyship in this sensible part (which was the destruction of my deare Mother); but y^r Ladyship's discretion ought to fortifie you against it before it become habitual and dangerous. Remember that you have an husband who loves you intirely; that you have other children who will neede your conduct; that you have many friends, and a prosperous family. Pluck up y^r spirits then, and at once vanquish these hurtfull tendernesses. It is the vote of all that honor & love you; it is what God requires of you, and what I conjure you to resolve upon; and I beseech y^r La'p, let this expresse bring us some fairer confidences of it, then the com'on report dos represent it to the griefe of,

Madame, y^r, &c.

Sayes-Court, 9 Sept. 1662.

To Mr. Vander Douse,

Grandson to ye greate Janus Dousa.

S^r,

I have to the best of my skill translated y^r Relation of China: if you find the Argument omitted, it is for that I thought it superfluous, being almost as large as the text; but I have yet left a sufficient space where you may (if you thinke good) insert it. In ye mean time, it would be consider'd, whether this whole piece will be to the purpose, there having ben of late so many accurate descriptions of those countries in particular, as what Father Alvarez Semedo has publish'd in the Italian;* Vincent Le Blanc in French;† and Mandelslo in high Dutch;‡ not omitting the Adventures & Travels of Pinto in Spanish;§ all of them now speaking the English language. At least I conceive that you

---

* History of the great and renowned Monarchy of China; translated from the Portuguese into English, by a Person of Quality; with cuts. Folio. 1655.

† Voyages fameux du Sieur Vincent le Blanc, Marseillois. 4to, Paris, 1658.

‡ Peregrinations from Persia into the East Indies, translated by John Davies. Folio.

§ Ferdinand Mendez Pinto, his Travels in the Kingdoms of Ethiopia, China, Tartaria, Cochin China, and a great part of the East Indies; translated out of Portuguese into English by Henry Cogan. Folio. 1663.

might not do amisse to peruse their workes, and upon comparing of them with this piece of yours, to observe what there is more accurate and instructive; least you otherwise seeme *actum agere*, as the word is: but this, Sir, I remit to your better judgement, who am,

S^r, y^r, &c.

Sayes-Court, 13: Sept^{tr}: 1662.

To Mr. (afterwards Dr.) CROONE, Professor of Rhetoriq, at Gresham College, London.*

S^r,

It has neither proceeded from the unmindfullnesse of y^r desires, or y^r deserts, that I had not long before this gratified y^r inclinations, in finding you out a condition, which it might become you to embrace, if you still continue y^r laudable curiosity, by wishing for some opportunity to travell, and see the world. There have pass'd occasions (and some which did neerely concerne my relations) when I might happily have engag'd you; but having long had a greate ambition to serve you, since I had this in prospect, I rather chose to dispence with my owne advantages, that I might comply with yours.

---

* He founded a course of Algebraic Lectures in seven colleges at Cambridge, and also a yearly anatomical Lecture in the Royal Society.

My worthy and most noble friend Mr. Henry Howard, has by my Co: Tuke signified to me his desires of some fit person to instruct and travell with his two incomparable children; and I im'ediately suggested Mr. Croone to them, with such recommendations and civilities as were due to his merits, and as became me. This being cherefully embrac'd on their part, it will now be yours to second it. All I shall say for y^r present encouragement is but this: England shall never present you with an equal opportunity; nor were it the least diminution that Mr. Croone, or indeede one of the best gentlemen of the nation, should have the tuition of an heire to the Duke of Norfolke, (after the Royal Family,) the greatest Prince in it. But the title is not the thinge I would invite you to, in an age so universally deprav'd amongst our wretched nobility. You will here come into a most opulent worthy family, and in which I prognosticate (and I have it assur'd me) you shall make your fortune, without any further dependances: For the persons who governe there, have both the meanes to be very gratefull, and as generous a propensity to it as any family in England: Sir, if you thinke fit to lay hold on this occasion, I shall take a tyme to discourse to you of some other particulars which the limits of an hasty letter will not permit me to insert. I have ben told to leave this for you at the Colledge; because I was uncertaine of seeing you, and that I have promis'd to give my friends an accompt of its reception. If your affaires could so far dispense with you as to afford me an afternoones visite at my poore villa, I should with more liberty conferr with you about it, and in hope of that favour I remaine,

S^r, y^r, &c.

Says-Court, 11: July: 1663.

To Dr. PIERCE, President of Magdalen Coll. in Oxford; & one of his M^{aties} Chaplaines in Ordinary.

Re^d Sir,

Being not long since at Somersett-house, to do my duty to her Ma^{ty} the Queene Mother, I fortun'd to encounter Dr Goffe.* One of the first things he ask'd me was, whither I had seene Mr Cressy's † Reply to Dr Pierce's so much celebrated Sermon? I told him, I had heard much of it, but not as yet seenc it: upon which he made me an offer to present me with one of the bookes, but being in hast, and with a friend, I easily excus'd his civility, that I could not well stay 'till he should come back from his lodging: in the meane time he gave no ordi-

---

* See vol. I. p. 23, and vol II. p. 188.

† Roman Catholic Doctrines no Novelties; or an Answer to Dr. Pierce's Court Sermon, miscalled, The Primitive Rule of Reformation. 8vo, 1663.

nary encomiums of y^t rare piece, which he exceedingly magnified, as beyond all answer; and to reinforce the triumph, he told me that you had written a letter to some friend of y^{rs} (a copy whereof he believed he should shortly produce) wherein (after you had express'd y^r greate resentment that some of ye Bishops had made you their property, in putting you upon that ungratefull argument) you totaly declin'd to engage any farther in ye controversy: intimating that you would leave it at the Bishops dores, and trouble your selfe no more with it. This (or words to this effect) being spoken to my selfe, and to some others who stood by, would have weigh'd more with me, had I not been as well acquainted with these kind of artifices to gaine proselytes by, as of your greater discretion never to have written such a Letter, and abilities to vindicate what you have publish'd, when you should see y^r time. Nor had I likely thought more of it, had not my Lord of Canterbury, the Bp: of Winchester, together with my Lord Chancelor (to whom upon some occasion of private discourse, I recounted the passage) expressly injoyned me to give you notice of it; because they thought it did highly concerne you; and that you would take it civily from me. And, S^r, I have don it faithfully; but with this humble request, that (unlesse there be very greate cause for it) you will be tender of mentioning by what hand y^r intelligence comes; because it may do me some injury.

Sʳ, I am perfectly assur'd, that you will do both yʳselfe and the Church of England that right which becomes you upon this occasion. I will not say that the burthen ought to be cast upon yʳ shoulders alone; but I will pronounce it a greater marke of yʳ charity, and zeale, and such as intitles you to the universal obligation which all men haue to you; upon confidence whereof I satisfie myselfe you will soone dismantle this douty battery, and assert what you haue gain'd so gloriously.

Thus I discharge my duty, in obedience to their com'ands. But it is upon another account that I was not displeas'd with having an opportunity by this occasion to expresse my thankes & great acknowledgements to you, for the present you made me of that yʳ incomparable Sermon, and which in my opinion is sufficiently impregnable; but something must be don by these buisy men, to support their credit, though at the irreparable expence of truth and ingenuity. The Epistle before Mr. Cressy's papers dos not want confidence: and we are very tame whiles we suffer our Church to be thus treated by such as being once her sons did so unworthily desert her. But pardon this indignation. I am,

Rᵈ Sʳ,
Yʳ most, &c.

Says-Court, 20 Aug. 1663.

To the Honourable ROBERT BOYLE.

Sir, Says-Court, Nov. 23, 1664.

The honour you design me by making use of that trifle which you were lately pleas'd to command an account of, is so much greater than it pretends to merit, as indeed it is far short of being worthy your acceptance: but if by any service of mine in that other business, I may hope to contribute to an effect the most agreeable to your excellent and pious nature, it shall not be my reproach that I did not my best endeavour to oblige it. I do every day, both at London and at home, put Sr Richard in mind of this suppliant's case; and, indeed, he needs no monitor, myself being witness that he takes all occasions to serve him in it; nor wants there any dispositions (as far as I can perceive), but one single opportunity only, the meeting of my Lord Privy Seal (who, for two or three Council days, has been indisposed, and not appeared), to expedite his request; there being a resolution (and which Sir Richard promises shall not slacken), both to discharge the poor man's engagements here, and afford him a competent viaticum.

As for that sacred work you mention, it is said there is a most authentic copy coming over, the laudable attempt of this person being not so fully approved. This is, in short, the account I have, why the impression is retarded. I should else esteem it one of the most fortunate adventures of my life, that by any industry of mine I might be accessary in the least to so blessed an undertaking.

If my book of architecture do not fall into your hands at Oxon, it will come with my apology, when I see you at London; as well as another part of the Mystery of Jesuitism, which (with some other papers concerning that iniquity) I have translated, and am now printing at Royston's, but without my name. — So little credit there is in these days in doing any thing for the interest of religion.

I know not whether it becomes me to inform you, that it has pleased his Majesty to nominate me a Commissioner to take care of the sick and wounded persons during this war with our neighbours: but so it is, that there being but four of us designed for this very troublesome and sad employment, all the ports from Dover to Portsmouth, Kent, and Sussex, fall to my district alone, and makes me wish a thousand times I had such a colleague as Mr. Boyle, who is wholly made up of charity, and all the qualifications requisite to so pious a care. But I cannot wish you so much trouble, the prospect of it would even draw pity from you, as well in my behalf, as for the more miserable, who foresee the confusion and importunities of it, by every article of our busy instructions. But the King has laid his positive commands on me, and I am just now going towards

Dover, &c. to provide for mischief. Farewel, sweet repose, books, gardens, and the blessed conversation you are pleased to allow, dear Sir,
Your most affectionate and most obedient servant,
J. Evelyn.

P. S. Mr. Goldman's Dictionary is that good and useful book which I mentioned to you.

Here is Mr. Stillingfleet's new piece in vindication of my Lord of Canterbury's. I have but little dipped into it as yet; it promises well, and I very much like the epistle; nor is the style so perplexed as his usually was.

Dr. Mer. Causabon, I presume, is come to your hands, being a touch upon the same occasion.

One Rhea* has published a very useful and sincere book, concerning the culture of flowers, &c. but it does in nothing reach my long since attempted design of that entire subject, with all its ornaments and accessories, which I had shortly hoped to perfect, had God given me opportunity.

Your servant, my Wife, most humbly kisseth your hands, as I do Dr. Barlow's, &c.

To Doct^r Pierce, &c.

S^r,
I receiv'd y^r favour of the first of this moneth wth very different passions, whiles in some periods

---
* Q.? the celebrated Ray.

you giue me reasons so convincing why you should rather consult y^r health, and gratifie y^r charge, & personal concernements, than reply to impertinent bookes; and in others againe make such generous and noble offers, that the Church of England, and the cause which is now dishonor'd, should not suffer through y^r silence: and I had (according to y^r com'ands) made my addresses to those h^{oble} persons with something of what you had instructed me, had either my Lord of Winchester, or my L: Chancellor been in towne. Since I received y^r lett^r my L: of Winchester is indeede gone to Farnham some few days past; but I was detain'd by speciall buisinesse in ye country 'til this very moment, when coming to London on purpose to waite on him, I miss'd him unfortunately, and unexpectedly. In the meane time, I was not a little rejoyc'd at something my Ld: of Salisbury did assure me, of some late kind intercourse betweene you and y^r Visitor, to the no small satisfaction of all those that love and honor you here.

In pursuance of y^r farther injunction, I was this very morning with Dr Goffe: after a short ceremony we touch'd upon Cressy's pamphlet: He tells me there are eight sheetes more printing (by a Revd Father of ye Society, as he named him), who has put Mr Cressy's Rhapsody into mode and figure, that so it might do ye worke amongst scholars, as it was like to do it wth his illiterate proselytes.

Upon this I tooke occasion to remind him of y̶e̶ lett̶r̶ which he lately pretended you had written, intimating y̶r̶ resolution not to reply. After some pause he told me that was a mistake, and y̶t̶ he heard it was onely a friend of yours which writt so. Whither he suspected I came a birding, or no, I cannot be satisfied, but he now blench'd what before (I do assure you) he affirm'd to me concerning y̶r̶ owne writing that lett̶r̶. This is the infelicity (and I haue observ'd it in more then one) that when men abandon their religion to God, they take their leave also of all ingenuity towards men. And what could I make of this shuffling, and caution, now turn'd to a mistake, & an heare-say? but so it seemes was not that of y̶r̶ being offended with the Bishops for the ingratefull taske they put upon you, which he often repeated; and the difference 'twixt you and y̶r̶ Visitor:—so after a short velitation, we parted. S̶r̶, I have nothing more to add to y̶r̶ trouble, then that I still persist in my supplication, and that you would at last breake through all these discouragements and objections for y̶e̶ publiq benefit. It is true, men deserve it not; but the Church, which is dearer to you then all their contradictions can be grievous, requires it. You can (in the interim) govern a dissorderly College which calls for y̶r̶ assiduous care; but so dos no lesse the needes of a despis'd Church; nor ought any in it concerne themselves so much as to this particular, without being uncivill to you: though (I confesse) after you have once chastis'd this insolence, no barking of the currs should provoke you for the future: S^r, I do not use a quarter of those arguments which y^r friends here suggest, why you ought to gratifie the Church by standing in this gapp; because I am confident you perfectly discerne them; and that though some particular persons may have unjustly injur'd you, yet she has been kind, and indulgent; and in a cause which concernes either her honor or veracity, it will be glorious (not to say gratefull) you should vindicate her wrongs. You are not the onely subject which that academiq Jack-pudding has reproach'd more bitterly personally: The drunkards made a song of holy David, yet still he daunc'd before the arke of God, and would be more vile. What are we Christians for? I do assure you, there is nothing I have a greater scorne & indignation against, then these wretched scoffers, and I looke upon our neglect of severely punishing them as an high defect in o^r politiques, and a forerunner of something very funest. I would to God vertue and sobriety were more in reputation: but we shall turne plainely barbarians, if all good men be discourag'd. S^r, you are of a greater mind then not to despise this. *Fa pùr bene e lascia dire.* But I run into extravagances, and I beseech you to pardon my zeale, and all other the impertinences of, S^r, y^r, &c.

Lond. 17th Septr. 1663.

To Mr. SPRAT, Chaplaine to the Duke of BUCKINGHAME, afterwards Bishop of Rochester.*

Upon receipt of the D^{rs} letter, and the hint of y^r designe, which I receiv'd at Oxford in my returne from Cornebery, I su'moned such scatter'd notices as I had, & which I thought might possibly serve you in some particulars relating to the person and condition of Sorbiere.

His birth was in Orange, where he was the sonn of a Protestant, a very indigent and poore man; but however making a shift to give him some education as to letters, he design'd him for a minister, and procur'd him to be pedagogue to a cadet of Monsr le Compte de la Suze, in whose family he liv'd easily enough, till being at length discover'd to be a rampant Socinian, he was discharg'd of employment, but in revenge whereof ('tis reported) he turn'd apostat, & renounc'd his religion, which had been hitherto Huguenot. I forgot to tell you that before this he obtain'd to be made a schoolemaster to one of the classes in y^t citty; but that promotion was likewise quickly taken from him upon the former suspition. He has pass'd through a thousand shapes to ingratiat himselfe in the world, & after having been an Aristarchus, physi-

---

* This letter alludes to Mons. Sorbiere's "Voyage to England," then just published; and also to Observations on the same Voyage by Dr. Sprat.

tian (or rather mountebanq) philosopher, critic, & polititian (to which last he thought himselfe worthily ariv'd by a version of some heterodox pieces of Mr Hobbes), the late Cardinal Mazarin bestow'd on him a pittifull canonicat at Avignon worth about 200 crownes p^r ann. wch being of our money almost 50 pounds, is hardly the sallary of an ordinary curat: but for this yet he underwent the basest drudgery of a sycophant in flattering ye Cardinal upon all occasions the most sordidly to be imagin'd, as where I can shew you him speaking of this fourb for one of the most learned persons of the age. He styles himself Historiograph du Roy, the mighty meede of the co'monest Gazetiere, as that of Conseiller du Roy is of every trifling petifoger, wch is in France a very despicable qualification. It is certaine that by some servile intelligences he made shift to skrew him selfe into ye acquaintance of many persons of quality, at whose tables he fed, & where he entertain'd them with his impertinences. A greate favourite of our late republiq he was, or rather the vilany of Cromwell, whose expedition at sea against Holland he infinitely extolls, with a prediction of his future glorious atchievements, to be seene in an epistle of his to Mons. de Courcelles, 1652, and upon other occasions, not to omitt his inciting of our Roman Catholiques to improve their condition under his Matie by some effort, which smells of a rebell spirit, even in this relation which he presumes to dedicat to ye French King.

Thus as to ye person of y^t man & his co'munications: for ye rest in which this audacious delator sufficiently exposes himselfe to y^r mercy, I forbeare to add; unlesse it be to put you in mind of what occurs to me in relation to your vindicating my L. Chancelor, whom all the world knows he has most injuriously vilified; and you haue an ample field to proceede on, by comparing his birth & education wth that of his Cardinal Patron, whom he so execssively magnifies, & even makes a demi-god.

My L: Chancelor* is a branch of y^t antient & honorable family of Norbery in Cheshire as it is celebrated by M^r. Camden in his Britannia, and so famous for ye long robe, that an uncle's son of his present Lo^p: came to be no lesse a man than L: Chiefe Justice of England not long since, wch. dignity runs parallel with their Premier President de Paris, one of the most considerable charges of that kingdome. Nor has this person ascended to this deserved eminency without greate & signal merits, having passed through so many superior offices; as Chancellor of ye Exchequer, Privie Counsellor, Ambass^r Extraordinary, &c. not to mention his early engagement wth his M^{atie} Charles ye I. in a period of so greate defection; the divers weighty

---

* Edward Hyde, Earl of Clarendon.

affaires he has successfully manag'd, fidelity to ye present King, his eloquent tongue, dextrous and happy pen, facetious conversation & obliging nature, all of them the products of a free & ingenious education, which was both at the University and Inns of Court, now crown'd with an experience & addresse so consum'at, that it were impossible this satyrist should have hit on a more unreasonable mistake, than when he refin'd upon the qualifications of this illustrious Minister. You will meete in a certaine lett^r of the old Kings to his consort ye Q. Mother, that his M^atie long since had him in his thoughts for Secretary of State. But these topics were infinite, and 'tis no wonder that he should thus defame a Chancelor, who has been so bold as to dare to censure a crown'd head, and to call in question the procedure of the K. of Denmark about the affaire of Cornlitz Ulefield,* for which Monsr l'Abbé de Paulmyr has perstring'd him to ye purpose, and publish'd it in French, together with some observations of an English Gent. upon the relation of Sorbiere, in wch those unworthy & malicious imputations of *lascheté* & bassesse in ye nation is perfectly vindicated, even by citations onely of their owne French authors, as namely André du Chesne, du Verdier, Philippe de Commines, and others of no meane name & esti-

---

* Count Cornelius Ulefield Oxenstiern, Danish Prime Minister.

mation amongst their most impartial historians, sufficient to assert the courage & gallantry of the English, without mentioning the brave impressions the nation has made even into ye very bowells of their country, which after the winning of severall signal battails, they kept in subjection some hundreds of yeares.

You cannot escape the like choice which he made, by which to judge & pronounce of the worth of English bookes, by the learned collection he carried over with him of ye workes of that thrice noble Marchionesse,* no more then of his experience of the English dyet by the pottage he cate at my L. of Devonshires: but it is much after the rate of his other observations; or else he had not pass'd so desultorily our Universities & the Navy, wth a thousand other particulars worthy the notice & not to be excused in one pretending to make relations; to omitt his subtil reflections on matters of state, & medling with things he had nothing to do with: such as were those false & presumptuous suggestions of his that the Presbyterians were forsooth the sole restorers of ye King to his throne, and the palpable ignorance of our Historiograph Royal, where he pretends to render an accoumpt of

---

* Margaret Cavendish, Marchioness, afterwards Duchess of Newcastle, a very voluminous writer both in verse and prose. There are fourteen volumes of her works in thin folios.

divers antient passages relating to the English Chronicle: the jurisdiction and legislative power of Parliaments, which he mingles & compares with that of ye Kings to celebrate & qualifie his politicks: upon all which you have infinite advantages. It is true he was civily received by the Royal Society, as a person who had reco'mended him selfe to them by pretending he was secretary to an assembly of learned men formerly meeting at Monsr. Monmors at Paris; so as he had been plainely barbarous not to have acknowledged it by the mention he makes; whiles those who better know whose principles the Mushroom* is addicted to, must needes suspect his integrity; since there lives not on ye earth a person who has more disoblig'd it.

S^r, I am, &c.

Says-Court, 31 Octob. 1664.

P. S.

I know not how you may have design'd to publish y^r reflexions upon this disingenuous Traveller; but it would certainely be most co'municative & effectual in Latine, the other particular of his relation co'ming onely to those who understand the French, in which language it is already going to be printed.

---

* Mr. Hobbes.

To my Ld Viscount Cornebery.

My Lord,

Being late come home, imagine me turning over y^r close printed memoires, and shrinking up my shoulders; yet wth a resolution of surmounting the difficulty, animated with my Ld Chancelors & y^r Lo^{ps} com'ands, whom I am perfectly dispos'd to serve, even in the greatest of drudgeries, the translation of bookes.* But why call I this a drudgery? who would not be proud of the service? By the slight tast of it, I find God & the King concern'd, and I will in due tyme endeavour to p'sent y^r Lord^p & the world with the fruites of my obedience, cherefully, & with all due regards: nor is it small in my esteeme that God directs you to make use of me in any thing which relates to ye Church, though in my secular station. I began indeede (as y^r Lo^p well remembers) with that Essay on St. Chrysostome some yeares since upon that consideration, though prompted by a lugubrous occasion, such a one (though in no respect so greate a one) as what I but too sensibly perceive afflicts my L^d y^r father; for as I last beheld his countenance, in thought I saw the very shaft transfixing him; though the greatenesse of his minde, and pious

---

* Mysterie of Jesuitisme, & its pernicious consequences as it relates to Kings & States, w'h I published this yeare.

resignation* suffer him to do nothing weakely, and with passion.

Besides the divine precepts, & his Lops greate example, I could never receive any thing from philosophy that was able to add a graine to my courage upon these irremediless assaults like that Enchiridion & little weapon of Epictetus, *Nunquam te quicquam perdidisse dicito, sed reddidisse,* says he: *Filius obijt? redditus est;* it is in his 15th chap. Repeate it all to my Lord, and to yr selfe; you cannot imagine what that little target will encounter; I never go abroad without it in my pocket. What an incomparable guard is that τὰ στίχ' ἐϕ ἡμῖν! cap. 1. where he discourses of the things which *are* & *are not* in our power: I know, my Lord, you employ yr retirements nobly; 'weare this defensive for my sake, I had almost sayd this Christian office.

But, my Lord, I am told, we shall have no Lent indicted this yeare. I acknowledge, for all Dr Gunning,† that I much doubt of its apostolical institution: but I should be heartily sorry a practise so neere to it, so agreeable to antiquity, so usefull to devotion, and in sum so confirm'd by or

---

* Upon ye death of his sonne Edward, a very brave & hopefull young man.

†. Dr. Peter Gunning, Bishop of Ely. He died July 6, 1684, æt. 71.

laws, should now faile, & sinke, that his Matie and his laws are restor'd. I know not what subtile & political reasons there may be: It were better, flesh should be given away for a moneth or two to the poore in some greate proportion, and that particular men should suffer, than a sanction & a costome so decent should be weaken'd, not to say abrogated; believe 'twill not be so easy a thing to reasume a liberty of this nature, wch gratifies so many humours of all sorts. Because God gives us plenty, must we always riot? If those who sit at the helme harken to the murmurs of impertinent & avaritious men, pray God they never have cause to repent of the facility when 'tis too late. I know religious fasting dos not so much consist in ye species and quality as the quantity; nor in the duration, as the devotion: I have always esteemed abstinence *à tanto* beyond the fulfilling of periods & quadragessimas; nor is this of ours every where observ'd alike by Christians; but since all who are under that appellation do generaly keepe it where Christ is nam'd (I do not meane among the Romanists alone) a few imperfect reformers excepted; methinks a reverend & antient costome should not so easily be canceld; for so I look on it, if once we neglect the indiction. But were that for one fortnight, with a strict proclamation, & lesse indulgence to the *faulty* (as they call that shop of iniquity) and some other pretenders to liberty; in my opinion it would greately become the solemn, & aproching station of the Passion-weeke: and I would to God it were reduced but to that, that the irksomenesse might not deterr the more delicat, nor the prohibition those whose interest it is to sell flesh. We in this island have so natural a pretence to mingle this concerne of devotion into that of the state, that they might be both preserv'd without the least shadow of superstition; and if once o^r fishery were well retriev'd (than which nothing could be more popular, nor indeare the person who should establish it) the profit of that alone would soone create proselytes of the most zealous of our carniverous Samaritans. Why should there be an interruption of our laws for a yeare, to the infinite disadvantage of the Church of England in many reguards?

My L: You are a pious person, and the Lenten abstinence minds me of another incongruity that you Parliament-men will I hope reforme, & that is the frequency of our theatrical pastimes during that indiction. It is not allow'd in any city of Christendom so much as in this one towne of London, where there are more wretched & obscene plays permitted than in all the world besides. At Paris 3 days, at Rome 2 weekely, & at the other cittys of Florence, Venice, &c. but at certaine jolly periods of the yeare, and that not without some considerable emolument to ye publique; whiles our enterludes here are every day alike; so as the ladys & the gallants come reaking from the play late on Saturday night, to their Sonday devotions; the ideas of the farce possesses their fantsies to the infinite prejudice of devotion, besides the advantages it gives to our reprochfull blasphemers. Could not Friday, & Saturday be spar'd; or, if indulg'd, might they not be employ'd for the support of the poore, or as well the maintenance of some worke-house, as a few debauch'd comedians? What if they had an hundred pound p^r ann. lesse com'ing in; this were but policy in them; more than they were borne too, & the onely meanes to consecrate (if I may use the tearme) their scarse allowable impertinences. If my Lord Chancelor would be but instrumental in reforming this one exorbitancy, it would gaine both the King and his Lo^p multitudes of blessings. You know, my L^d, that I (who have written a play* & am a scurvy poet too some times) am far from Puritanisme; but I would have no reproch left our adversaries in a thing which may so conveniently be reform'd. Plays are now wth us become a licentious excesse, & a vice, & neede severe censors that should looke as well to their morality, as to their lines and numbers. Pardon

---

* *Thyrsander*, a tragi-comedy, mentioned in Evelyn's list of MSS. at the end of the third volume, which he would " write our faire and reforme if he had leasure."

this invective, my L: nothing but my perfect affection for y^r person & y^r vertue could have made me so intemperate; & nothing but my hopes that you will do the best you can to promote the greate interest of piety, & things worthy y^r excellent opportunities, could have render'd me thus prodigal of my confidence. Season my L^d y^r father with these desiderata to our consu'mat felicity; but still with submission & under protection for the liberty I assume; nor let it appeare presumption irremissable, if I add, that as I owne my Lord o^r illustrious Chancelor for my patron & benefactor; so I pay him as tender & awfull respect (abstracted from his greatenesse & the circumstances of that) as if he had a natural as he had a virtual & just dominion over me; so as my gratitude to him as his beneficiary, is even adopted into my religion, and 'till I renounce that, I shall never lessen of my duty; for I am ready to professe it, I have found more tendernesse, & greater humanity from the influences of his L^{op} than from all the relations I have now in the world, wherein yet I have many deare & worthy friends. My L. pardon againe this excesse, which I sweare to you, proceedes from the honest, & inartificial gratitude of,

    My Lord,
      Y^r &c.

London, 9 Feb. 1664-65.

To Sr Tho. Clifford
(afterwards Lord High Treasurer).

S^r,

Upon receipt of yours of the 17th instant, I repair'd to my L. Arlington, and from him to his Matie, who on sight of y^r lett^r added his particular com'ands, that upon arrival of ye prisoner I should im'ediately bring young Everse to him, and that then he would instruct me farther how he would have him treated; w^h I perceive will be wth greate respect, and some thinke wth liberty: for the other Captaine, that I should pursue his R^l Highnesses directions: and in order to this, I haue com'anded my Martial to be ready. I am sorry we are like to haue so many wounded men in their company, but I have taken all the care I can for their accom'odation: I pray send me a list of the names & qualities of our prisoners, they being so apt to contrive & forme stories of themselves, that they may pass for Embdeners or Danes: I thanke God all our affaires here are in good order: I did yesterday repaire to ye Commiss^rs of the Navy to remove the obstruction wch hinder'd our Receiver from touching the effects of o^r Privy Seale, they pretending a defect in the order, wch I have been faine to carry back to ye Council: Coll. Reymes writes for 700^l: S^r, here haue ben an host of women, making moane for their losse in the unfortunat

London:* I have wth much artifice appeas'd them for ye present, but they are really objects of much pitty; and I have counsel'd them to make choyce of some discreete person to represent to us their respective losses & expectations, that we may consider their cases without clamor and disturbance. S^r, I am ravish'd to heare o^r fleete is in so flourishing a condition, I pray God continue it and give you all successe. I would beg the presentment of my most humble duty to his Royall Hig^ss, and that you will grace wth y^r more particular com'ands,

S^r, y^r &c.

London, 2 Apr. 1665.

To D^r (afterwards Sir) CHRISTOPHER WREN, &c.

S^r,

You may please to remember that some tyme since I begg'd a favour of you in behalfe of my little boy: he is now susceptible of instruction, a pleasant, and (though I speake it) a most ingenious and pregnant child. My designe is to give him good education; he is past many initial difficulties. and conquers all things with incredible industry: do me that eternal obligation, as to enquire out and recom'end me some young man for a preceptor. I

---

* The London frigate, blown up by accident, with above 200 men. See vol. II. pp. 236, 240.

will give him £20 per ann. sallary, and such other accom'odations as shall be no ways disagreeable to an ingenuous spirit; and possibly I may do him other advantages: in all cases he will find his condition with us easy, his scholar a delight, & the conversation not to be despised: this obliges me to wish he may not be a morose, or severe person, but of an agreeable temper. The qualities I require are, that he be a perfect Grecian, and if more than vulgarly mathematical, so much the more aecomplish'd for my designe: myne owne defects in ye Greeke tongue and knowledge of its usefulnesse, obliges me to mention that particular with an extraordinary note: in sum I would have him as well furnish'd as might be for the laying of a permanent & solid foundation: the boy is capable beyond his yeares; and if you encounter one thus qualified, I shall receive it amongst the greate good fortunes of my life that I obtain'd it by the benefit of y^r friendship, for which I have ever had so perfect an esteeme. There is no more to be said, but that when you have found the person, you direct him im'ediately to me, that I may receive, and value him.

S^r, I am told by S^r Jo: Denham that you looke towards France this somer: be assur'd I will charge you wth some addresses to friends of mine there, that shall exceedingly cherish you; and though you will stand in no neede of my recom'endations, yet I am confident you will not refuse the offer of those civilities which I shall bespeake you.

There has layne at Dr Needham's a copy of ye Parallel* bound up for you, & long since design'd you, which I shall entreate you to accept; not as a recompence of your many favours to mee, much lesse a thing in the least assistant to you (who are y^rselfe a master), but as a toaken of my respect, as the booke itselfe is of the affection I beare to an art which you so happily cultivate.

Dear S^r, I am
Y^r &c.

Says-Court, 4 Apr. 1665.

To his Grace the Duke of ALBEMARLE.

May it please y^r Grace,

Being here at Douer for ye examining & auditing my accoumpts, as one of his M^aties Commissioners in this Kentish district; and finding that o^r prisoners at the Castle here, since their late attempt to escape through ye Magazine (over which till then they had a very spacious & convenient roome to lodge in) are now for want of accom'odation neces-

---

* " A Parallel of the Ancient Architecture with the Modern," written by Roland Freart, sieur de Cambray, and translated by Mr. Evelyn.

sitated to be kept in a very straite place, by meanes whereof they grow miserably sick, and are indeede reduced to a sad condition, which cannot be remedyed without extraordinary inconvenience to ye Lieutennant: My most humble suite to y^r Grace is, that you will be pleas'd to give order that they be conveyed to Chelsey Colledge; and the rather, that there being no greate number of them, it will be hardly worth the while & charge to maintaine officers for them here & particular guards: the condition of the poor men (who suffer for ye attempt of their more daring fellowes) is very deplorable, nor can it be prevented without enlargement of their quarters, which the Governor cannot spare them without danger. I have already inform'd y^r Grace how much we suffer by ye scruples of those vessels, who refuse to transport our recover'd men to ye fleete, which makes me againe to supplicate y^r Grace's fresh orders; it would infinitely conduce to his M^{aties} service: but of this, as of severall other particulars I shall render y^r Grace a more ample accoumt at my returne to London; where I shall not faile to do my duty as becomes,

   May it please y^r Grace,
      Y^r Grace's, &c.

Dover, 30 May, 1665.

To Sr Thomas Clifford.

S^r,

I was in precinct for my journey when y^r lett^r arriv'd, wch imparted to us that most glorious victory, in which you have had the honor to be a signal atchiever.* I pray God we may improve as it becomes us: his Royall Highn^ss being safe, becomes a double instance of rejoyceing to us; and I do not know that ever I beheld a greater and more sollem expression of it, unlesse it were that on his M^a^ties Restauration, than this whole City testified the last night, & which I cannot figure to you without hyperbolies. I am heartily sorry for those heros that are fallen, though it could not have been on a more transcendant occasion. S^r, I co'municated y^r lett^r to my L^d: Arlington, and to his M^a^tie, who read it greedily. My greatest solicitude is now how to dispose of ye prisoners in case you should be necessitated to put them in at the Downes, in order to which my Lord Duke of Albemarle has furnished me with 400 foote & a troop of horse, to be co'manded by me for guards if neede require; & I am just going to put all things in order. His Grace concludes wth me, y^t Dover Castle would be the most convenient place for their custody, but would by no meanes invade his R: Hig^sses particular

---

* For an account of this victory, see vol. II. p. 368.

province there without his Hig^sses: consent, & therefore advises me to write his High^ss: for positive co'mands to the Lieutenant. It is therefore my humble request that you will move him therein, it being of so greate importance at this time, & not onely for his Castle of Dover, but for the forts likewise neere it; & that (besides my owne guards) he would be pleas'd y^t a competent number of land souldiers might be sent with them from on board, to prevent all accidents, till they come safe to me; for it was so likewise suggested by his Grace, who dismiss'd me wth this expedient: "Mr. Evelyn," says he, "when we have fill'd all the goailes in ye country wth our prisoners, if they be not sufficient to containe them, as they sent our men to ye East Indies last yeare, we will send them to the West this yeare by a just retaliation." S^r, I thinke fit to let you understand, that I have 3 days since obtayn'd of the Council a Privy Seale, wch I moved might be £20,000, in reguard of ye occasion; together wth the use & disposal of the Savoy-Hospitall (w^h I am now repairing and fitting up, having given order for 50 beds to be new made, & other utensils), all which was graunted. I also obtain'd an Order of Councill for power both to add to our servants, & to reward them as we should see cause. His Matie: has sent me 3 chests of linnen, which he was pleas'd to tell me of himselfe before I knew they were gon; so mindfull & obliging he is, that nothing may be wanting. S^r, have no more to add, but the addresses of my most humble duty to his Royal Hig^{ss}: & my services to Mr Coventry from,

S^r, y^r &c.

Paynters Hall, Lond. 16 June, 1665.

To Sr Peter Wyche, Knt.*

S^r,

This crude paper (which beggs y^r pardon) I should not have presum'd to transmit in this manner, but to obey y^r co'mands, and to save the imputation of being thought unwilling to labour, though it be but in gathering straw. My greate infelicity is, that the meeting being on Tuesdays in ye afternoone, I am in a kind of despaire of ever gratifying myne inclinations, in a conversation w^h I so infinitely honor, & that would be so much to mine advantage; because the very houre interferes wth an employment, w^h being of publiq concernement, I can in no way dispense with: I mention this to deplore myne owne misfortune onely, not as it can signfie to any losse of yours; w^h cannot be sensible of so inconsiderable a member. I send you notwithstanding these indigested thoughts, and that attempt upon Cicero, wch you enjoin'd me.

---

* Chairman of a Committee appointed by the Royal Society to consider of the improvement of the English tongue.

I conceive the reason both of additions to, and the corruption of the English language, as of most other tongues, has proceeded from the same causes; namely, from victories, plantations, frontieres, staples of com'erce, pedantry of schooles, affectation of travellers, translations, fancy and style of Court, vernility & mincing of citizens, pulpits, political remonstrances, theatres, shopps, &c.

The parts affected wth it we find to be the accent, analogy, direct interpretation, tropes, phrases, and the like.

1. I would therefore humbly propose, that there might first be compil'd a Gram'ar for the præcepts; which (as did the Roman, when Crates tranferr'd the art to that city, follow'd by Diomedes, Priscianus, and others who undertooke it) might only insist on the rules, the sole meanes to render it a learned, & learnable tongue:

2. That with this a more certaine Orthography were introduc'd, as by leaving out superfluous letters, &c.: such as *o* in woomen, people; *u* in honour; *a* in reproach, *ugh* in though, &c.

3. That there might be invented some new periods, and accents, besides such as our gram'arians & critics use, to assist, inspirit, and modifie the pronunciation of sentences, & to stand as markes before hand how the voice & tone is to be govern'd; as in reciting of playes, reading of verses, &c. for the varying the tone of the voyce, and affections, &c.

4. To this might follow a Lexicon or collection of all the pure English words by themselves; then those w^h are derivative from others, with their prime, certaine, and natural signification; then, the symbolical: so as no innovation might be us'd or favour'd; at least 'till there should arise some necessity of providing a new edition, & of amplifying the old upon mature advice.

5. That in order to this, some were appointed to collect all the technical words; especialy those of the more generous employments: as the author of the " Essaies des Merveilles de la Nature, et des plus nobles Artifices," has don for the French; Francis Junius and others have endeavor'd for the Latine: but this must be gleaned from shops, not bookes; & has ben of late attempted by Mr. Moxon.*

6. That things difficult to be translated or express'd, and such as are as it were, inco'mensurable one to another: as determinations of weights and measures; coines, honors, national habits, armes, dishes, drinkes, municipal constitutions of courts; old, and abrogated costomes, &c. were better interpreted than as yet we find them in dictionaries, glossaries, and noted in the lexicon.

7. That a full catalogue of exotic words, such as are daily minted by our *Logodædali,* were exhibited,

---

* In the second volume of his " Mechanick Exercises."

and that it were resolved on what should be sufficient to render them current, *ut Civitate donentur;* since without restraining that same *indomitam novandi verba licentiam,* it will in time quite disguise the language: there are some elegant words introduc'd by physitians chiefely and philosophers, worthy to be retained; others, it may be, fitter to be abrogated; since there ought to be a law, as well as a liberty in this particular. And in this choyce, there would be some reguard had to the well sounding, and more harmonious words, and such as are numerous, and apt to fall gracefully into their cadences and periods, and so recommend themselves at the very first sight as it were; others, which (like false stones) will never shine, in whatever light they be placed; but embase the rest. And here I note, that such as have lived long in Universities doe greately affect words and expressions no where in use besides, as may be observed in Cleaveland's Poems for Cambridg: and there are also some Oxford words us'd by others, as I might instance in severall.

8. Previous to this it would be enquir'd what particular dialects, idiomes, and proverbs were in use in every several county of England; for the words of ye present age being properly the *vernacula,* or classic rather, special reguard is to be had of them, and this consideration admits of infinite improvements.

9. And happly it were not amisse, that we had a collection of ye most quaint and courtly expressions, by way of *florilegium,* or phrases distinct from the proverbs: for we are infinitely defective as to civil addresses, excuses, & formes upon suddaine and unpremeditated (though ordinary) encounters: in which the French, Italians, & Spanyards have a kind of natural grace & talent, which furnishes the conversation, and renders it very agreeable: here may come in synonimes, homoinymes, &c.

10. And since there is likewise a manifest rotation and circling of words, which goe in & out like the mode & fashion; bookes would be consulted for the reduction of some of the old laydaside words and expressions had formerly *in delicijs;* for our language is in some places sterile and barren, by reason of this depopulation, as I may call it; and therefore such places should be new cultivated, and enrich'd either wth the former (if significant) or some other: for example, we have hardly any words that do so fully expresse the French *clinquant, naïveté, ennuy, bizarre, concert, façoniere, chicaneries, consummé, emotion, defer, effort, chocq, entours, débouche;* or the Italian *vaghezze, garbato, svelto,* &c. Let us therefore (as ye Romans did the Greeke) make as many of these do homage as are like to prove good citizens.

11. Something might likewise be well translated out of the best orators & poets, Greek and

Latin, and even out of ye moderne languages; that so some judgement might be made concerning the elegancy of ye style, and so a laudable & unaffected imitation of the best reco'mended to writers.

12. Finaly, there must be a stock of reputation gain'd by some public writings and compositions of ye Members of this Assembly, and so others may not thinke it dishonor to come under the test, or accept them for judges and approbators: and if ye designe were ariv'd thus far, I conceive a very small matter would dispatch the art of rhetoric, which the French propos'd as one of the first things they reco'mended to their late academitians.

I am, S^r:

Y^r most, &c.

Says-Court, 20 June, 1665.

To my Lord Viscount CORNEBERY.

My Lord,

Those who defin'd history to be *Disciplina composita de bono practico obtinendo* pointed us to that use of it which every wise man is to make of it by his reading of authors. But as it is the Narration *Rerum gestarum* (for whatever is matter of fact is the subject of history), your L^p cannot expect I should at this distance from my study, & bookes of that kind, be able to present you with so compleate a series of authors as you require of me; much lesse such a method as y^r affection for so noble a resolution, and so becoming a greate person, does truely merit. However, that this may not be looked on as an excuse, and that I may in some measure obey y^r L^ps com'ands, I shall as far as my talent, and my faithlesse memory serves me at present, give y^r Lo^p the names of those authors which haue deservedly been esteemed the most worthy and instructive of those greate and memorable actions of the ages past.

A Recention of y^r Greeke Historians from the reigne of Cyrus (before which we have nothing of credible in any prophane history) 'til after Justinian, and ye confusion of ye Roman Empire by the Goths and Vandals:

1 Herodotus.
2 Thucydides.
3 Xenophon.
4 Polybius.
5 Diodorus Siculus.
6 Dionysius Halicarnassus.
7 Josephus.
8 Arrianus.
9 Appianus.
10 Dion-Cassius.
11 Herodian.
12 Zosimus.
13 Procopius.
14 Agathias, &c.

The Latine Historians from ye foundation of Rome to the death of the Emperor Valens: Sallust, Cæsar, Titus Livius, Vellejus Paterculus, Quintus Curtius, Tacitus, Florus, Suetonius, Justinus, Ammianus Marcellinus, &c.

To these may be superadded, Plutarch, Diogenes Laertius, Philostratus, and Eunapius, among the

Greekes; Cornelius Nepos, Æmilius Probus, Spartianus, Lampridius, and the Augustæ Scriptores, of the Latine, &c.: but for being more mix'd, and lesse methodical, they would haply be read in another order; and if the Greekes have happly written more even of the Roman story than the Romans themselves, it is what is universaly knowne and acknowledg'd by the learned; which has made the enumeration of the one, to exceede the mention of ye latter. These are, my L^d. sufficient to afford y^r L^p: a fairer & more ample course, then any of y^r quality usualy pretend to; being the best, & most worthy consideration both as to ye grandeur of examples, and politure of the language. As to the later period, from Valens and the Gotie Emperors to our times, I shall furnish y^r curiosity, when you have finish'd this stage; for it were now, my L^d. to discourage you, the very calling over the names of so many; how much more, should I add (what y^r L^{sps} curiosity will desire to dip into, to emerge a compleate historian) the Biographi, or writers of particular lives, relations, negotiations, memoires, &c. which are things apart, and that properly come within the series of ye more solid and illustrious historians: onely as to that of Chronologie, I conceive it of absolute necessity, that y^r L^{sp} joyne it with all y^r readings together with some geographical author & guide, whose tables, mapps, and discoveries both for the antient & modern names, situations & boundaries of ye places, you shall with incredible advantage consult, to fix and make it y^r owne. Scaliger's Emendatio Temporum, Petavii Rationarium, Calvisius, Helvicus, or our Isaacson,[*] may suffice to assist you, with Cluverius, our Peter Heylin, and the late accurate atlasses set forth by Bleau. To these may be added as necessary subsidiaries; H. Stephens's Historical Dictionary set lately forth in London; and if your L^p thinke fit to pursue the cycle with more expedition, which were likewise to gratifie y^r curiosity by a preparation that will furnish you with a very useful prospect, before you engage y^r selfe on ye more particulars, there is in English one Howel (not James) who has published a very profitable Compendium of Universal History, so far as he has brought it; to which you may joyne what Bp. Usher has set forth in two volumes, containing the annales of all the memorable actions & passages which have happened in the Church from the creation, mingled wth divers secular passages of rare remarke, and which may serve you instead of Baronius, or any of his voluminous epitomizers, Spondanus, Peruginus, &c. And by that time y^r L^p is arriv'd thus far, you will have perform'd more than any man of y^r quality can pretend to in Court, by im'ense degrees, according to my

---

[*] Henry Isaacson, author of the " Chronological Series of the four Monarchies." Folio, London, 1633.

weake observation, who sometimes passe my time at the circle where the gallants produce themselves with all their advantages, & (God knows) small furniture, Nor will it be difficult for you to goe through the rest with delight & ease, whether you would begin at ye present age, and reade upwards, 'till you meete wth the period where you left off (which is Grotius's advise to Mon^r Maureliq), or proceede in that order in which you began: but, my Lord, of this, as of whatever else you shall judge me worthy to serve you in, I shall endeavour to p'sent y^r Lo^p with something more material, & better digested, when you please to co'mand, my L^d,

Y^r Lordship's, &c.

Cornebery, 21 June 1665.

To my Ld. Viscount CORNEBERY, Ld Chamberlaine to her Matie, &c.

My Lord,

I should be exceedingly wanting to my duty, and to the interest you pleas'd to allow me in y^r friendship, not to preserve it by such acknowledgements as are due to you by infinite obligations: and if this have not been done oftener, distance, and the many circumstances of a jealous intercourse, will easily obtaine y^r mercy; for I sweare to you, my Lord, there breathes not a man upon earth who has a greater value for y^r noble person; because I have establish'd it upon y^r virtues, and that which shines in you above titles, and adjuncts, wch I reguard but as the shadows of greate men; nothing constituent of good & realy permanent. But, my L^d: I intend not here a panegyric, where haply an epithalamium were due, if what has been lately told me, of y^r L^{ps} being newly married, or shortly re-entring into those golden-fetters, be true.* But can y^r L^p think of such a felicity, and not com'and me to celebrate it? not as a poet (for I know not w^t it meanes) but as one perfectly devoted to y^r good fortune; since that glory must needes be in my mouth, which already is so profoundly engraven in my heart. I thought indeede that golden key which I saw ty'd to y^r side by that silken riban, was the forerunner of some other knot, constant as the colour, and bright as the mettall. My L^d: I joy'd you at Hampton-Court for ye one, and I

---

* Henry Hyde, Lord Cornbury, eldest son of Sir Edward Hyde, Earl of Clarendon, whom he succeeded in his titles and estate Dec. 29, 1674, had two wives. The first was Theodosia, daughter of Arthur Capel, Earl of Essex, beheaded for his loyalty to King Charles I.; and the second, alluded to by Evelyn, was Flower, widow of Sir William Backhouse of Swallowfield, Berks, Bart. by whom he had no issue. By this marriage Lord Cornbury became possessed of the manor and house at Swallowfield. The celebrated Lord Chancellor Clarendon resided at his son's house after his retirement from public life, and there wrote his great work " The History of the Rebellion."

would joy you from Says-Court for the other; you have in the first a dignity conspicuous for ye ornament it receives from y^r vertues; but in the second onely, a reward of them above the pearles, & the rubies: 'tis a price which Fortune owes y^r L^p: and I can celebrate her justice without flattery. Long may you live under her happy empire. When I am certaine of ye particulars, I will string more roses on this chaplet, and make you a country gardener's present; if the anxiety of being at this distance from a person whose influence is so necessary, do not altogether wither my genius.

But, my Ld. give me now leave to entertaine you a little wth mine owne p^{r}ticular condition; since as contraries illustrate one another, it cannot but improve y^r happinesse.

After 6978 (and possibly halfe as many more conceil'd) which the pestilence has mow'd downe in London this weeke; neare 30 houses are visited in this miserable village, whereof one has beene the very neerest to my dwelling: after a servant of mine now sick of a swelling (whom we have all frequented, before our suspicion was pregnant) & which we know not where will determine; behold me a living monument of God Almighty's protection and mercy! It was Saturday last 'ere my courageous wife would be persuaded to take the alarme; but she is now fled, with most of my family; whilest my conscience, or something which I would have taken for my duty, obliges me to this sad station, 'till his M^atie take pitty on me, and send me a considerable refreshment for the comfort of these poore creatures, the sick & wounded seamen under mine inspection through all the ports of my district. For mine own particular, I am resolv'd to do my duty as far as I am capable, & trust God with the event; but the second causes should coöperate: for in sum, my L^d, all will, and must fall into obloquy & desolation, unlesse o^r supplys be speedily settled on some more solid fonds to carry this important service on. My Bro: Com^r S^r W^m D'Oily after an accoumpt of £17,000 is indebted about £6000, and my reckoning comes after it apace. The prisoners of warr, our infirmatories, and the languishing in 12 other places; the charge of sallaries to physitians, chyrurgeons, officers, medicaments, & quarters, require speedy & considerable supplies;—lesse than £2000 a weeke will hardly support us. And if I have been the more zealous & descriptive of this sad face of things, & of the personal danger I am expos'd to, it is because I beg it may be an instance of y^r goodnesse & charity to reade this article of my letter to my Ld: y^r Father, who I know has bowels, and may seriously represent it to his M^atie and my L: High Treasurer. For, my L^d, having made mine attempts at Court by late expresses on this occasion, I am driven to lay this appeale at his Lo^ps feete, because having had

experience of his favour in mine owne concerne
& private affaires, I addresse my selfe wth a confidence I shall succeede now that it imports the
publiq. I dare not apply w^t St Paule sayd to Timothy (because it dos not become me), but give me
liberty to alude: I know none (amongst all o^r
Court great-ones) like minded, who dos naturaly
care for our state. The consectary is ———; for
all seeke their owne. 'Tis, my L^d, a sad truth, & this
no time to flatter; we should succumb under the
poiz but for some few such Atlasses as are content
to accept of the burthen wth the honor; which
though it makes it sit heavy, makes it sit with a
good conscience, & the expectation of a blessing.
I am a plaine country gent^n: yet heare, & see, and
observe, as those in the valies best discerne the
mountaines; this nation is ruin'd for want of acti-
vity on our parts; religion & gratitude on all.
But, my L^d, I tirannize y^r patience; pardon the
excesse; I have not often ye opportunity, and God
knows when I may enjoy another, who daily carry
my life in my hands. If the malignity of this sad
contagion spend no faster before winter, the calamity will be indicible.—But let me now acquainte
y^r Lo^p how I passe those moments wch my assiduous prayers to God for y^r prosperity, & my service
of his M^atie do not take up. It is now about 2
moneths since I consign'd a large epistle to Royston: for y^t piece y^r Lo^p enjoyn'd me to publish in

consequence of the former, and which I have made bold to inscribe to my Ld: Chancellor, under somewhat an ænigmatical character, because of the invidiousenesse of ye argument. The booke it selfe was quite finish'd, & wrought off; but Royston being fled, and the presses dissolv'd, we cannot hope to get o^r freedome, till it please God in mercy to abate ye contagion. This is that w^h hinders us from y^t most incomparable piece of Mr. Stillingfleete's friend against Searjeant, and divers other particulars, w^h though printed will not as yet be publish'd;—both venders, & buyers, & readers, being universaly scathed. As to o^r philosophical concernes, Dr Wilkins, Sr Wm Petty, & Mr. Hooke, wth our operator, live all together at my Ld Geo. Barclay's at Durdans neere my Brother, where they are excogitating new rigging for ships, new charriots, & new ploughs, &c. so as I know not of such another happy conversation of Virtuosi in England. And now I mention'd my Bro: I were ungratefull to omit my acknowledgement of the infinite honor he tells me my Ld: Chancelor was pleas'd to do me, before so many persons of quality and gent: of our county of Surrey as came in to waite on him at Farnham, at my Ld Bishops of Winchester table; when his Lo^p was pleas'd to mention me with an eulogy, and kindnesse so particular & obliging, as I can never hope to merite from his goodnesse. But I would esteeme it the most fortunate day in my

life y^t should present me with an occasion, in which I might signalize my prone & most ardent inclynations to his service, as being professedly more engag'd to his Lo^p than to any person living in this world. And if God heare the humble prayers w^h I poure out for the continuance of y^r prosperity, I shall have perform'd but my duty, who am wth a most unfained resignation,   My Ld:
Y^r, &c.

Says-Court, 9th Sepr. 1665.

To my Ld Viscount CORNEBERY, Ld Chamberlaine to her Matie.

My L^d:

By this most agreeable opportunity I continue to p'sent y^r Lo^p with my faithfull service, and if it arrive seasonably to supplicate y^r L^{ps} pardon for the style, the mistake, and the length of mine of the ninth instant: it will excite in you different passions, and *one*, my L^d, not an unpleasant one. Smile at my intelligence, and pity all the rest; for it will deserve it, and find a way to y^r noble breast. My servant (whom I there mention to have sent from my house for feare of the worst) will recover, and proves sick only of a very ougly surfeit; wch not only frees me fro' infinite apprehensions, but admitts me to give my Wife a visite, who is at my Brother's, and within a fortnight of bringing me my seaventh sonne: and it is time, my L^d, he were borne; for they keepe us so short of monys at Court, that his Maties Commiss^rs had neede of one to do wonders, and heale the sick and wounded by miracle, 'till we can maintaine o^r chyrurgeons. My Ld: I do not forget y^r injunction of waiting on you this moneth at Cornebery; but I am momentarily threatned to be hurried to the sea-side againe, after this conflict of my Ld Sandwich;—and the woman in the straw I would gladly see out of perill. I will not question y^r L^sps being at Oxford this approaching reconvention of Parliam^t: My Father-in-law waites there, and it must go ill wth me if I kisse not y^r hands. Just now I heare the gunns from the Tower: this petty triumph revives us much; but the miserably afflicted Citty, and euen this o^r poore village, want other consolations; my very heart turnes within me at the contemplation of our calamity. God give the repentance of David, to ye sinns of David! We have all added some weights to this burthen; ingratitude, and luxurie, and the too, too soone oblivion of miracles.

The Almighty preserve y^r Lo^p, and my best friend in the world my most hon^rd Ld Chancelor. I would say a thousand affectionate things more to conjure y^r Lop^s belief, that I am,

My L:, y^r &c.

Says-Court, 12 Sepr 1665.

Sir Philip Warwick to John Evelyn, Esquire.

Cousen,

I am to seek how to answere your letter; for without passing any compliment vpon you how much I am concern'd in yo{r} safty, w{ch} I find endangered by y{r} employment—without professing how sensible I am, that scarce any perticular in the Nauy ought to haue that care & tendernes wait vpon it as the sick and wounded men, and the prisoners, though a lesse regard in respect I heare ours are not soe well used; and that the Emb{r} serv{t} seems to take such little care for exchanges, as if he meant to burthen vs w{th} them: and that these fellowes are soe stuborne they will not worke, nay beat any that will—yet a shame it is if they be not in the proportion the King allowes them prouided for. The ill effect of both these I acknowledge if they be neglected. And when I haue said this you'll wonder what I can say next, that my Lord Treas'r makes not the prouision. S{r}: I must say, though I offend my good friend S{r} George Carteret, that from the first my Lord Treasurer told him this charge was a cheife part of the expence of the Nauy, & by his assignm{ts} to be prouided for. It was the first sin transferring faults one from another; & therefore I am asham'd to be making such returnes, & know that will as little feed the hungry & cloath the naked, as a mouth that's open w{th} a benediction & a hand closed wth the money. And yet how to make you judge of this I cannot, w^thout showing you how the whole Royall ayde is distributed. (And this I assure you, the distribution of the whole 2,500,000^li is not of perticular concerne vnto me, fine p'd

	£.
Of the Citty for the Nauy before the Parl^t borrowed - - - - - - - - -	200000
Of the Dunkirk mony - - - - -	050000*
13 Counties wholy assigned - - - -	1277604
County of Bucks for the Nauall Reg^t -	0047346
The first 3 months of all the other counties	0096047
Vpon 17 other counties 102^milli & 40^milli	
And now lately the dispute being that he had noe proper assignm^t for the sick & wounded, my Lord told him he would assigne him 28,000^li of those counties particularly for them - - -	0170000
but I feare that will not doe you any seruice, Sr George saying the assignm^t being upon the 3^d yeare, he cannot borrow vpon it.	
This hath bin already the Nauys portion of the Royal ayde - - - - - -	1840997

---

* This to be repaid.

		£.
Ordnance hath had assigned vnto it	-	0367686
Guards hath counties sett out for	- -	0170616
Garrisons - - - - - - - - -		0045121
Wardrobe had on Wales - - - - -		0025000

Rem: on the 17 counties 50^{mli} } 109^{mli} 0608423
     on Wales - - 59

And now do you see by whose friendship you have receiued that small refreshment, wch I say not to diminish his kindnes, but to shew you that properly you were a care of Mr. Vice Chamberlin's.

                 Totall   2449420
                 Rem: 0109000
                           2558420

All I can adde is, my Lord T'rer will endeavor to dispose the Vice Chamberlin; & if it be in his power, for I thinke him as much overlayed as others, I doubt not he'l vnd^{r}take yor charge. And because the assignm^t wch remaynes to be made vpon Wales, wch is about 30,000^{li} for the second yeare & the first quarter of the third, may better please him, my Lord T'rer will offer him that, or offer it to S^r W^m D'Oyly & yo^{r}selfe, if you can procure credit vpon it. He'l make an essay whether out of the present prizes (wch if his Ma^{t}y will not employ to this vse, being a better fond of credit, he may be repaied from this assignm^t) he can get you a consid^ble sum. His Lo^p is ready to assigne out of Wales or the 17 counties 50,000^li for this seruice singly. And if I could give you a better & more perticular account I would, for I valew both yours and Sr William's integrities & informations soe much, you may both assure yo^rselues I'l not be wanting. And am really sensible of your cares & dangers, wch we want not (being for all comers) euen here; but being in our station & depending on Prouidence, I hope none of vs shall miscarry. Wee are now seperated & in motion, but I'l hast the resolution. In the mean time you may reserue this to y^rselfe. Only co'municate it to S^r W^m D'Oyly, to whom I cannot at present write, for hauing receiued yor l'res but late this night, and the post goeing away in the morning, & I have to send my l'r six myle thither. I begge his pardon & yours, & remayne, wth all truth & affection,

Y^r most faithf^l
kinsman & serv^t,
P. WARWICK.

Stratton, Sept. 16, 1665, 8 at Night.

To Sir PHILIP WARWICK, Secretary to my Lord High Treasurer.

S^r,

Your favour of the 16th current from Stratton, has not only inlightened mine eyes, but confirm'd my reason; for sure I am I durst write nothing to you which would cary in it the least diffidence of y^r most prudent œconomy; and you are infinitely mistaken in me if y^u thinke I have not establish'd my opinion of y^r sincerity & candor in all that you transact, upon a foundation very remote from what the world dos ordinarily build upon: I am sufficiently satisfied to whose care our supplies did naturaly belong: for I do not believe the sums we have received to carry on our burthen thus far (trifling as they have been compar'd to ye occasion) proceeded from his (Sir George's) good nature (w^h I have been much longer acquainted with then you), but to shift the clamor wch our necessities have compell'd us to; whilst our task-masters exacted brick without allowing us straw. And if I have express'd any thing to you in a style more zealous then ordinary, it has been to lay before you a calamity wch nothing can oppose but a suddaine supply; and for that my Ld Arlington (to whom I have frequently said as much) directed me to the proper object. Nor was what I writ a prophesy at adventure: One fortnight has made me feele the uttmost of miseries that can befall a person in my station and wth my affections : To have 25,000 prisoners, & 1500 sick & wounded men to take care of, without one peny of mony, and above £2000 indebted : It is true, I am but newly acquainted wth buisinesse, and I now find the happy difference betwixt speculation and action to the purpose; learning that at once, wch others get by degrees; but I am sufficiently punish'd for the temerity, and I acknowledge the burthen insupportable: Nor indeede had I been able to obviate this impetuous torrent, had not his Grace the Duke of Albemarle and my L^d: Sandwich (in pure compassion of me) unanimously resolv'd to straine their authority, and to sell (though not a full quorum) some of ye prizes, & breake bulke in an Indian ship, to redeeme me from this plunge: and all this, for the neglect of his personal care—whom you worthily perstringe, though for domestiq respects & other relations they were not willing to expresse their resentiments. S^r, I am in some hopes of touching y^e £5000 some day this weeke; but w^t is that, to ye expense of £200 ye day? Is there no exchange or pecuniary redemption to be propos'd? or is his Matie resolv'd to maintaine the armies of his enemyes in his owne boosome? whose idlenesse makes them sick, and their sicknesse redoubles the charge! 'I am amaz'd at this method, but must hold my tongue. Why might not yet the French, who are numerous in this last action (and in my conscience have enough of the sea) be sent home to their master, not to gratifie but plague him wth their unprofitable numbers?

S^r, I most humbly acknowledge your goodnesse for the confidence you have in me, and for that *Arcanum,* the accoumpt of the disposure & assignement of this prodigious Royall ayd of £2,500,000 which you have so particularly imparted to me, & that I should have preserv'd wth all due caution, though you had enjoyn'd me none. If I obtaine this small sum of £5000 it will be a breathing till I can meete my Bro: Commis^rs at Oxford, whither I am sum'on'd to joyne for ye effects and settlements of some of those more solid appointments mention'd in y^r audit, & which you have promis'd to promote, & therefore I will trouble you no further at present, then to let y^u know, that upon that account of y^r encouragement (I meane the providence of God & my sole desires of serving him in any thing which I hope he may accept, for I sweare to you no other consideration should tempt me a second time to this trouble) I am resolv'd to maintaine my station, and to refuse nothing that may contribute to his Mat^ies service, or concerne my duty, who am, S^r, y^r, &c.

Says-Court, 30 Sepr 1665.

England where we have supported this burthen, there should not have been a sufficient fond consecrated & assign'd as a sacred stock for so important a service; since it has been a thing so frequently & earnestly press'd to their Lo^ps; and that this is not an affaire which can be menag'd without p^rsent monyes to feede it; because we have to deale with a most miserable indigent sort of people, who live but from hand to mouth, & whom we murther if we do not pay daily or weekely; I meane those who harbor our sick and wounded men and sell bread to our prisoners of war. How we have behav'd o^rselves for his M^aties advantage and honor, we are most ready to produce the accoumpts, and to stand to ye comparison of what it cost a former Usurper, & a power which was not lavish of their expenses. Let it please y^r Honor to consider of ye premises, and if you can believe I retaine so much of servile in me, as to informe you of tales, or designe to magnifie my owne merits (whatever my particular & private sufferings have been), let me be dismiss'd wth infamy; but let me beg of y^r Hon^r to receive first the relation of his M^aties principal Officers & Commiss^rs of the Navy which accompanies the paper of,

     Right Honble,
       Y^r, &c.

Says-Court, 2 Octob: 1665.

To SAMUEL PEPYS, Esq. Clerk of the Admiralty, and one of the principal officers of his Majesty's Navy, &c.

S^r,

I have according to your com'ands sent you an hasty draught of the Infirmary, and project for Chatham, the reasons, & advantages of it; which challenges your promise of promoting it to the use design'd: I am myselfe convinc'd of the exceeding benefit it will every way afford us. If, upon examination of the p^{r}ticulars, and y^r intercession, it shall merit a recom'endation from ye rest of the principall officers, I am very confident the effects will be correspondent to the pretence of the papers which I transmit to accompany it. In all events, I have don my endeavour; and, if upon what appeares demonstrable to me (not without some considerable experience, and collation with our officers, discreete & sober persons) I persist in my fondnesse to it, from a prospect of the singular advantages wch would be reaped by setting it on foote, I beseech you to pardon my honest endeavours, wth the errors of,

S^r, Y^r, &c.

Says-Court, 3 Jan. 1665-6.

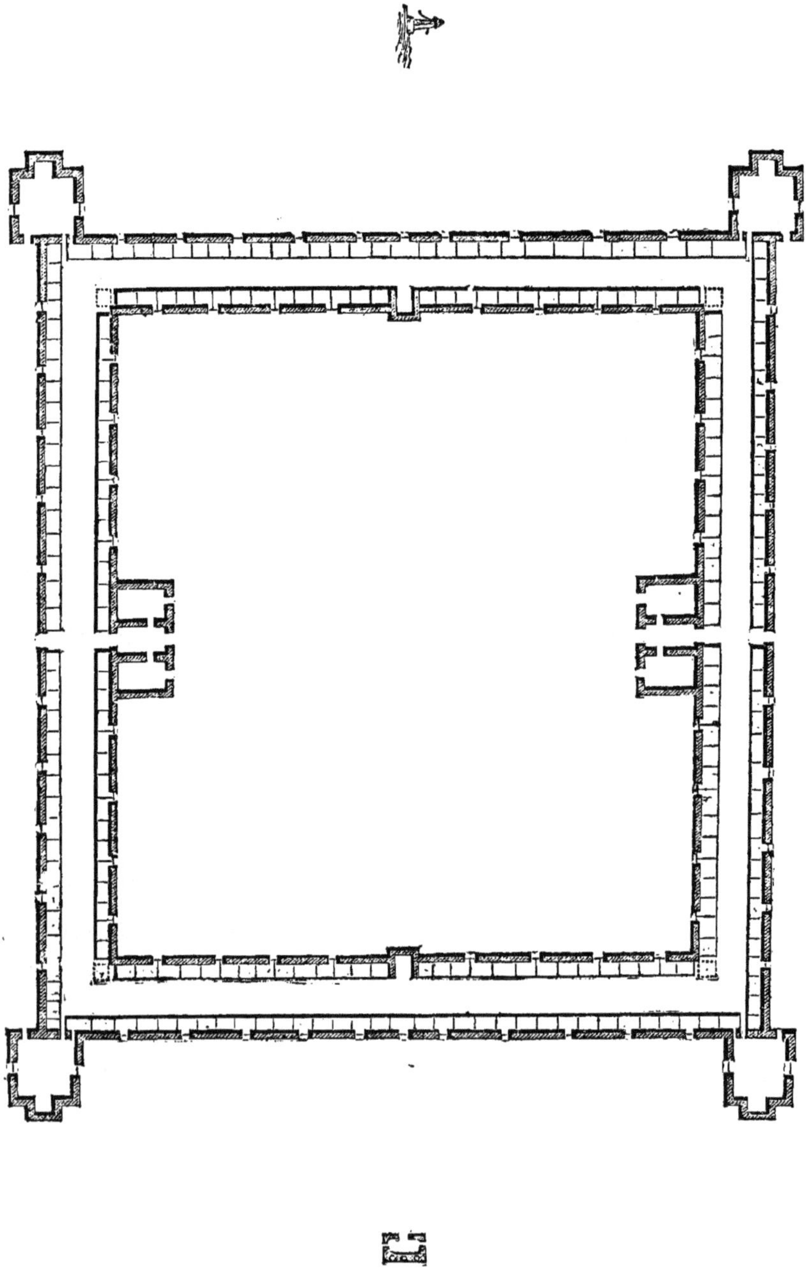

S$^r_;$ Sayes Court, 26 Mar. 1666.

I know not wth what successe I have endeavord to performe y^r com'ands; but it has ben to the uttmost of my skill, of wch you are to be my judges: The favour I bespeake of you is, y^r pardon for not sending it before: I have not enjoy'd one minute's repose since my returne (now a fortnight past) 'till this very morning; having ben ever since soliciting for a little monye to preserve my miserable flock from perishing. On Saturday, very late, I dispatch'd Mr. Barber towards my Kentish circle, where our sick people are in quarters; and at his returne, I hope to present you a compleate accompt; but 'till this instant morning I had not written one line of those tedious papers; so that if through hast (the parent of mistakes) there may happly appeare some escapes, giue pardon to y^r servant; or let me purchase it with this small present of fragments (such yet as you haue been pleas'd to accept) and a little booke, that I also recom'end to excuse my expense of such leasure as I can redeeme from the other impertinences of my life. As to ye report w^h I send you, I would receive it as a favour; howeuer y^r resolutions of putting it in execution may succeede, (the tyme of yeare being so farr elaps'd, in reguard of action, and more im'ediate vse) it might yet be gracefully presented to his Royall H^{sse}, or rather indeede, to his Matie himself, who has so frequently ben pleas'd to take notice of it to me as an acceptable project, because it would afflict me to have them thinke I haue either ben remisse, or trifling in my proposall. This obligation I can onely hope for from your dexterity, addresse, and friendship, who am,

  S^r,
    Y^r most affectionate
     and humble servant,
       J. EVELYN.

S. Pepys, Esq.

S^r, there is nothing in ye other paper w^h y^u com-'anded me to returne; but what is included in these, wth ample and (I hope) considerable improvements.

I must beg a copy of those papers when ye clearkes are at leasure, hauing never a duplicate by me; and it may happly neede a reviewe.

S^r, the bearer hereoff, Roger Winne, being o^r messenger (and without whose services I cannot possibly be, hauing so frequent occasions of sending him about businesse belonging to my troublesome employment) dos by me supplicate y^r protection, that he may not be pressed, of which he is hourely in danger as he travells about o^r affaires, without y^r p^{r}ticular indulgence w^h I therefore conjure you to let him have under y^r hand and signature.

S^r, Sayes-Court, 26 Mar: 1666.

If to render you an account of the progresse of my late proposal be any testimony of my obedience to y^r com'ands; be pleas'd to belieue that I most faithfully present it in these papers according to the best of my talent. And if you find the estimate considerably to exceede the first calculation, you will remember that it was made to ye meridian of London; that the walles were both by his M^{atie} and the directions of the principall officers to be made thicker and higher; that the materials and workemen were presum'd to be found much cheaper in the country; and that the place and area to build on was suppos'd a level. But it has fallen out so much to our prejudice, and beyond all expectation in these particulars; that to commence with the ground, we could not in 4 or 5 miles walking about Chatham and Rochester, find one convenient spot that would beare a level of 200 foote square, vnlesse it were one field beyond the dock, in the occupation of Mr. Commissioner Pett neere the bogg and marsh, which has neither solid foundation, nor fresh water to it. There is a very handsome greene close at the end of the Long Rope-house towards Chatham: but the declivity is so suddaine and greate to the west, that lesse then a ten foote raising will not bring it to such a rectitude as that we can lay our plate vpon the wall, which will be a considerable trouble and charge to reforme, as may easily be demonstrated: ffor either the earth must be so much abated towards the east, or the wall advanc'd to the height of neare 20 foote, whiles one extreame of the roofe will touch the superficies of the earth: Besides the field is not above 150 feet wide. But supposing all this might be encounter'd (as indeede it might wth charge) it bordures so neere to the rope-houses, the dock, and that ample way leading to it from the hill-house and Chatham, as might endanger his M^{aties} people in case of any contagion, because it will be impossible to restraine them from sometimes mingling amongst the workemen and others, who haue employment in the dock, when ye convalessent men shall be able, or permitted to walke abroad. This, and some other difficulties, made vs quit the thoughts of that otherwise gracefully-situated place. After many other surveyes, we at last pitch'd on a field call'd the Warren, just beneath the Mill, and reguarding the north towards the river. The accesse is com'odious; it has a well of excellent water, ready dugg, and wanting onely repaires; and though this ground be likewise somewhat vneven, yet, with helpe, it will carry about 240 feet in length, and 150 in breadth, allowing the filling vp of some vallies and depressures of about 4 or 5 foote deepe, to be taken from severall risings. This, for many reasons, I conceive to be the fittest for our purpose, it having also a solid foundation on ye chalke, and being at a competent distance from all dangerous commerce with the towne, which will greately contribute to ye health of the sick, and protection of the inhabitants; but being at present in lease to the Chest, leaue must be obtayn'd, and the tennant, who now rents it, satisfied; in all which Mr. Commissioner Pett (whose direction and assistance I tooke, according to y^r injunctions) informes me, there will be no difficulty.

Vpon examination of the Materials on the place:

	£.	s.	d.
Bricks will not be delivered at the place under	00	18	00
Lime p^r load cont. 32 bushells, p^r M -	00	16	00
Drift sand, by tonn - - -	00	00	14
Tyles, p^r M delivered - - -	01	01	00
Heart lathes, p^r load, cont. 36 bundles -	02	10	00
Sawing, p^r c - - - -	00	03	04
Workmen sufficient, in wch was our greate mistake	00	02	06

Vpon those Materials we conceiv'd thus of the Scantlings:
Walles at 1 brick ½.

Walle-plates	-	-	9 in. 5				
Pr p^ll rafters	-	-	9	6 middle 16½ f. long.			
			11	7 ends.			
Single rafters	-	-	4½	3½			
Purlins	-	-	9	6	-	-	17
Binding-beames	-	-	12	12			
Windo-frames	-	-	4½	3½	-	4	2
Dore-cases in brickwork, single							in.
doores	-	-	-	7	6 - - 6	2	8

The two outward double, w^th
architrave - - 7 6 - - 9 9 4
Ground-flo. g'ist - - 4 4 - - 18
  And if stone-floares to the 4 corner-roomes, as has been since judg'd more co'modious, the
G'ists - - - - 8 3
So' men - - - - 14 11
  Besides partitions, posts, interstisse, quartarage.

At those scantlings, together wth the alteration of the walles for height and thicknesse, &c.

Every rod of square brick-worke solid, at 1½ br. thick, cont. in br. of 9 inch. aboue 12 br. long, to 16½ f. in height; 15 br. to every 3 f. high, which to 16½ is about 83; so that 83 by 21 is 1743 br. supercial. This, at the design'd thicknesse, is every square rod 5229 bricks, which I suppose at 17 (the lowest we can expect) delivered at the place, is every rod sq. 09*l.* 08*s.* 01*d.* The total of br. worke then, cont. about 118 sq. rodd, without defalcations of doores, windoes (being 8 doors at 6 and 3 f.; windoes 114 at 3 and 2 f, reduc'd to measure, cont. doores 24 f. by 48, wch is 1152 sq. foote; windoes 342 f. by 228 f. is 77,976 f. sq.); both these reduc'd to sq. rodds, are almost 30 rodds square; whereof allow 10 sq. r. for inequality of the foundation and chimnies (if upon ye warren-ground), and then the br. of the whole (without lime and sand) will cost for 98 sq. rodd, at 04*l.* 08*s.* 01*d.* - - 431 12 02

And every rodd after the rate of 18*d.* for one
  foote high, in workmanship, to - - 01 04 09
Which for 98 rodd is - - - 122 06 00

So as the brick-worke for the whole will come to 650 00 00
Tyling at 36 p^r sq. - - - 450 00 00
Timber at 46 p^r sq. - - 600 00 00
Glasse, about 684 f. at 6*d.* p^r foote - - 17 00 00
Windoe-frames, at 4*d.* each - - 22 00 00

Single doores and cases, at 20s. each; double doores and cases (for the more com'odious bringing in of the sick, being frequently carried) at 36s. wth ye casements, locks, hinges, &c. - - - - 30 00 00
Stone-floores - - - 32 00 00
Stayres, p^r step 3s. 76 in all - - 11 08 00
Levelling the ground as computed vpon view 46 10 00

Total £1859 18 00

But this erection, reduc'd to 400 bedds, or rather persons (which would be a very competent number, and yet exceedingly retrench his M^aties charge for their maintenance) and the whole abated to neere a 5th part of the expense, which amounts to about - - - 371 00 00
The whole would not exceede - - 487 18 00

Whereoff the timber and roofe - - 480 00 00
The timber alone to - - - 360 00 00
Which, if furnish'd from the yard, the whole charge of the building will be reduc'd to 127 18 00
So as the number of beds diminish'd cradles, and attendance proportionable, the furniture compleate will cost - - - 480 00 00

Total £1607 18 00

According to the formerly-made estimate, and which whole charge will be sav'd in quarters of 400 men onely, within 6 moneths and about 15 dayes, at 6d. p^r head, being no lesse then 10l. p^r die., 70l. p^r weeke, 280l. p^r moneth, 3640l. p^r ann.; which is more then double w^t his M^atie is at in one yeare's quarters for them in private-houses; besides all the incomparable advantages enumerated in the subsequent paper, wch will perpetually hold vpon this, or any the like occasion: the quartering of so many persons at 6d. p^r di', amounting to no less then 7280d. p^r an.

If this shall be esteem'd inconvenient, because of diffurnishing the yard, or otherwise a temptation to imbecill the timber of the yard:

All the materials bought as above -	- 1487	18 00
Furniture - - -	- 480	00 00
Total	£1967	·18 00

The whole expense will be reimburs'd in 8 moneths, viz. in 400
men's diet alone by 6d. p^r die'   -   378d. p^r moth
           4536 p^r an^m

Whereas the same number at his
 Maties ordinary entertainment is 627 00 00 p^r moth
             7526 08 00 p^r an^m

So as there would be saved yearely £2990 08 00

Note, y^t the sallary of the stuard (who buyes all provisions, payes and keepes the acc'p^t, takes charge of the sick when set on shore, and discharges them when recovered, &c.) is not computed in this estimate; because it is the same wch our clearkes and deputies do by ye p'sent establishment.

Thus I deduce the p^{rt}iculars:

Chirurgeons 7: viz. 3 Mr Chir. at 6s. p^r diem   £
each; mates 4, at 4s. each; diet for 400,   280
280l.; 1 matron p^r weeke 10s.; 20 nurses   56
at 5s. p^r weeke; fire, candles, sope, &c.   42
3d. p^r weeke   -   -   -
                £378 p^r moth

Cradles-bedds, 200 at 11s. p^r cradle at 4½ f.
  wide, 6 long   -   -   -   110 00 00
Furniture, wth bedds, rug, blanquetts, sheetes, at
  30s. p^r bed   -   -   -   300 00 00
Vtensils for Hospital, &c.   -   70 00 00
                                 ─────────────
                                 £480 00 00

But I do farther affirme, and can demonstrate, that supposing the whole erection, and furniture (according to my first and largest project, and as his Matie and the p^rp^ll Off^rs did thinke fit to proportion the height and thicknesse of the walles) for the entertainment of 500 men, should amount to   1859 18 00
                Furniture to   -   -   -   582 10 00
                                           ─────────────
                         Total   £2442 08 00

Then would be saved to his Matie 332*l*. 18*s*. p^r mo^th; 3994*l*. 16*s*. p^r an^m.

So that in lesse than 8 moneths tyme there will be saved in the quarters of 500 men alone, more monye than the whole expense amounts to; five hundred men's q^rs at 1*s*. p^r die' coming to 25*l*. p^r die', 175*l*. p^r weeke, 700*l*. p^r mo^th, 9408*l*. p^r an'.

Vpon which I assume, if £3994, by five hundred men; or £3640 in foure hundred men; or lastly if but £2990 be saved in one yeare in the quarters of 400 sick persons, &c. there would a farr greater sum be saved in more than 6000 men; there having ben sent 7000 sick and wounded men to cure in my district onely; and of those 2800 put on shore at Chatham and Rochester, for which station I proposed the remedy; five hundred sick persons quarter'd in a towne at the victualers, and scatter'd ale-houses (as ye costome is) will take up at least 160 houses, there being very few of those miserable places which afford accom'odation for about 2 or 3 in an house; wth being frequently at greater distances, employ of chirugeons, nurses, and officers, innumerable; so as when we have ben distress'd for chirugions, some of then (upon computation) walked 6 miles every day, by going but from quarter to qr, and not ben able to visite their patients as they ought: whereas in or hospital, they are continually at hand. We have essay'd to hire some capacious empty houses, but could never meete wth any tollerably convenient; and to have many, or more than one, would be chargeable and very troublesome. By our infirmary, then we have these considerable advantages:

At 6d. pr die' each (in ye way of Com'ons) the sick shall have as good, and much more proper and wholesome diet, then now they have in ye alehouses, where they are fed wth trash, and embecil their monye more to inflame themselves, retard and destroy their cures out of ignorance or intemperance, whiles a sober matron governs ye nurses, lookes to their provisions, rollers, linnen, &c. And ye nurses attend the sick, wash, sweepe, and serve ye offices, the coock and laundrer comprehended in ye numbr and at ye same rate, &c. By this method, likewise, are the almost indefinite number of chirurgions and officers exceedingly reduc'd; the sick dieted, kept from drinke and intemperance, and consequently from most vnavoidably relapsing. They are hindred from wandring, slipping away and dispersion. They are more sedulously attended; the physitian better inspects the chirurgions, who neither can, nor will be in all places, as now they are scattered in the nasty corners of the townes. They are sooner and more certeanely cur'd (for I have at p'sent neere 30 bedds employ'd in a barne at Graues-end, which has taught vs much of this experience) they are receiv'd and discharg'd wth infinitely more ease. Our accp^{ts} better and more exactly kept. A vast and very considerable sum is saved (not to say gain'd) to his Matie. The materialls of the house will be good if taken downe; or if let stand, it may serve, in tyme of peace, for a store or workhouse; the furniture will (much of it) be vsefull vpon like occasion; and what is to be esteem'd none of the least virtues of it, 'till totaly cure the altogether intollerable clamor, and difficulties of rude and vngrateful people, their landlords and nurses, raysed by their poverty vpon the least obstruction of constant and weekly payes; for want of which, they bring an ill repute on his Maties service, incense the very magistrates and better sort of inhabitants (neighbours to them) who too frequently promote (I am sorry to speak it) their mutinies; so as they have ben sometimes menacing to expose our men in the streetes where some have most inhospitably perish'd. In fine, this would encounter all objections whatsoever; is an honourable, charitable, and frugal provision; effectual full of encouragement, and very practicable; so as, however for the p'sent, it may be consider'd, I cannot but persist in wishing it might be resolu'd vpon towards autumne at the farthest; Chatham and Rochester alone, having within 17 or 18 monethes cost his M^atie full £13,000 in cures and quarters; halfe whereof would have neere been saved had this method ben establish'd: add to this, the almost constant station of his M^aties shipps at the buoy in the Noore, and river of Chatham; the clamor of that place against o^r quartering these, this crazy tyme, and the altogether impossibility of providing else-where for such numbers as continualy presse in vpon vs there, more than any where else after actions, or the returne of any of his M^aties fleete; which, with what has ben offer'd, may reccomend this project, by y^r favourable representation of ye premises, for a permanent establishment in that place, especially, if his M^atie and R. H^sse so thinke meete. This account, being what I have ben able to lay before you, as the effects of my late inspection vpon the places, by com'ands of the Hon^l the

Prp^{ll} Offr^s I request through y^r hands may be address'd to them from,

   S^r,
  Y^r most obedient servant,
      J. Evelyn.

We might this sum'er burne o^r owne bricks, and procure timber at ye best hand, w^h would save a considerable charge.

To my Lord Viscount Cornbery.

My Lord,

Ubi Amor, ibi Oculus, excuses ye glaunces we cast upon desireable objects; my hand cannot containe itselfe from this presumption, when I have any thing to write which affords me the least pretense; and though you should not answer my lett^rs, yet, till you forbid me writing, I please myselfe that you vouchsafe to reade them. Great persons pay deare for such addresses, who afford them that honor; and especialy those that (like y^r Lo^p) know so well to value their tyme. One period more, my L^d, and *beso los manos*.

Upon Wednesday last I went to London, and spent the whole afternoone in viewing my Ld: Chancel^rs *new house*,* if it be not a solecisme to give a palace so vulgar a name. My uncessant buisinesse had 'till that moment prevented my passionate desires of seeing it since it was one stone advanc'd: but I was plainely astonish'd when I beheld w^t a progresse was made. Let me speake ingenuously; I went with prejudice, and a critical spirit; incident to those who fancy they know any thing in art: I acknowledge to y^r L^p that I have never seene a nobler pile: my old friend and fel-

---

* Clarendon House, built by Mr. Prat; since quite demolished by Sir Thomas Bond, &c. who purchased it to build a street of tenements to his undoing. J. E.—See vol. III. pp. 85. 95—97. 117.

low traveller (cohabitant & contemporarie at Rome) has perfectly acquitted himselfe. It is, without hyperbolies, the best contriv'd, the most usefull, gracefull, and magnificent house in England,—I except not Audly-end; which, though larger, and full of gaudy & barbarous ornaments, dos not gratifie judicious spectators. As I sayd, my Ld: here is state and use, solidity & beauty most symetricaly combin'd together: Seriously there is nothing abroad pleases me better; nothing at home approches it. I have no designe, my Ld: to gratifie the architect, beyond what I am oblig'd, as a profess'd honorer of virtue wheresoever 'tis conspicuous; but when I had seriously contemplated every roome (for I went into them all, from the cellar to the platforme on ye roofe) seene how well and judiciously the walls were erected, the arches cut, & turn'd, the timber braced, their scantlings and contignations dispos'd, I was incredibly satisfied, and do acknowledge myselfe to have much improved by what I observed. What shall I add more? *rumpatur invidia*, I pronounce it the first Palace of England, deserving all I have said of it, and a better eneomiast.

May that greate & illustrious person, whose large & ample heart has honor'd his country wth so glorious a structure, and by an example worthy of himselfe, shew'd o^r nobility how they ought indeede to build, and value their qualities, live many long yeares to enjoy it; and when he shall be pass'd to that upper *building, not made w*th *hands,* may his posterity (as you my L^d) inherite his goodnesse, this palace, and all other circumstances of his grandure, to consu'mate their felicity; with which happy augure, permitt me in all faithfullnesse, and sincerely, to subscribe my selfe, my L^d,

Y^r, &c.

Says-Court, 20th Jan. 1665-6.

To the Dean of Rippon (Dr. WILKINS) afterwards Lord Bishop of Chester.

S^r,

I have read Mr. Tillotson's " Rule of Faith," and am oblig'd to render him thankes for the benefit I acknowledge to have receiv'd by it: Never in my life did I see a thing more illustrated, more convincing, unlesse men will be blind because they will be so. I am infinitely pleas'd with his equal style, dispassionate treatment, & Christian temper to that importunat adversary: for my part, I looke upon that buisinesse as dispatch'd, and expect onely the grimaces and agonies of dying & desperate men for the future: plainely the wound is mortal.

S^r, that I presume to send you the consequence of what I formerly publish'd in English, in the Controversy 'twixt the Jesuits and Jansenists, speakes rather my obedience to a com'and from that greate person,* than my abilities to have undertaken, or acquitted my selfe of it as I ought: I have annexed an Epistolary Preface, not to instruct such as you are in any thing which you do not know: but for their sakes, who reading the booke, might possibly conceive the French Kings to have ben the onely persons in danger; & because I hope it may receive y^r suffrage as to the pertinence of it *pro hic et nunc.*

I am heartily sorry that some indispensable avocations frequently deprive me of your meetings at Gressham-Colledge, & particularly that I cannot be there on Wednesday; his Matie having enjoyn'd me to repaire to-morrow to Chatham, for the taking order about erecting an infirmary, capable to entertaine about 500 sick persons, & all to be finish'd against the next occasion. If Almighty God do not vouchsafe to accept this service, as well as the King my master, I shall be an intollerable looser, by being so long diverted from a conversation so profitable and so desirable. But warrs will once have a period; and I now & then get a baite at philosophy; but it is so little and jejeune, as I despair of satisfaction 'till I am againe restor'd to the Society, where even y^r very fragments are enough to enrich any man that has the honor to approach you. S^r, I thinke I have at last procured the

---

* My Lord Chancellor.

mummia wch you desired: be pleas'd in ye name & wth authority of the Royal Society to challenge it of the injurious detainers, therein using the addresse of Mr. Fox; Sr Sam. Tuke having written most effectually in our behalfe, who deserves (together with the Hon. Mr. Hen Howard of Norfolk) a place among our benefactors.

Sir, I am, &c.

To Sir SAMUEL TUKE, Knt. & Bart.

S^r,

It was some foure days before the most fatal conflagration of the (quondam) Citty of London y^t I addressed a few lines to you; little thinking I should so soone have had two such dissolutions to deplore: the burning of the best towne in the world: and the discease of the best ffriend in the world, your excellent lady. S^r, you know they are but small afflictions that are loquacious—greate ones are silent: & if ever greate ones there were, mine eyes have beheld, & mine eares heard them, with an heart so possess'd with sorrow, that it is not easily expressed; because ye instances have ben altogether stupendous & unparallel'd. But it were in vaine to entertaine you with those formal topics, w^h are wont to be applied to persons of lesse fortitude & Christian resignation, though I cannot but exhort you to what, I know, you do—looke upon all things in this world as transitory & perishing; sent us upon condition of quitting them cherefully, when God pleases to take them from us. This consideration alone (wth the rest of those graces w^h God has furnish'd you w^thall) will be able to aleviate y^r passion, & to preserve you from succumbing under y^r pressures, w^h I confesse are weighty: but not insupportable: Live therefore, I conjure you, & helpe to restore y^r deare Country, & to consolate y^r ffriends. There is none alive wishes you more sincere happinesse than my poore family.

I suppose I should have heard ere this from you of all y^r concernments; but impute y^r silence to some possible miscarriage of y^r lett^rs; since the usual place of addresse is wth the rest reduc'd to ashes & made an heape of ruines. I would give you a more particular relation of this calamitous accident; but I should oppresse you with sad stories, and I question not but they are come too soone amongst you at Paris with all minutenesse, & (were it possible) hyperbolies. There is this yet of lesse deplorable in it: that, as it has pleas'd God to order it, little effects of any greate consequence have been lost, besides the houses:—That o^r merchands at the same instant in w^h it was permitted y^t ye tidings should flie over seas, had so settled all their affaires, as they complying wth their forraine correspondence as punctualy as if no disaster at all had happen'd; nor do we heare of so much as one that has fail'd. The Exchange is now at Gressham Colledge. The rest of the Citty (which may consist of neere a 7th part) & suburbs peopl'd with new shopps, the same noyse, buisinesse, & com'erce, not to say vanity. Onely the poore booke-sellers have ben indeede ill treated by Vulcan; so many noble impressions consum'd by their trusting them to ye churches, as the losse is estimated neere two-hundred thousand pounds: wch will be an extraordinary detriment to ye whole republiq of learning. In ye meane time, the King & Parliament are infinitely zealous for the rebuilding of our ruines; & I believe it will universally be the employment of ye next spring: They are now busied wth adjusting the claimes of each proprietor, that so they may dispose things for the building after the noblest model: Every body brings in his idea, amongst the rest I p'sented his M^{atie} my owne conceptions, wth a Discourse annex'd. It was the second that was seene, within 2 dayes after the conflagration: But Dr. Wren had got the start of me.* Both of us did coincide so frequently, that his M^{atie} was not displeas'd with it, & it caus'd divers alterations; and truly there was never a more glorious phœnix

---

* These Plans were afterwards printed by the Society of Antiquaries, and have been repeatedly engraved for the various Histories of London; that by Mr. Evelyn is erroneously inscribed Sir John Evelyn.

upon earth, if it do at last emerge out of these cinders, and as the designe is layd, with the present fervour of ye undertakers. But these things are as yet im'ature;. & I pray God we may enjoy peace to encourage those faire dispositions: The miracle is, I have never in my life observ'd a more universal resignation, lesse repining amongst sufferers; which makes mee hope, y^t God has yet thoughts of mercy towards us: Judgments do not always end where they begin; & therefore let none exult over our calamities:—We know not whose turne it may be next. But, S^r, I forbear to entertain you longer on these sad reflections; but persist to beg of you not to suffer any transportations unbecoming a man of virtue; resolve to preserve y^r selfe, if it be possible, for better times, the good & restauration of y^r country, & the comfort of y^r friends & relations, and amongst them of, S^r,

Y^r, &c.

Says-Court, 27th Sepr 1666.

To my Lord Chancellor:
Sir EDWARD HYDE, afterwards Earl of CLARENDON.

My L^d:
I did the other day in West^r Hall give my Ld Cornbery, y^r L^{ps} sonne, my thoughts briefely concerning a most needefull reformation for the transmitting a clearer streame for the future from the

presse, by directing to imaculate copys of such bookes as being vended in greate proportions do for want of good editions amongst us export extraordinary sums of mony, to our no lesse detriment than shame: and I am so well satisfied of the honor which a redresse in this kind will procure even to posterity (however small the present instance may appear to some in a superficial view) that I thinke my selfe obliged to wish that y^r Lo^p may not conceive it unworthy of y^r patronage. The affaire is this:

Since the late deplorable conflagration, in wch the stationers have been exceedingly ruin'd, there is like to be an extraordinary penury & scarcity of Classic authors, &c. us'd in our Grammar Scholes; so as of necessity they must suddainely be reprinted: My Ld: may please to understand, that our book-sellers follow their owne judgement in printing the antient authors according to such text as they found extant when first they entred their copy; whereas, out of MSS. collated by the industry of later critics, those authors are exceedingly improved. For instance, about 30 yeares since, Justine was corrected by Isaac Vossius, in many hundreds of places most material to sense & elegancy; & has since ben frequently reprinted in Holland after the purer copy: but wth us, still according to the old reading. The like has Florus, Seneca's Tragedys, & neere all the rest: which haue in the meane time been castigated abroad by severall learned hands, which, besides that it makes ours to be rejected, & dishonors our nation, so dos it no little detriment to learning, & to the treasure of the nation in proportion: The cause of this is, principaly the stationer driving as hard & cruel a bargain with the printer as he can; and the printer taking up any smatterer in the tongues, to be the lesse looser; an exactnesse in this no wayes importing the stipulation: by which meanes errors repeate & multiply in every edition, & that most notoriously in some most necessary schole-bookes of value, which they obtrude upon the buyer, unlesse men will be at unreasonable rates for forraine editions. Y^r Lo^p: dos by this perceive the mischievous effects of this avarice, & negligence in them.

And now towards the removing these causes of the decay of typography, not onely as to this particular, but in generall: It is humbly propos'd to consider whether it might not be expedient: First, that inspection be had what text of the Greeke & Latine authors should be follow'd in future impressions: 2^{ly}, That a censor be establish'd to take care and caution of all presses in London, that they be provided with able correctors, principaly for scholebookes, which are of large & iterated impressions. 3dly, That the charge thereof be advanc'd by the Company, which is but just, and will be easily reimburs'd, upon an allowance arising from better &

more valuable copys; since 'tis but reason that whoever builds an house be at the charges of surveing: and if it stand in relation to the publiq (as this dos), that he be obliged to it.

My L^d; these reflections are not crudely represented, but upon mature advise & conference wth learned persons with whom I now & then converse; & they are highly worthy y^r Lo^ps interesting y^r power & authority to reforme it, & will be inserted into the glorious things of y^r story, & adorne y^r memory; greate persons heretofore did take care of these matters, & it has consecrated their names. The season is also now most proper for it, that this sad calamity has mortified a Company wch was exceedingly haughty & difficult to manage to any usefull reformation; & therefore (well knowing the benefit wch would accrue to ye publiq by so noble an attempt) I could not but reco'mend it to y^r Lo^p: out of the pure sense of gratitude I have to wish y^r Lo^p all the happy occasions of increasing y^r honor, for the favors you always shew me, and the obligations I haue to y^r p^rticular friendship & kindnesse. My L^d: if this paper find acceptance, I would be bold to add some farther hints for ye carying it on to some perfection; for besides all I have sayd, there will neede paines in reading, consulting MSS. & conference wth learned men, good indexes, apt divisions, chapters & verses, as the *Dutch Variorum*, embellishments of Roman and Italiq letters, to seperate inserted speeches (especialy in historians and sententious authors), and which adds to the use and lustre, together with a choyce of succinct notes after more terse & profitable copys. For 'tis a shame, that ever such as our owne countryman Farnaby has publish'd, should be sold us from other countries; because our owne editions are so much inferior to them. If y^r Lo^p: would set y^r heart upon other particulars, concerning the reformation of our English Presse, I could give instance in some of high reputation, & no meane advantage. But I would rejoice to see but this take effect. My L^d, I kisse y^r L^{ps} hands, &c.

Sayes-Court, 27 Nov^r: 1666.

To Abraham Cowley, Esq.

S^r,

You had reason to be astonish'd at the presumption, not to name it affront, that I who have so highly celebrated recesse, and envied it in others, should become an advocate for the enemie, which of all others it abhorrs and flies from. I conjure you to believe y^t I am still of the same mind, & that there is no person alive who dos more honor and breathe after the life and repose you so happily cultivate and adorne by your example: But as those who prays'd dirt, a flea, and the gowte,* so have I *Publiq Employment* in that trifling Essay,† and that in so weake a style compar'd to my antagonists, as by that alone it will appeare I neither was nor could be serious; and I hope you believe I speake my very soule to you: but I have more to say, which will require your kindnesse. Suppose our good friend were publishing some Eulogies on the Royal Society, and by deducing the originall, progresse, and advantages of their designe, would bespeake it some veneration in the world? Has Mr. Cowley no inspirations for it? Would it not hang the most heroic wreath about his temples? Or can he desire a nobler or a fuller argument either for the softest aires or the loudest echoes, for the smoothest or briskest strokes of his Pindaric lyre?

There be those who aske, What have the Royal Society done? Where their Colledge? I neede not instruct you how to answer or confound these persons, who are able to make even these informe blocks and stones daunce into order, and charme them into better sense. Or if their insolence presse, you are capable to shew how they have

---

* Dornavius's "Amphitheatrum Sapientiæ Socraticæ Jacoseriæ." contains a large collection of those facetiæ, in prose and verse, with which the scholars of those times relieved their serious studies.

† "Public Employment, &c. preferred to Solitude," 1667. Printed in "Miscellaneous Writings," 1825, 4to, pp. 501—509.

layd solid foundations to perfect all noble arts, and reforme all imperfect sciences. It requires an history to recite onely the arts, the inventions, and phænomena already absolved, improved, or opened. In a word, our Registers have outdon Pliny, Porta, & Alexis, and all the experimentists, nay, the great Verulam himselfe, & have made a nobler and more faithfull collection of real seacrets, usefull and instructive, than has hitherto been shewn.—S^r, we have a Library, a Repository, & an assembly of as worthy & greate persons as the world has any; and yet we are sometimes the subject of satyr and the songs of drunkards; have a King to our founder, and yet want a Mæcenas; and above all a spirit like yours, to raise us up benefactors, & to compell them to thinke the designe of the Royall Society as worthy their reguards, & as capable to embalme their names, as the most heroic enterprise, or any thing antiquity has celebrated; and I am even amaz'd at the wretchednesse of this age that acknowledges it no more. But the Devil, who was ever an enemy to truth, and to such as discover his præstigious effects, will never suffer the promotion of a designe so destructive to his dominion, which is to fill the world with imposture & keepe it in ignorance, without the utmost of his malice and contradiction. But you have numbers and charmes that can bind even these spirits of darknesse, and render their instruments obsequious; and we know you have a divine hymne for us; the luster of the R¹ Society calls for an ode from the best of poets vpon the noblest argument. To conclude: here you have a field to celebrate the greate and the good, who either do, or should favour the most august and worthy designe that ever was set on foot in the world: and those who are our real patrons and friends you can eternize, those who are not you can conciliate & inspire to do gallant things.—But I will add no more, when I have told you with very greate truth that I am,

S^r, &c.

Sayes-Court, 12 March, 1666-7.

From ABRAHAM COWLEY to J. EVELYN, Esq.

S^r,   Chertsea, May 13, 1667.

I am asham'd of ye rudenesse I have committed in deferring so long my humble thanks for y^r obliging letter wch I received from yow at ye beginning of ye last month: my laziness in finishing ye copy of verses vpon ye Royal Society, for wch I was engag'd before by Mr Sprat's desire, & encouraged since by yow, was the caus of this delay, haueing designed to send it to yow enclosed in my letter; but I am told now y^t ye History is almost quite printed, & will bee published so soon, y^t it were impertinent labour to write out y^t wch you will so suddenly see in a better manner, and in ye company of better things. I could not comprehend in it many of those excellent hints wch yow were pleas'd to give mee, nor descend to the praises of particular persons, becaus those things affoord too much matter for one copy of verses, and enough for a poem, or the History itself: some part of wch I have seen, & I think yow will bee very well satisfied wth it. I took ye boldness to show him y^r letter, & hee says he has not omitted any of those heads, though hee wants y^r eloquence in expression. Since I had ye honour to receive from yow ye reply to a book written in praise of a solitary life,* I haue sent all about ye town in vain to get y^t author, haveing very much affection for ye subiect, wch is one of the noblest controversies both modern and ancient, & you have delt so civily wth your adversary, as makes him deserve to bee look'd after. But I could not meet wth him, the books being all, it seems, either burnt or bought up. If yow pleas to do mee ye favour to lend it to mee, & send it to my brothers hous (y^t was) in the King's Yard, it shall bee return'd to yow w^thin a few days wth ye humble thanks of y^r most faithfull obedient serv^t,

A. COWLEY.

---

* Sir George Mackenzie's " Moral Essay upon Solitude, preferring it to Public Employment," &c. 1665.

To HENRY HOWARD, Esq. of Norfolk, heir apparent to that Dukedom.*

S^r,

It is not without much regret and more concernement as it reguards y^r honorable & illustrious family, that I have now so long a time beheld some of the noblest antiquities in the world, & which y^r grandfather purchased with so much cost & difficulty, lye abandoned, broken, & defaced in divers corners about Arundel House & the gardens belonging to it. I know y^r Honour cannot but have thoughts and resolutions of repairing & collecting them together one day; but there are in the meane tyme certaine broken inscriptions, now almost obliterated with age, & the ill effects of the weather, which will in a short time vtterly be lost & perish, vnlesse they be speedily removed to a more benigne & lesse corrosive ayre. For these it is, I should be an humble suitor that you would think fit to make a present of them to the University of Oxford, where they might be of greate vse and ornament, and remaine a more lasting record to posterity of your munificence, than by any other application of

---

* This Letter procured all the Marmora Arundeliana, Greek and Latin Inscriptions, Urns, Altar Tables, &c. now at Oxon. J. E. See his Dedication to this gentleman, prefixed to Roland Freart's "Idea of the Perfection of Painting," reprinted in Evelyn's "Miscellaneous Writings," 1825, 4to, p. 555.

them whatsoever; and the University would thinke themselves oblig'd to inscribe y^r name, and that of y^r illustrious family to all significations of gratitude.

I have also long since suggested to y^r Hon^r that you would cause the best of y^r statues, basso-relievos, & other antiquities standing in y^r gallery at Arundel House, to be exquisitely design'd by some skillfull hand, and engraven in copper, as Mons: Liancourt did those of Rome by Perrier, & long before him Raphael himselfe, Sadeler, and other incomparable sculptors: because by this meanes they would be co'municated to the world, and diuers greate & learned persons, studious of antiquity, might be benefited by them; and if such a thing were added to the impression of the *Marmora Arundeliana* (which I heare the University of Oxon are now preparing for a second impression), how greately would it adorne that admirable work, & do new honors to y^r illustrious name & family, as it has formerly, & yet dos to divers noble Italians, & others, who have not ben able to produce such a collection as you are furnished with, but which perish in obscurity, & yield not that to ye publiq, who would be obliged to celebrate you, for want of a small expence! Methinkes, whilst they remaine thus obscur'd & neglected, the very marbles are become vocal, and cry to you for pitty, & that you would even breathe life into them. S^r, you will easily see I have no other designe in this then to expresse the honour I have for y^r person and for y^r illustrious family; and because I find this would be one of the most glorious instances to augment and perpetuate it, I cannot but wish that it might take effect. I have no more to add but that I am, &c.

Says-Court, 4 Aug. 1667.

To Doctor BATHURST,
President of Trinity College, Oxon.

S^r,

I heartily wish I had the good fortune to be as serviceable to you in particular for the many favours I have received, as I doubt not but I shall be to a place, which for y^r sake as well as my owne, I have so much reason to honour, I meane the University; if at least it may be esteemed a service to have obtained of Mr. Henry Howard of Norfolk, the freely bestowing upon you all those learned monuments which passe vnder the famous names of *Marmora Arundeliana*. This, S^r, the interest wch that illustrious person has allowed me in his friendship has wrought for you; and I dare pronounce it highly worthy your acceptance. For you shall not onely be masters of some few, but of all; and there is nothing more to be don, than after you have taken notice of his munificence (which I desire, and wish may be speedily don in a publiq addresse as from the body of the University) to take order for their transportation to you; for which effect, I conceive it would be worth your while to delegate Mr. Obadiah Walker, or Dr. Wren (Sir Christopher), persons that I much honor, who may take care, and consult about the best expedients for their removall; for they being marble & some of them basse-relievos rarely cutt, will deserve to be guarded from injuries: And when they are at Oxford, I conceive they can no where be more fittly placed than in some part about the new theatre, except you should think fit to protect some of the more curious & small ones, as urnes, &c. in the galleries next the library, where they may remaine secure. I haue assured Mr. Howard that the University will not faile in their sense of this noble gift and munificence, by decreeing him a publiq and conspicuous inscription which shall consecrate his memory: And if I have hinted it more particularly to Mr. Walker, it is what I think will become y[r] justice & such gratefull beneficiaries. I shall intreate you to acquainte Mr. Vice-Chancellor with what I have don, as also Dr. Barlow, & Dr. Pierce, the Warden and Presidents of Queenes & Magdalen Coll: my worthy friends, and beg that through your addresse this service of mine may be acceptable to the University from,

S[r], your, &c.

Lond: 9th Sept. 1667.

To the Earl of SANDWICH,
Lord Ambassador in Spain, at Madrid.
My Lord,

I could hardly obtaine of my selfe to give y^r Exc^y this trouble, or dare to mingle my impertinencies amongst your publiq and weighty concernes, 'till reflecting on the greatesse of y^r genius, I concluded it would neither be disturb'd, nor disdaine my humble addresse, that confident of y^r com'unicative nature, I adventur'd to supplicate y^r Exc^s favour in behalfe of a worke of mine upon the Hortulan subject; and in particular, that y^r Exc^y would vouchsafe by the meanest of y^r servants to give me some short descriptions of the most famous gardens and villas of Spaine,* and what other singularities of that kind might occur to the adorning of a labour wherein I chiefely pretend to gratifie greate & illustrious persons, and such as like y^r L^p are the most worthy to cultivate and enjoy these amœnities. The catalogue which I here presume to send y^r Exc^y, and the paines I have already taken to render it no trifling or un-usefull speculation, will in some degree com'ute for this bold addresse; especialy since I could never hope to receive so much light from

---

* Which he sent me from Madrid, many sheets of paper written in his owne hand, together with the *Sembrador* or plough itselfe, wch I gave to ye R: Society, & is describ'd in their " Transactions."—J. E.

any but y^r Ex^{cy}, to whom I am confident there can be nothing curious in this argument conceal'd, how close & reserv'd so ever the Spaniards are. I have heard that there is lately a German at Madrid, who pretends to a successful invention for the setting of corne by a peculiar sort of plow. This, I am sure cannot have escaped y^r Ex^{cy}: and it will be due to the R: Society, the History whereof, now at last publish'd here wth infinite applause, I doubt not is come to y^r hands, and that you will judge it worthy the most accurate translation. But, my Lord, I shall leave that to the joynt request of the Society, and accumulate no more to these extravagances of mine, after I have supplicated your Ex^{cys} pardon, who am,

May it please y^r Ex^{cy}, y^r, &c.

Says-Court, 13 Decr 1667.

To the Rev. JOSEPH GLANVIL, Chaplain in Ordinary to his Majesty, and F.R.S. a native of Devonshire,* and a distinguished writer of the seventeenth century.

S^r,

I received so wellcome, and so obliging a toaken from y^u by ye hands of Mr: Oldenburgh, that after

---

* He sent me his booke, intituled, " Plus Ultra; or the Progress and Advancement of Knowledge, since the Days of Aristotle," octavo, Lond. 1668. J. E.—An account of this may be seen in the Philosophical Transactions, No. 36.

all I can say in this lett^r in acknowledgement of that particular favour, I must continue to subscribe myselfe y^r debtor: For what have you seene in any of my productions, which should make you augure so favourably of that trifle of mine, upon so trite and humble a subject; or mention me amongst the heros whom you so meritoriously celebrat! I cannot find any thing to support it, but your most obliging nature, of which the comely and philosophic frame is aboundantly conspicuous, by this worthy vindication both of y^r selfe and all usefull learning, against the science (falsely so called) of your snarling adversary.* I do not conceive why the Royall Society should any more concern themselves for the empty and malicious cavells of these delators, after what you haue say'd; but let the moon-dogs bark on, 'till their throats are drie; the Society every day emerges, and her good Genius will raise up one or other to judge & defend her; whilst there is nothing which dos more confirme me in the noblenesse of the designe, than this spirit of contradiction which the devil (who hates all discoveries of those false & præstigious ways that have hitherto obtain'd) dos incite to stirr up men against it. But, S^r, you have

---

* Henry Stubbe, an inveterate enemy of the Royal Society, which he set forth in many pamphlets. He also wrote an Answer to Mr. Glanvil, intituled, " The *Plus Ultra* reduced to a *Non Plus;* or a Specimen of some Animadversions upon the *Plus Ultra* of Mr. Jos: Glanvil." Quarto, 1670.

discours'd this so fully in this excellent piece of yours, that I have no more to add, but the suffrage and subscription of, S^r,

Y^r, &c.

Says-Court, 24 June, 1668.

To the Earle of SANDWICH, Ambass^r Extraordinary in the Court of Spaine, at Madrid.

My Lord,

I am plainely astonish'd at y^r bounty to me, and I am in paine for words to expresse the sense I have of this greate obligation.*

And as I have ben exceedingly affected with the descriptions, so have I ben greately instructed in the other particulars y^r Lo^p mentions, and especialy rejoice that y^r Ex^{cy} has taken care to have the draughts of the places, fountaines, & engines for ye irrigation & refreshing their plantations, which may be of singular use to us in England. And I question not but y^r Ex^{cy} brings with you a collection of seedes; such especially as we may not have com'only in our country. By y^r Lo^{ps} description, the *Encina* should be the *Ilex major aculeata*, a sucker whereoff yet remaines in his M^{aties} Privie-Gardens at White Hall, next the dore y^t is opposite to the

---

* Upon his communicating particulars of horticultural matters in Spain.

Tennis-Court. I mention it the rather, because it certainly might be propagated with us to good purpose, for the father of this small tree I remember of a goodly stature; so as it yearely produc'd ripe acorns; though Clusius, when he was in England, believ'd it to be barren: & happly, it had borne none in his tyme. I have sown both the acorns of the tree, and the cork with successe, though I have now but few of them remaining, through the negligence of my gardiner; for they require care at the first raising, 'till they are accustom'd to the cold, and then no rigour impeaches them. What y^r Exc^y: meanes by the *Bama de Joseph,* I do not comprehend; but the *Planta Alois,* which is a monstrous kind of *Sedum,* will, like it, endure no wett in winter, but certainely rotts if but a drop or two fall on it, whereas in summer you cannot give it drink enough. I perceive their culture of choyce & tender plants differs little from ours in England, as it has ben publish'd by me in my *Calendarium Hortense,* which is now the third time reprinting. Stoves absolutely destroy our conservatories; but if they could be lin'd with cork, I believe it would better secure them from the cold & moisture of the walls, than either matrasses, or reedes with which we co'monly invest them. I thinke I was the first that ever planted Spanish Cardôns in our country for any culinerie use, as y^r Ex^{cy}: has taught the blanching; but I know not whether they serve themselves in Spaine with the purple beards of the thistle, when it is in flower, for the curdling of milk, which it performes much better than reinet, and is far sweeter in the dairy than that liquor, which is apt to putrifie.

Your Excell^y has rightly conjectur'd of ye pomegranad: I have allways kept it expos'd, and the severest of our winters dos it no prejudice; they will flower plentifully, but beare no fruit with us, either kept in casès & in the repository, or set in ye open ayre; at least very trifling, with ye greatest industry of stoves & other artifices.

We have aspargus growing wild both in Lincolnshire & in other places; but y^r L^p observes, they are small & bitter, & not comparable to the cultivated.

The red pepper, I suppose, is what we call ginny-peper, of which I have rais'd many plants, whòse pods resemble in colour the most oriental & polish'd corall: a very little will set ye throat in such a flame, as has ben sometimes deadly, and therefore to be sparingly us'd in sauces.

I hope y^r L^p will furnish y^r selfe wth melon seedes, because they will last good almost 20 years; & so will all the sorts of garavances, calaburos, & gourds, (whatever Herrera affirme,) which, may be for divers oeconomical uses.

The Spanish onion-seede is of all other the most excellent: and yet I am not certaine, whether that which we have out of Flanders and St. Omers, be all the Spanish scede wch we know of. My Lady Clarendon (when living) was wont to furnish me with scede that produc'd me prodigious cropps.

Is it not possible for y^r Ex^cy to bring over some of those quince and cherry-trees, which y^r L^p so celebrates? I suppose they might be secur'd in barells, or pack'd up, as they transport other rarities from far countries. But, my Ld: I detaine y^r Ex^cy too long in these repetitions, & forget that I am all this while doing injury to ye publiq, by suspending you a moment from matters of a higher orb, the interest of states, & reconciling of kingdomes: and I should think so of another, did I not know withall, how universal y^r comprehensions are, & how qualified to support it. I remaine, my L^d,

Y^r, &c.

Says-Court, 21 Aug. 1668.

To Doctor Beale.

S^r,

I happn'd to be wth Mr. Oldenburg some time since, almost upon the article of his receiving the notice you sent him of y^r fortunate and useful invention; and I remember I did first of all incite him, both to insert it into his next Transactions, and to provoke y^r farther prosecution of it;

which I exceedingly rejoice to find has ben so successfull, that you give us hopes of y^r farther thoughts upon *that*, and those other subjects which you mention.* You may happly call to remembrance a passage of the Jesuite Honorati Fabri, who speaking of perspectives, observes, that an object looked on through a small hole appears magnified; from whence he suggests, the casting of two plates neately perforated, & fitted to looke through, preferrable to glasses, whose refractions injure the sight. Though I begin to advance in yeares (being now on the other side of 40) yet the continuance of the perfect use of my senses (for which I blesse Almighty God) has rendred me the lesse solicitous about those artificial aydes; which yet I foresee I must shortly apply my selfe to, and therefore you can receive but slender hints from me which will be worth y^r acceptance upon that argument: onely, I well remember, that besides Tiberius of old (whom you seeme to instance in), Joseph Scaliger affirmes the same happned both to his father Julius and himselfe, in their younger yeares. And sometimes methinkes, I my selfe have fansied to have discern'd things in a very dark place, when the curtaines

---

* The paper alluded to is intituled, "An Experiment to examine what Figure and Celerity of Motion begetteth or encreaseth Light and Flame." Philosophical Transactions, vol. I. p. 226.

about my bed have ben drawne, as my hands, fingers, the sheete, and bed-clothes; but since my too intent poring upon a famous eclipse of the sun, about 12 yeares since, at which time I could as familiarly have stared with open eyes upon that glorious planet in its full lustre, as now upon a glowworme (comparatively speaking), I have not onely lost that acuteness of sight, but much impair'd the vigour of it for such purposes as it then serv'd me. But besides that, I have treated myne eyes very ill neere these 20 yeares, during all which tyme I have rarely put them together, or compos'd them to sleepe before one at night, & sometimes much later: that I may in some sort redeeme my losses by day, in which I am continually importun'd with visits from my neighbours & acquaintance, or taken up by other impertinences of my life in this place. I am plainely asham'd to tell you this, considering how little I have improv'd myselfe by it, but I have rarely ben in bed before 12 o'clock as I sayd, in the space of 20 yeares; and yet I reade the least print, even in a jolting coach, without other assistance* save that I now & then use to rub my shut eye-lids over with a spirit of wine well rectified, in which I distill a few rose-marie flowers, much after the pro-

---

* The Editor is thankful to God that he can and does do this at double the age of Mr. Evelyn, mentioned in the preceding page.—W. B.

cesse of the Queene of Hungarie's water, which dos exccedingly fortifie not onely my sight, but the rest of my senses, especialy my hearing and smelling; a drop or two being distill'd into the nose or cares, when they are never so dull; and other κολλουριον I never apply. Indeede, in ye sum'er-time, I have found wonderfull benefit in bathing my head with a decoction of some hot & aromaticall herbs, in a lixivium made of the ashes of vine-branches, and when my head is well washed wth this, I im'ediately cause aboundance of cold fountaine-water to be poured upon me *stillatim*, for a good halfe-hour together; which for the present is not onely one of the most voluptuous and gratefull refreshments imaginable, but an incredible benefit to me the whole yeare after: for I never neede other powdering to my hair, to preserve it bright and cleane, as the gallants do; but which dos certainly greately prejudice transpiration by filling up, or lying heavy upon the pores. Those therefore, who (since the use of perrucqs) accustome to wash their heads, instead of powdering, would doubtlesse find the benefit of it; both as to the preventing of aches in their head, teeth, and cares, if the vicissitude & unconstancy of the weather, and consequently the use of their monstrous perrucqs, did not expose them to the danger of catching colds. When I travell'd in Italy, and the Southern parts, I did sometimes frequent the publiq bathes (as the manner is), but seldome without peril of my life, 'till I us'd this frigid affusion, or rather profusion of cold water before I put on my garments, or durst expose my selfe to the ayre; and for this method I was oblig'd to the old and noble Rantzow, in whose booke *de conservanda valetudine* I had read a passage to this purpose; though I might have remember'd how the Dutchmen treate their labouring horses when they are all over in a froth, which they wash off with severall bucketts of cold water, as I have frequently observ'd it in the Low Countries.*

Concerning other aydes; besides what the masters of the catoptrics, phonocamptics, otacoustics, &c. have don, something has ben attempted by the R[l]. Society; and you know the industrious Kircher has much labour'd; as the rest of those artificial helps are sum'd up by the Jesuite And. Schottus. I remember that Mons[r] Huygens (author of the pendulum), who brought up the learned father of that incomparable youth Mons[r] de Zulichem, who us'd to prescribe to me the benefit of his little wax taper (a type whereof is, with the history of it, in some of our Registers) for night elucubrations preferable to all other candle or lamp light whatsoever. And because it explodes all glaring of the flame, which by no meanes ought to dart upon the eyes,

---

* The common practice with post-horses in England, in the present day.

it seemes very much to establish your happy invention of tubes instead of spectacles, which have not those necessary defences.

Touching the sight of catts in the night, I am not well satisfied of the exquisiteness of that sense in them. I believe their smelling or hearing dos much contribute to their dexterity in catching mice, as to all those animals who are born with those prolix smelling haires. Fish will gather themselves in sholes to any extraordinary light in the darke night, & many are best caught by that artifice. But whatever may be sayd of these, and other senses of fish, you know how much the sagacity of birds & beasts excelle us: how far eagles and vultures, ravens & other fowles will smell the carcase; *odorumq; canum vis*, as Lucretius expresses it, & we daily find by their drawing after the games. Gesner affirmes that an otter will wind a fish four miles distance in the water, and my Ld: Verulam, cent: 8, speakes of that element's being also a medium of sounds, as well as ayre: celes do manifestly stirr at the cracking of thunder, but that may also be attributed to some other tremulous motion; yet carps and other fish are known to come at the call and the sound of a bell, as I have ben inform'd. Notorious is the story of Arion, and of Lucullus's lamprys which came *ad nomen;* and you have formerly minded me of Varro's Greeke-pipe, of which Lucian and Cicero *ad Atticum* take occasion to speake.

Pliny's dolphin is famous, and what is related of the American Manati: but the most stupendous instance, that of the xiphia or sword-fish, which the Mamertines can take up by no other stratagem than a song of certaine barbarous words, as the thing is related by Thom: Fazzello. It is certaine, that we heare more accurately when we hold our mouthes a little open, than when we keepe them shut; and I haue heard of a dumb gentleman in England, who was taught to speake (and therefore certainely brought to heare in some degree) by applying the head of a bass-viole against his teeth, & striking upon the strings with the bow: you may remember the late effect of the drum extending the tympanum of a deafe person, to greate improvement of his hearing, so long as that was beaten upon; and I could at present name a friend of mine, who though he be exceedingly thick of hearing, by applying a straite stick of what length soever, provided it touch the instrument and his eare, dos perfectly, and with greate pleasure heare every tune that is playd: all which, with many more, will flow into your excellent work, whilst the argument puts me in mind of one Tom Whittal, a student of Christ Church, who would needes maintaine, that if a hole could dexterously be boar'd through the skull to the brain in the midst of the fore-head, a man might both see, and heare, & smell without the use of any other organs; but you are to know, that this learned problematist was brother to him who preaching at St. Maries, Oxford, tooke his text out of the history of Balaam, Num. 22: " Am I not thine asse?" Deare S^r, pardon this rhapsody of,

S^r, y^r, &c.

Sayes-Court, 27 Aug.1668.

To the Right Honourable Sir THOMAS CLIFFORD, Treasurer of his Majesty's Household, &c.*

R^{gt} Honb^{le},

In my conversation sometimes amongst bookes to redeeme my tyme from other impertinencies, I think it my duty to give yor Ho^r notice of some pieces which have come to my hands, the subjects whereof I cannot but esteeme highly prejudicial to the honor of his M^{atie} and the whole nation, especialy two bookes, the one written in French, the other in Latine (not inelegantly) both with approbation of their superiors, the States of Holland licencing their publication. The argument of them is a remonstrance to all the world of the occasion, action, and successe of the late war betweene the English & the Dutch; but with all the topics of reproach and dishonor as to matter of fact; every period being filled with the dissembled instances of our in-

---

* Afterwards Lord High Treasurer of England.

justice, ingratitude, cruelty, and imprudence; and the persons of divers particular gallant men engag'd in that action, injuriously treated and accus'd, & in summ, whatever they can else suggest to render his M^(atie) and people cheap and vile, the subjects of derision and contempt. I should think in my poore judgment (under submission to a better) that there is nothing which ought to be more precious to a Prince, or his people, than their reputation: sure I am, it is of more value with a man of honor than his life; and certainely, a greate kingdom, which comprehends so many individuals as have been one way or other concern'd in the publiq interest, ought to be tender of their fame, and consequently oblig'd to vindicate it, and cannot without a crime do lesse, without being wanting to themselves in a most necessary defence.

I know it may be say'd, that this is but a paper quarrell; but y^r Hon^r dos consider, what effects such malevolent suggestions do produce, & with what a black & deepe malice contriv'd, how far they flie, and how universaly understood the Latine & French tongues are, the one amongst the grave and more intelligent sort (not by way of pamphlet, but of a formal & close treatise), and the other amongst ye vulgar; to which is also joyn'd, for the better fixing their injurious ideas, the several types & figures cut in brasse, to represent our misfortunes; as in particular our want of conduct (as they terme it) in the first encounter, our basenesse in surprising a few poore fishermen, and the firing of Schelling, revenged in the dire conflagration of London, the metropolis of our nation, the descent they made on Sheer Nesse, and their glorious exploit at Chatham, where they give out we so ridiculously lost, or betraid the creame of our fleete, and bullwarks of the kingdom, by an unparalleled supinenesse: nor this crudely, or in a trifling way of writing; but so as may best affect the passions & prepossesse the judgement and beliefe of the reader. I say nothing of some personal reflections on my Ld Arlington, Sr Rob: Holmes, and even the King himselfe, whom they represent deliberating in a paniq consternation of a flight to Windsor, &c. nor many other particulars pointed at; nor of a thousand other notorious indignities plainely insupportable: But I have sayd enough to inflame a breast sensible of honor, and generous as I know yours to be, to approve, or at least to pardon the proposal which I shall humbly submit to y^r consideration and encouragement, for the vindication of his M^{atie} and the nation's honor, and especialy of an action in which your H^r bore so greate & so signal a part. And that were doubtlesse by employing an able pen, not to a formal, or studied reply to any particular of this egregious Libell (which might now happly be thought unseasonable), but to compose a solid and usefull History of the late War, according to the truth of circumstances, and for the honor of those very many brave men who were actors in it, whose names deserve as well to be transmitted to posterity as our meaner antagonists; but which must else dye in obscurity, and what is worse, with obloquy and scorn, not of enemyes alone, but of all that shall reade what these men are permitted to scatter abroad in ye world, whilst there is no care taken amongst us at home to vindicate them from it.

When I have mention'd to y^r Ho^r the employment of an able pen upon this occasion, I prevented all pretences to it as relating to myselfe; who have neither the requisite talents, nor the least presumption for it.* But I would humbly suggest, how worthy and glorious in y^r Ho^r it would be, to moove my L^d: Arlington, and with him, to provoke his Matie to impose this province upon some sober and well instructed person, who, dignified with the character of his Royal Historiographer, might be oblig'd to serve and defend his Maties, honor, and

---

* Mr. Evelyn was however appointed to write this History, and had made considerable progress, when upon the conclusion of the war he was ordered to lay it aside. What he had written is unfortunately lost, except the Preface, which he published in 1674, as a distinct treatise, under the title of " Navigation and Commerce, their Original and Progresse:" (reprinted in Evelyn's " Miscellaneous Writings," 1825, 4to. pp. 625—687). This highly pleased the King, but because it gave great offence to the Dutch, it was for a time suppressed. See vol. II. pp. 287. 293. 295. 296. 332; and succeeding Letters.

that of the publiq, with his pen ; a thing so carefully and so industriously observed by ye French King, and other greate potentates, who have any reguards or tendernesse to their owne or their people's glory, the encouragement of gallant men, and prospect of their future stories, as there is nothing more notorious. It is history alone (however the writers of them may be esteem'd) which renders the greatest princes, and the most deserving persons, what they are to the present age; which perfumes their names to posterity, inspires them to an emulation of their vertues, and preserves them from being as much forgotten as the co:mon dust in which they lie mingled. If y^r Ho^r: thinke this worthy y^r thoughts (and worthy of them I pronounce it to be), all that I shall humbly supplicate to you is, that through y^r favour I may present his Matie: wth a person highly deserving it ; as being one, who has not onely ben a sufferer in his capacity, but one who is perfectly able and accomplish'd to serve his Matie : a learned industrious person, and who will esteeme himselfe gratified with a very modest subsistence, to be allways at hand, and allways laborious : and not to weare a title (as some triflers have lately don) to the reproch of it. If there be already a tollerable honorary appendant to the place of Historiographer, we have no more to beg, but the graunt of it ; if not, that through y^r mediation, some encouragement may be procur'd. It will not be one of y^r least noble things, for which you will merit a just veneration of y' memory. But I shall add no more at present, because I will beg the grace of a particular permission to discourse this affaire to you, and with the joynt request of my worthy friend Mr. Williamson* (who will likewise present y^r Ho^r: with a specimen of the persons abillities) bespeake y^r Ho^{rs} favourable encouragement, who remaine,

Y^r Ho^{rs}: &c.

Sayes-Court, 1 Feb. 1668-9.

To my Ld Henry Howard of Norfolk.

My Lord,

I am not prompted by the success of my first addresse to y^r Hon^r, when, as much for y^r owne glory, as that of the University's, I prevail'd with you for the Marbles, which were inscriptions in stone; to solicit you now on the same account for ye Books, which are inscriptions but in parchment: but because I am very confident y^r Hon^r cannot consult a nobler expedient to preserve them, and the memory of y^r name and illustrious family, than by wishing that the Society (on whom you have so generously bestow'd y^r Library) might exchange the MSS: (such onely, I meane, as concerne ye civile lawe, theologie,

---

* Afterwards Sir Joseph Williamson, Principal Secretary of State.

and other scholastical learning) for mathematical, philosophical, and such other books, as may prove most usefull to the designe and institution of it: especialy, since the University do not onely humbly desire it (as I can testifie by divers letters which I have seene from the Vice-Chancellor, and other eminent persons there), but desire it with a designe of owning it yours, and of perpetuating y^r munificence, by dignifying y^t appartment where they would place them, with the title of Bibliotheca Arundeliana, than which, what can be more glorious and conspicuous? The learned Selden, Sr Ken: Digby, Archbp. Laud (not to mention Sr Tho: Bodley their founder, and severall others, who are out of all exception) esteem'd this a safer repository, than to have consign'd them to their mansions and posterity; and we have seene, that when their persons, families, and most precious moveables have suffer'd (some of them the uttmost violences and dispersion), their bookes alone have escaped untouch'd in this sacred asylum, and preserv'd the names of the donors through all vicissitudes. Nor in saying this do I augure lesse of the R^l: Society, should they thinke fit to keepe them in their owne library; but, because by thus parting with such as are foraigne to their studies to the University, your illustrious name and library will be reserv'd in both places at once with equal zeal, and no lesse obligation; when as many as shall have recourse to such bookes at Oxon, as are under the Arundelian title, will have occasion to mention it in their workes and labours to your eternal honour. For my part, I speake it with greate sincerity, and due veneration of y^r L^{ps} bounty, that if I would to the uttmost of my power consult the advancement of y^r L^{ps} glory in this gift, it should be by declaring my suffrage in behalfe of the Uniuersitie's request. I sayd as much in the late Council, where I must testifie that even those who were of a contrary sense to some others of us, were yet all of them equally emulous of y^r L^{ps} honour. But, since it was the unanimous result to submit this particular to y^r L^{ps} decision, I cannot, upon most serious reflection on the reasons which I have aledged, and especialy that of preserving y^r name and library by a double consignation, but implore y^r L^{ps} favour and indulgence for ye University, where y^r munificence is already deeply ingraven in their hearts, as well as in their marbles; and will then shine in letters of a more refulgent lustre: for, methinkes I hear their Publiq Orator, after he has celebrated y^r name amongst the rest of their glorious benefactors and heros, end his panegyric in the resounding theater, as once the noble poet, in the person of the young Arcadian,

Ecl: 7: *Nunc te Marmoreum pro tempore fecimus*—
We yet, greate Howard, thee but in marble mould,
But if our bookes increase, thou shalt be gold.

I am y^r L^{ps}: &c.

Sayes-Court, 14 Mar: 1669.

To Dr. Meric Casaubon, Is. Fil.
Prebend of Canterbury, &c.

Reverend S^r,

Tho' I am a stranger to y^r person, yet the name & the learning wch you derive both from inheritance, as well as acquisition, draw a just veneration to them. S^r, whilst it has ben lately my hap to write something concerning the nature of forest trees, & their mechanical uses, in turning over many books treating of that & other subjects, I met with divers passages concerning staves, which have in a manner obliged me to say something of them in a treatise which I am adorning: but whilst I was intent on this, I began to doubt whether I should not *actum agere*; remembring this passage of y^r father (τοῦ μακαριτοῦ) in his Com'ent on Theophrastus, p. 172. edit. 1638: *Sed hæc hactenus; nam de Baculis et eorum forma, multiplicique apud veteres usu, plurima quæ observavimus ad lucem multorum Scriptorum veterum, alibi,* ἐαν ὁ Θεὸς ἐθέλῃ, *co'modius proferremus.* That which I now would entreate of you, S^r, is to know whether y^r learned father did ever publish any expresse treatise concerning this subject, & if not, that you'l be pleas'd to afford me some short hints of what you see noted in his Adversaria about it: by which meanes you will infinitely oblige me, who shall not faile to let the world know to whose bounty & assistance I am indebted. S^r, that worthy & communicative nature of yours, breathing in y^r excellent writings, prompts me to this great confidence; but, however my request succeedes, be pleased to pardon the liberty of, R^d Sir, your most humble, tho' unknowne servant, &c.

Sayes-Court, 17 Jan. 1669-70.

To JOHN EVELYN, Esquire.

S^r,

You might have had a more speedy answer to your kind letter, but y^t soon after ye receipt of it, I fell into my ordinary distemper, which is ye stone, but with more then ordinary extremities, which hath continued these 3 or 4 dayes already, and what will be ye end God knows; to whom, for either life or death, I heartily submit.

Presently after ye reading of your's I set my selfe to search my father's Adversaria and Papers, and after a little search I found a proper head, or title *de Baculis,* as an addition to what he had written upon Theophrastus; and under y^t title, many particular references to all kind of ancient authours, but soe confusedly y^t I thinck noe man but I, y^t have been used to his hand and way, can make any thing of it. There are 2 full sides in q^rto. S^r, if God grant me life, or some respite from this present extremitie, it shall be one of ye first things I shall doe, to send you what he hath written, copyed out in ye same order as I find it.

Whilst I was searching my father's papers, I lighted on a note concerning Plants and Trees, which I thought fit to impart unto you, because you tell me you have written of trees; you have it here enclosed. Besides this I remember I have, but know not where to find it at this time, Wormij Literatura Danica, where, if I be not much mistaken, he hath somewhat *de Baculis,* there, or in some other treatise I am pretty confident. S^r, I desire you to beleeve y^t I am very willing to serve any gentleman of your quality in soe reasonable a request. But if you be ye gentleman, as I suppose, who have set out ye first booke of Lucretius in English, I must needes confesse myselfe much indebted to you, though I never had ye opportunitie to professe it, for y^t honourable mention which you were pleased to make of me in your preface. Whatsoever I should thinck of your work or translation, yet civility would engage me to say soe much. But truly, S^r, if you will beleeve me, who I thinck was never accounted a flatterer by them y^t have known me, my iudgement is, y^t you have acquitted yourselfe of y^t knotty business much better then I thought could be done by any man, though I thinck those excellent parts might deserve a more florid and proper subiect; but I submit to your better iudgement.

S^r, it hath been some taske to me to find soe

much free time to dictate soe much: if there be any thing impertiment, I desire you will be pleased to consider my case. Soe I take my leave, and rest,

Your very humble servant,
Meric Casaubon.*

January 24, 1669-70.

To Dr. Meric Casaubon, Isaaci Fil.

Rev^d S^r,

There was no danger I should forget to return you notice of the favour I yesterday received, where I find my obligations to you so much improv'd, by the treasure they convey'd me; and that it is to you I am to owe the greatest and best of my subsidiaries. There are many things in your paper which formerly I had noted; but more which I should never have observ'd; and therefore both for confirming my owne, and adding so many more, and so excellent, I think my selfe sacredly engag'd to publish my greate acknowledgements, as becomes a beneficiarie. As to the crude and hastie putting this trifle of mine abroad into the world, there is no danger;† since I should thereby deprive my

---

* This Letter is not written by Mr. Casaubon, but only bears his signature.

† Amongst Mr. Evelyn's papers there is a small fragment of this treatise in Latin, consisting only of 2 or 3 pages; it does not appear that it was ever finished. From an introductory pa-

selfe of those other assistances which your generous bounty has in store for me ; nor are those materials which lie by me, brought into any tollerable order yet, as not intended for any worke of labour, but refreshment, when I am tired with other more serious studies. Thus, S^r, you see me doubly oblig'd to returne you my thanks for this greate humanity of yours, and to implore the divine goodnesse to restore you to your health, who am, Revd S^r,

Y^r, &c.

Sayes-Court, 24 Jan. 1669-70.

To my Lord High Treasurer of England
[CLIFFORD].

Rig^t hon^{ble},

I should much sooner have made good my promise of transmitting to y^r Hon^r, ye inclosed synopsis (containing the briefe, or heads of the work I am travelling on) if, besides ye number of bookes & papers that I have ben condemn'd (as it were) to reade over and diligently peruse, there had not lately ben put into my hands a monstrous folio, written in Dutch,* which containes no lesse than

---

ragraph, it should seem to have been intended as a jocular piece ; but the small part which is written is grave and solemn. It begins with the staff which Jacob used when he met his brother Esau.

* " Saken van Stuet en Oorlogh door d'Heer Lieuwe Van Aitzema," &c.

1079 pages, elegantly and carefully printed at the Hague this last yeare; and what fills me with indignation, derogating from his M^{atie} & our Nation: the subiect of it being principaly ye warr with Enggland not yet brought to a period, which prompts me to believe there is another volume preparing on the same argument. By the extraordinary industrie used in this, and the choice pieces I find they have furnish'd the author with, his M^{atie} and y^r L^p will see that to write such an historie as may not onely deliver truth and matter of fact to posterity, but vindicate our prince and his people from the prepossessions & disadvantages they lie under (whilst, remaining thus long silent, we in a manner justify their reproches), will require more time to finish than at the first setting out could well have ben imagin'd. My Lord, I dare affirme it without much vanity, that had I been ambitious to present his M^{atie} with a specimen onely of my diligence, since first I received his com'ands, I could long ere this have prevented these gent. who, I am told, are already upon the Dutch war. There had nothing ben more easy than after a florid preamble to have publish'd a laudable description & image of the severall conflicts, & to have gratified aboundance of worthy persons who were actors in them; but since my Lord Arlington and y^r L^p expect from me a solemn deduction and true state of all affaires & particulars from his M^{aties} first entring into treaty with the States at his arrival in England, to the yeare 1667, nay to this instant period (which will comprehend so greate & so signal a part of his glorious reigne), I easily believe his M^atie will neither believe the time long nor me altogether indilligent, if he do not receive this historie so soone as otherwise he might have expected. All I will add in relation to myselfe is this; that as I have not for many moneths don any thing else (taking leave of all my delightfull studies), so by God's help I intend to prosecute what I have begun, with the same fervour & application. Your Lo^p will consider how irksome a taske it is to reade over such multitudes of books, remonstrances, treatises, journals, libells, pamphlets, letters, papers, & transactions of state, as of necessity must be don before one can set pen to paper. It would affright y^r Lo^p to see the heapes that lie here about me, & yet is this the least part of the drudgerie and paines, which consists in the judgment to elect and cull out, and then to dispose & place the materials fitly; to answer many bitter and malicious objections, & dextrously, & yet candidly, to ward some unlucky points that are not seldome made at us; and after all this the labour of the pen will not be inconsiderable. I speake not this to inhaunce of the instrument, but rather that I may obtaine pardon for the lapses I may fall into, notwithstanding all this zeale & circumspection: and that his M^atie will graciously accept of my endeavours, and protect me from the unkindnesses of such as use to decry all things of this nature for a single mistake; or because some lesse worthy men find not themselves or relations flatter'd, and be not satisfied that (tho' they deserve not much) they are no way disoblig'd. As to the method, I have bethoughte myselfe of this (if y^r L^p confirme it) namely, to transmit the papers (as fast as I shall bring them to any competent period) to my Lo: Arlington and y^r L^p: that so being com'unicated (thro' both y^r favours) to his Matie before they swell into enormous bulke, he may cast his royal eye over them with lesse trouble, and animadvert upon them 'til they are refin'd and fit for his gracious approbation; since by this meanes I shall hope to attaine two greate things; the performing of his Maties pleasure, and that part of a true historian, which is to deliver truth; and he (I think) who attaines to this, *omne tulit punctum.*—But, my Lord, there are yet divers considerable papers and pieces which I want; letters, treaties, articles, and instructions to ambassadors, &c. which I can only receive from Mr. Secretarie and from y^r L^p, that so I may not be impos'd on by such memoires and transactions of state as I find to my hand (if I durst adventure on the coyne) in the books of our antagonists publish'd with a confidence so frontlesse. But since I may not well hope for these and other personal and living assistances (as I shall also have neede of) 'till the more urgent afaires of Parliament are over, I do in the meane time employ my selfe in adorning a preface (of which I here inclose y^r L^p a sum'arie) and go on in reading, and collection of materials, that when I shall have receiv'd those other desiderates, I may proceede to ye compiling part, and of knitting together what I have made some progresse in.

I am, my Lord, y^r Ho^{rs}, &c.

Sayes-Court, 20 Jan. 1670.

To my Lord Treasurer.

My Lord,

It is not my fault, but misfortune, that you have not 'ere this received a full account of the time which (by y^r particular favour to me) I acknowledge to be wholy yours: your L^p has sometime since justified ye quæries which I first drew up, that they were material, & promis'd I should not want y^r assistance in the solution of them; but the recesse of the Court, and consequently y^r Lo^{ps} absence, & otherways want of opportunity, & pressure of affaires, has depriv'd me of receiving those necessarie directions which so important a subject as that under my hand dos require: but tho' this might serve somewhat to extenuate what may be thought wanting to my industrie, yet I hope I shall not be found to have trifled in that which I am preparing to put shortly into y^r hands; namely, the two former parts of the Historie, which (if y^r Lo^p likewise approve) I think of disposing into the following periods. The first (giving a succinct account of their original, for methods sake) comprehends the state of the Hollanders in relation to England, especially their defection from ye Crowne of Spaine, a^o 1586, til his present Maties happy Restauration, 1660; and herein, a deduction of all the notorious injuries & affronts which ye English have suffer'd from the Dutch, and what rebukes they have received for them from the powers who first made warr against them, & from his Matie, whom they compell'd to make another. The second sets forth at large the course and progresse of the late differences, from his Maties returne a^o 1660, to the year 1666 (inclusively) by which time (his Maties Ambass^rs being recal'd from their respective ministeries abroad) the warr was fully indicted. This period more especially relates his Maties endeavor to have compos'd matters in dispute between his subiects and the Dutch: answers all their cavells, vindicates his honor, states the aggression, treaties wth Munster; describes the first battail, the action at Bergen; transacts with the Dane, with the French, the rupture with both; together with all the intercurrent exploits at Guiny, the Mediterranean, West Indies, and other signal particulars, in 169 paragraphs or sections; and thus far it is already advanced. The third and last period includes the *status* or height of the warr (against the three greate potentates we named) to the conclusion of it in the Treaty at Breda, 1667, in wch I shall not omit any of those numerous particulars presented to his Matie thro' my Lord Arlington's hands, in my first project of the work, nor any thing else which y^r Lo^p shall com'and me to insert.

The two former parts being already dispatch'd, want nothing save ye transcribing, which I therefore have not thought convenient to hasten, 'til I receive your Lo^ps directions in the difficulties which I herewith transmit; upon returne whereof, I shall soone present his Matie with the better part of this worke; and then, as his Matie shall approve of my dilligence, proceede with the remainder, which I hope will not take up so long a time. If it shall be thought fit hereafter to cast it into other languages, especialy Latine or French, it may be considerably contracted, so very many particulars in the English relating onely to companies & more domestiq concernes, in a legal style, full of tedious memorials and altercations of merchants; which (tho' now requisite to deduce somewhat more at large for the justification of his Maties satisfaction of his subiects, and as a testimonie publish'd from authentiq records amongst ourselves) will be of little importance to forrainers, and especialy greate persons, curious & learned men, who are to be entertain'd with refin'd and succinct narratives, & so far with the cause of the warr, as may best imprint the sense of the wrongs we have sustain'd, take off the prejudices our enemies have prepossess'd them with, together with the most shining matter of fact becoming the style of historie.

I now send y^r Lo^p my Preface; it is in obedience to a particular suggestion of my Lord Arlington's, requiring of me a compleate deduction of the progresse of navigation &.com'erce, from its first principle to ye present age: and certainely not without greate judgement; since (as his Lo^p well observ'd) all our contests & differences wth the Hollanders at sea derive onely from that sourse: and if the Introduction (for a page or two) seeme lesse severe than becomes the fore-lorne of so rude a subject.as follows it, I have this to say, that as no man willingly embarks in a storme, so I am perswaded y^r Lo^p will not condemne me when you have perus'd it to the end, & consider'd how im'enee an ocean I have pass'd to bring it home to the argument in hand, and yet in how contracted a space I have assembl'd together that multitude of particulars the most illustrious; taken in all that is material, and more (permit me to affirme) then is to be found in many authors of greate bulke, much lesse in any one single treatise, antient or modern; by which y^r Lp. may perhapes a little estimate the dilligence that has ben used, and that I can do nothing which your

Lordshipe thinks fit to com'and me, superficialy. I confesse it were yet capable of politure, and would shew much brighter in another dresse among the curious, to whom singly it might happly prove no unacceptable entertainement: I could yet also add considerably to it, but some perhaps may think it already too large for a *vestibule,* tho' that will best appeare when the superstructure is finish'd, which, if my calculation abuse me not (from the model already fram'd, & in good part advanc'd) will amount to at the least 800 or 1000 pages in folio, notwithstanding all the care I can apply to avoid impertinences, as far as consists with integrity, & the numerous particulars which necessarily crowd into so active and extensive a warr. Sure I am (whatever may be objected) 'tis apposite & proper to the subject and the occasion of it, & stands & falls by y^r Lo^{ps} suffrage. His Ma^{ty} has yet two sheetes, which I beseech y^r Lo^p to retrieve for me; and after y^r animadversions on this, I will waite upon your Lo^p, & receive your farther directions to,

My Lord, &c.

Sayes-Court, 31 Aug. 1671.

From JOHN EVELYN to the Rev. Father PATRICK.

R: Father,
Sayes-Court, 27 Sept. 1671, hoc Sanctum Benedictum.

You require me to give you an account in writing, what the doctrine of the Church of England is concerning the B. Eucharist? and in particular, whether there be any thing in it signifying to adoration? which, I conceive, an expression of mine one day at Mr. Treasurer's, might occasion. Though I cannot suppose you to be at all ignorant of what her opinion is in these matters; and that indeede you ought to enquire concerning them of some of our learned Prelates and Doctors, whose province it is to unfold these mysteries; yet since you command it, and that I reade in the Apostle* how every one is obliged to render an answer to those who demand a reason of the hope which is in them: I do with all alacrity comply with your desires, as far as my talent reaches.†

1. The doctrine of the Church of England is, or at least to my best understanding, imports, that after the prayer, or words of consecration, the symbols become changed into the body and blood of Christ, after a sacramental, spiritual, and real manner; and that all initiated, or baptized persons, of competent age and capacity, who by unfained repentance, and a faithful consideration of the life,

---
* 1 Peter, ch. 3. v. 15.   † See note on this passage in p. 235.

doctrine, and passion of our B. Saviour, resolve to undertake his holy religion, and to persist in it, are made realy participants of the benefits of his body and blood for the remission of their sins, and the obtaining of all other spiritual graces; inasmuch, as it is a revival of the sacrifice of Christ on the crosse, *once* offered for sin, and for ever effectual; and a renewing of the covenant of grace to the penitent.

But she who affirmes this, holds also, that even after the words of consecration (or, rather, efficacy of the benediction) the bodily substance of the elements remaine; yet so as to become the instruments of the Divine Spirit, conveying its influence and operation to the prepared recipient : and therefore she dos not behold the elements altogether such as naturaly they are to the corporal refection; but (as Theodoret speakes) upon the change of the names, the change which grace superinduces. Or, if you like it better; not merely bread and wine, naked figures and representations; but such as exbibite Christ himselfe, and puts the worthy communicant into sure possession of him. In a word, they are seales to superiour excellencies, give fœderal title to God's promises; and though they are not changed in natural qualities, yet are applicable of divine benefits, and a solemn profession of our faith, &c. And upon this account, the mysterious presence of Christ she holds to be a greate miracle, engaging the infinite power of God, to render the flesh and blood of Christ so present in the elements by effect and benediction, as that the worthy receiver as really communicates in reference to his spirit, as he sacramentaly communicates in reference to his body; the mystical presence being present with the material, by a supernatural conjunction realy tendered to the faithfull.

I could add infinite other formes to expresse the same thing, but this I take to be the cleare sense of the article; and can, when you command me, defend it by the best and noblest instances of Scriptures, Fathers, and reason;[*] but you have not required it, and it were too tedious for a letter. Let it suffice, that the difference between us and the Church of Rome consists chiefly in the definition of the manner of the change; the *quomodo* or *modus;* about which (not to recite here what Ockham, Cajetan, Biel, &c. say) when P. Lombard had (as himselfe professes) collected the opinions and sentences of all the antients, he ingenuously acknowledges he could no way make out that there was any substantial conversion; for the doctrine was then in the cradle; and when afterwards it grew up, and became an article of faith, Durandus says, plainly, the matter of bread remained, *Modum nescimus, præsentiam credimus,* and so says the Church of England: it was then left free. Why should it not be so still? We both affirm a change

---

[*] See note on this passage in p. 235.

and the reality of it; onely we retaine the antient and middle belief, and presume not to determine the manner of it; because we find it no where revealed; and can produce irrefragable testimonies for 1200 years, to explode the gross and material sense which the later age has forced upon it, when to assert it they tell us that a body consisting of all its physical dimensions and parts, occupies neither place nor space, but is reduced to a point invisible: that meer accidents can inhere without subject: that colour, tast, smell, and the tactile qualities can subsist after the destruction of the substance: that bodys are penetrable: that the same individual thing may be at the same time in different places visible and invisible at the same period: that the same proposition may be absolutely true and false in the same instance: that contradictions may consist with God's veracity: that Christ devoured himselfe, and that his body was broaken and torne with teeth, when it was yet whole and entire: that Christ's body may be eaten, though only accidents be manducated and chewed: that a sacrifice should be made without the destruction of the oblation, and a thousand other incompossibilities, riddles, and illogical deductions extinguishing the eye of reason, and making an errour necessary to salvation. In brief, this new-minted transubstantiation, abhorring from the genuine and rational sense of the text, substitutes a device not only incredible, but impossible; so as Christians, who are enjoyned to offer up a rational liturgy and service, or reason of the hope which should be in them, must bid defyance to it; for they must not believe their eyes, nor tast, nor touch, nor smell (the criterions by which St. John confirms the Christian doctrine, *quod vidimus oculis nostris, quod perspeximus, et manus nostræ contrectaverunt, &c.)* But they must renounce them all, and not onely quit the common principles of sciences, but even common sense. I will say nothing of those who have taken in these strang impressions with their milk, considering the incredible force of education: and that the profoundest learned amongst the heathen were not secured by it from the grossest errours upon this account. One would yet have thought the wise Athenians† needed not a lecture from St. Paule upon the topicks he preached; but that persons enlightened as the Doctors of the Church of Rome pretend to be, should fall into absurdities so illogical and destructive to the very definition of that which discriminates men from bruits, is plainely stupendious; and seemes, methinks, to be pointed at by the greate apostle, where he tells us in the later days, that God shall send some of them strong delusions,‡ and you know what follows. He would be thought a thick-skinn'd doctor in any of their owne, as well as our scholes, who skill'd

---

* 1 Jo. ch. 1. v. 1—3; 4 Acts, v. 20.
† 7 Acts, v. 22, &c. ‡ 2 Thess. ch. 2. v. 11.

not to discern how a thing might be real, and yet spiritual, or, as if nothing were real, but what were corporeal and natural. These do not consider how God himselfe operates on the conscience and soules of men, and that the gifts of his sacred spirit are real graces, and yet not things intelligible and sensible as bodys are. That the Church of England believes a *real presence*, she expresses in the Canon of her Eucharistical office,* *verily* and *indeede*, and than *that*, what can be more *real?*

To object, that the faith in the Holy Trinity obliges us to as greate a difficulty as the Pontifician modalitie, is very trifling, since that is onely matter of beliefe indefinite. We are not required to explaine the manner of the mysterie; nor have we, or the most metaphysical wit living, faculties and adequate instruments to dissolve that knot: spiritual things belong to spirits; we can have no notices proportionable to them; and yet, though they are unfathomable by our reason, they are not inconsistent with it, nor do they violate our understanding by enjoining non-sense. They indeede exceede our explications, but disparage not our Religion; rather they procure it veneration; since there are in nature and common objects, things which we know to be, but know not how they be. But when the dispute (as in this of the Holy Eucharist) is of bodyes and material things, we can define, and may pronounce concerning their affections and possibi-

---

* See ye Catech: in Book of Common Prayer.

lities; they are obnoxious to sense, and fall justly under our cognizance and explication. But y^r R: enjoyns me to say what our Church permits her sons to believe concerning Adoration; I will tell you, the very same that St. Augustine, *Nemo digne manducat, nisi prius adoraverit*: she holds therefore, that the Holy Eucharist is an homage, and an Act of Adoration, and receives it in that humble gesture; for Christ being there present in an extraordinary manner, she worships him at a-tyme when he exhibits himselfe to her in so extraordinary and mysterious a manner, and with so greate advantages; but then this Act is to her Blessed Lord, as God's right hand; or, if it please you better, she adores the flesh and blood of her Saviour in the mysterie, and venerable usage of the symbols, representing and imparting it to our soules: but she gives no divine honours to the bare symbols, without that signification: since it is certain, had the primitive Christians don otherwise,* their enemies would have said, they worshipped the work of their own hands too, and so retorted their reproches. The Church of England, and we her sons, worship what we know; you worship what you know not; and whatsoever is not of faith is sin. Species, and accidents, representations and meere creatures, though consecrated to holy uses, are not proper objects of adoration; God is a jealous God, and it would be seriously considered how innumerable the contingences

---

* See Minutius Felix Octav.

are (though your opinions were tollerable) that render your manner of worshiping the Host extreamely obnoxious and full of perill; since the possible circumstances and defects of the priest's ordination, consecration, recitation of the words, want of intention, impuritie of the elements, their disproportion and mixture; if the priest be illegitimate, simoniacal, or irregular, and severall other impediments of the like nature, render the adorers grosse idolaters by your owne tenets and confession.

I have but a word to add, and that is concerning the Oblation, in which the Church of England differs from that of Rome. She affirmes, that the notion amongst the antients imported onely *Oblatum celebrare, et memoria renovare;* and, that if Christ were realy offered (as you pretend) he must every time be put to death againe. But St. Paule tells us plainely he was but once* offered, as now shortly on Good Friday he is sayd to be crucified, and at Christmas to be borne, &c. But we add, if Christ delivered his holy body, and sacrific'd it in a natural sense, when he instituted the h: Sacrament, before his real passion on the Crosse (as, according to you, indisputably he did), it could not be propitiatory; and if were not propitiatory, what becomes of your Masse? For if it was propitiatory when he instituted it, his blessed Father was reconciled before his suffering, which I think we neither dare to affirme. It was then representative

---

* Compare 6 Romans, and 9 Heb.

and memorative onely, of what *was to be*, as now it is to us, of what it has already ben: and yet the Church of England dos for all this acknowledge it in another sense to be a sacrifice, both propitiatory and impetratory; because the oblation of it to God with and by the prayers and praises of her members, dos render God propitious, by obteining the benefits which the death of our Lord dos represent; and therefore over it we beseech God for the universal peace of the Churche; for the state of the world; for Kings, Priests, and Magistrates; for the sick; for a glorious resurrection of the saints.* In sum, with St. Cyrill, we implore that it may moove God to grant all that is desired by the regular and assiduous offices of the Catholiq Church, especialy of those who at that time offer and communicate:

This, R: F., is the best account I am able for the present, and in so short limits, to give you: it is what our Church will owne, what I believe, and what I endeavour to practise, and who in greate charity and humility subscribe myselfe,

R. Fr.
Your most faithfull servant,
J. Evelyn.

S^r, you must pardon my frequent blotts, &c.
For the R. F. Patrick.

---

* See ye prayer in our Com'union Office, for ye whole state of Christ's Church militant, &c.

Note to page 226.

If it be transubstantiated, tis a miracle; now our b: Saviour never did miracles (that we read of), but the visible change was apparent to all the world, as from blindness to sight, from sickness to health, from death to life; so the loaves were augmented, the water converted to wine, &c.: but here is a miracle wrought without any visible change, which we never read he did, and is indeed a contradiction, and destroys the effect of our common sense and reason, by which alone we have assurance of all that Christ did and suffered; and if we may not credit these, we may justly doubt of the whole Chr: Religion itselfe; which God would never tempt his rational creatures to do.

Note to page 228.

And now we mentioned Fathers, there occurs to me one passage in that excellent treatise of St. Aug: "De Doctrina Christ:" B. 3. c. 6. upon that famous period in St. John, on which our antagonists put so much stresse, that as it instructs us how to interpret the literal sense of divers the like places in Scripture, so has it perfectly convinced me as to the meaning of that pretended difficulty: I say so fully, as I dare oppose it to whatsoever can be produced out of all the Fathers of the Church (as they call them) put all together. The words are these—*si preceptiva,* &c. If a preceptive speech or expression seemes to injoyne a thing that is flagitious or wicked, or to prohibite a beneficiall or profitable thing, it is figuratively to be taken; *e. g.* 'Except ye eate the flesh of the Son of man, and drink his blood (says our Saviour), ye shall have no life in you.' This seems to com'and a flagitious and unlawful thing, 'tis therefor figurative, injoyning us to communicate in the passion of our Lord, and sweetely and profitably to keep in mind that his flesh was crucified and wounded for us: and this is plainely the sense and the voice of the Church of England, that I think men must be out of their witts to contend against it. I could yet augment the number of as plain testimonys and suffrages from more of those good men; but it is unnecessary.

To my Lord Treasurer.

My Lord,

I was yesterday at Whitehall to waite on y^r Lo^p, and a little to expostulate with you upon the work enjoin'd me, for want of that assistance which Mr. Secretary promis'd from time to time; so as unlesse y^r Lo^p interpose and procure those papers, I must desist, and go no further: 'tis, my Lord, a grave and weighty undertaking in this nice & captious age, to deliver to posterity a three-years war, of three the greatest powers and potentates of Europe against one nation newly restor'd, and even at that period conflicting with so many calamities besides. If this deserve no application extraordinary, I have taken but ill measures when I entred on it; but I rely on y^r L^p, whose com'ands first animated, & by whose influence onely I care to proceede. If the materials I have amass'd lie still in heapes, blame not me, who write not for glory, unlesse you approve of what I write, and assist the deferrent, for I am no more. Tis matters of fact his Ma^{ty} would have me deliver to the world; let me have them authentic then, and now especialy in this crisis of exinanition (with griefe & indignation I speake it), and that the whole nation is sinking. As to the action at Bergen, I am ready to transmit what I have drawn up, but it shall go no further 'til you cast your eye upon it, since without y^r Lo^{ps} approbation (after the measures I have taken of y^r comprehensive and consum'ate judgement, *quorumq; pars ipse fuisti*, I neither can nor ought to like any thing I do: but this, either your modestie or buisenesse denys me, & unlesse I overcome it, let all I have don wither & rise no more. Augustus Cæsar had weighty affaires on his hand, but he suffer'd nothing to pine of lesser concerne, when he sometimes heard poems recited; and Scipio would converse with Lælius, and often with Lucullus too; and will you let your country suffer, and that which you with so much earnestnesse and vigour press'd might be publish'd with the greatest expedition, languish now for want of your assistance? My Lord, what you were wont to say was

EPISTOLARY CORRESPONDENCE.   239

English to rise as one man in rescue of our honour, the whole world will blush at our stupid *lacheté*, and the ingratitude of our foes be styl'd a vertue. Let me, therefore, my Lord, receive y[r] further directions seasonably, that whilst you still incite me to dispatch, your Lo[p] not furnishing me those pieces, render it impossible to advance.

I am, my Lord, &c.

Sayes-Court, Nov. 14, 1671.

Desiderata.—The particulars of the Treaty with the Dutch after the first war w[th] y[e] Parliam[t], to be found (I suppose) in the Paper Office.

2. What com[m]ission was given De Ruyter when he went to Ginne, of which we charge the States?

3. Mr. Hen. Coventries instructions for Sweden, so far as concernes the action at Bergen.

4. Coll. Nichols's instruction, &c. with the Articles of the reddition of New Amsterdam.

5. Lord Fitz Harding's instructions, which I suspect are corrupted in the Dutch relations.

6. The instructions of S[r] Walter Vane sent to the Duke of Brandenburg.

7. His Ma[ties] treatie with the Bishop of Munster.

8. By whose importunitie was the saile slacken'd in the first encounter with the Dutch, or whether I am to blanch this particular?

9. What particular gent. volunteers, &c. am I

240   EPISTOLARY CORRESPONDENCE.

more especialy to mention for their behaviour in the first engagement.

10. Was Mr. Boyle's head carried into the sea from the trunk?

11. Did there no wound or bruise appeare upon my Lord Falmouth's body?

12. On whom is the breaking bulke of the E. India prizes to be realy charged?

13. Did Bastian Senten board the Earle of Sandwich, take downe the blew flag, set up the orange, & possesse him 3 houres, as the Dutch relations pretend?

14. Sir Gilbert Talbot's letter to the Commander in Chiefe at Bergen, which I find not in y'r Lo'ps papers.

15. I desire the order y'r Lo'p promis'd me, to the Cleark of y'e Parliament, that I may search the Journals for those important particulars your Lo'p mentioned, &c.

To my Lord High Treasurer (CLIFFORD).*

My Lord,

According to my duty, I send y'r L'p the lett'rs and papers which your L'p has ben pleas'd to trust

* Mr. Evelyn wrote a congratulatory letter to Sir Tho. Clifford on his being made a Peer, and in the margin added this note: "Who was ever a most obliging friend to me in partime withall, for the compiling of that part of yᵉ History of the late Warr, which (having receiv'd both his Maᵗⁱᵉˢ and yʳ Lᵒᵖˢ approbation) I designe to publish, and the rather because I have no other meanes to expresse my greate obligations to yʳ Lᵖ than to set that forth, in which yʳ Loᵖˢ courage & virtue has ben so conspicuous. And now, my Lord, the greate abilitie, uprightnesse, and integritie which yʳ Lᵖ has made to give lusture thro' the rest of those high offices and charges which you have rather dignified, than they your Lᵖ, makes me perfectly deplore yʳ Lᵖˢ so solemn, so extraordinary, & so voluntarie a recesse. I am deeply sensible of my owne greate losse by it, because I have found yʳ Lᵖ has ever ben the most obliging to me; but much more of the publiq. I pray God to blesse yʳ Lᵖ, and humbly beg this favour, that you will still regard me as yʳ most gratefull beneficiary, & reckone me amongst the number of those who not onely make the sincerest professions, but who realy are what they professe, wᶜʰ is to be,

My Lord, &c.

Sayes-Court, 21 Aug. 1672.

cular, and after Treasurer (whatever his other failings were), a person of as cleane hands and generous a mind, as any who have succeeded in that high trust."

more especialy to mention for their behaviour in the first engagement.

10. Was Mr. Boyle's head carried into the sea from the trunk?

11. Did there no wound or bruise appeare upon my Lord Falmouth's body?

12. On whom is the breaking bulke of the E. India prizes to be realy charged?

13. Did Bastian Senten board the Earle of Sandwich, take downe the blew flag, set up the orange, & possesse him 3 boures, as the Dutch relations pretend?

14. Sir Gilbert Talbot's letter to the Commander in Chiefe at Bergen, which I find not in y[r] Lo[ps] papers.

15. I desire the order y[r] Lo[p] promis'd me to the Cleark of y[e] Parliament, that I may search the Journals for those important particulars your Lo[p] mentioned, &c.

To my Lord High Treasurer (CLIFFORD).*
My Lord,

According to my duty, I send y[r] L[p] the lett[rs] and papers which your L[p] has ben pleas'd to trust

---

* Mr. Evelyn wrote a congratulatory letter to Sir Tho. Clifford on his being made a Peer, and in the margin added this note: "Who was ever a most obliging friend to me in partime withall, for the compiling of that part of ye History of the late Warr, which (having receiv'd both his Maties and y^r Lo^ps approbation) I designe to publish, and the rather because I have no other meanes to expresse my greate obligations to y^r L^p than to set that forth, in which y^r Lo^ps courage & virtue has ben so conspicuous. And now, my Lord, the greate abilitie, uprightnesse, and integritie which y^r L^p has made to give lusture thro' the rest of those high offices and charges which you have rather dignified, than they your L^p, makes me perfectly deplore y^r L^ps so solemn, so extraordinary, & so voluntarie a recesse. I am deepely sensible of my owne greate losse by it, because I have found y^r L^p has ever ben the most obliging to me; but much more of the publiq. I pray God to blesse y^r L^p, and humbly beg this favour, that you will still reguard me as y^r most gratefull beneficiary, & reckone me amongst the number of those who not onely make the sincerest professions, but who realy are what they professe, wch is to be,

My Lord, &c.

Sayes-Court, 21 Aug. 1672.

---

cular, and after Treasurer (whatever his other failings were), a person of as cleane hands and generous a mind, as any who have succeeded in that high trust."

To the Lord Viscount CORNBERY.

My Lord,

I think it is not unknown to y^r L^p that I have sometime since ben com'anded by his Ma^ty to draw up a narrative of the occasions of the first Dutch Warr; in order to which my Lord Clifford acquaints me he did formerly and dos still continue to desire of you, that you would be pleas'd to give me the perusal of Sr Geo: Downings dispatches to my Lord Chancelor y^r father, which (as I remember) you told me were at Cornbery, where now you are. My Lord, 'tis an extraordinary mortification to me, that my untoward employments here have not suffer'd me to waite upon you all this time of y^r sweete recesse, that I might also have seen how that place is adorn'd and improv'd since I was there, & where I might likewise have seene those papers, without giving y^r Lo^p this trouble; but y^r L^p will consider my present condition, & may be assur'd that I shall make use onely of such particulars as conduce to ye province impos'd on me by his Matie. I would likewise be glad to know what light y^r Lo^p can give me out of the lett^rs & dispatches of my Lord Holles, Mr. Coventrie, & Sr Gilbert Talbot, which have all of them an influence into that affaire, as it concern'd France, Denmark, and Sweden, upon which I am also directed to touch, but shall not be able to do it with any satisfaction, unlesse y^r Lo^p favour me with the com'unication of the subsidiaries in y^r Cabinet, who am, my Lord, &c.

Whitehall, 17 Sept. 1672.

To the Duchesse of NEWCASTLE, &c. at Bolsover*
(when she sent me her Works),

May it please y^r Grace,

I go not into my study without reproch to my prodigious ingratitude, whilst I behold such a pile of favours & monuments of y^r incomparable spirit, without having yet had the good fortune, or the good manners indeede, to make my recognitions as becomes a person so immensely oblig'd. That I presume to make this small present to y^r Grace (who were pleas'd to accept my collection of Archi-

---

* This letter might be considered as a banter on this extraordinary lady (of whom see vol. II. pp. 283, 285, 286), were it not remembered, that the homage paid to high rank and riches at that time of day was excessive; and that Mr. Evelyn was himself very profuse of compliment in his dedications and letters of acknowledgment. If the reader will turn to a very scarce and curious volume, entitled, "A Collection of Letters and Poems, written by several Persons of Honour and Learning upon divers important subjects to the late Duke and Duchess of Newcastle, London, 1678," he will find that not only learned men, but learned bodies of men, made use of the same terms in celebrating the talents and accomplishments of these noble authors.

tects, to whom timber and planting are subsidiaries) is not for the dignitie of the subject (tho' Princes have not disdain'd to cultivate trees & gardens with the same hands they manag'd sceptres), but because it is the best expression of my gratitude that I can returne. Nor, Madame, is it by this that I intend to pay all my homage for that glorious present, which merits so many encomiums, or write a panegyric of y^r virtues, which all the world admires, least the indignitie of my style should prophane a thing so sacred; but to repeate my admiration of y^r genius, & sublime witt so comprehensive of the most abstracted appearances, & so admirable in your sex, or rather in your Grace's person alone, which I never call to mind but to rank it amongst ye Heroines, and constellate with the Graces: such of ancient daies were Zenobia, Queene of Palmyra, that writ the Historie of her country, as y^r Grace has don that of my Lord Duke y^r husband, worthy to be transmitted to posteritie. What should I speak of Hilpylas, the mother-in-law of young Plinie, & of pis admirable wife! of Pulcheria, daughter to the Emp. Arcadius; or of Anna, who call'd Alexius father, & writ 15 books of historie, &c.! Your Grace has title to all their perfections. I passe Cornelia, so neere the greate Scipio, & mother of the Gracchi, to come to the later wits, Isabella, Queene of Castile, wife of Ferdinand, K. of Arragon, of which bed came the first Charles, &

the mother of foure learned daughters, of whom was one Catherine, wife to our Henry the 8th; Mary of Portugal, wife to John Duke of Braganza (related to her Matie the Queene Consort), rarely skill'd in the mathematical sciences; so was her sister, espoused to Alexander Duke of Parma; Lucretia d'Esté, of the house of Ferrara; Dutchess of Urbin, a profound philosopher; Vittoria Colonna, wife of Ferdinand d'Avila, Marquis of Pescaria, whose poetrie equal'd that of ye renowned Petrarch; Hippolita Strozzi, daughter to Fran: Duke of Milan; Mary of Arragon; Marques de Vasco, Fabiala, Marcella, Eustochium, St. Catharine of Sienna, St. Bridget & Therese (for even the greatest saints have cultivated the sciences), Fulvia Morata, Isabella Andreini, Margarite of Valois (sister to Francis the First, and grand-mother to the greate Henry of France), whose novells are equal to those of ye witty Boccaccio, & the memoires of another Margarite, wife of this greate Prince, that name having ben so fertil for ladys of the sublimest genius. Catharine de Roches of Poictiers was a celebrated wit, & Claudia de Cleremont, Dutchesse of Retz, Mary de Gournay, & the famous Anna M. Schurman: and of our owne country, Queene Elizabeth, Queene Jane, the Lady Weston, Mrs. Philips our late Orinda, the daughters of Sr Tho: More; the Queene Christina of Sweden, & Elizabeth, daughter of a Queene also, to whom the renowned Des

Cartes dedicated his learned worke, & the profound researches of his extraordinary talent. But all these, I say, sum'd together, possesse but that divided, which y^r Grace retaines in one; so as Lucretia Marinella, who writ a book (in 1601), *dell' Excellenzia delle Donne, con difetti é mancamenti de gli huomini,* had no neede to have assembled so many instances & arguments to adorne the work, had she lived to be witnesse of Margarite, Dutchesse of Newcastle, to have read her writings, & to have heard her discourse of the science she comprehended: I do, Madame, acknowledge my astonishment, & can hardly think too greate of those soules, who, resembling y^r Grace's, seeme to be as it were wholy separate from matter, & to revolve nothing in their thoughts but universal ideas. For what of sublime & worthy in the nature of things, dos not y^r Grace comprehend, and explaine! What of greate & noble, that y^r illustrious Lord has not adorn'd, for I must not forget the munificent present of his very usefull book of Horsemanship, together with y^r Graces works upon all the profound as well as politer subjects, which I receiv'd of Sr Fran: Tapps from both y^r Graces hands; but this accumulation ought to be the argument of a fresh and more ample acknowledgement, for which this paper is too narrow. My wife (whom you have ben pleas'd to dignifie by the name of y^r daughter, & to tell her that you looke upon her as your owne, for a mother's sake of hers, who had so greate a veneration of y^r Grace) presents her most humble duty to you by, Madame,

Y^r Grace's, &c.

Sayes-Court, 15 June, 1674.

To Doctor Meric Casaubon, Isaaci Fil.[*]
Rev^d S^r,

I am infinitely oblig'd to you for y^r civil reply to my lett^r; but am not a little tr^{o}ubl'd, that it should importune you in a time when you were indispos'd. The stone is an infirmity, which I am daily taught to co'misserate in my poore afflicted & deare Brother who languishes under that torture, and therefore am much concern'd when I heare of any that are exercis'd under that sad affliction: I will therefore beg of you, that no impertinence of mine (for truely that trifle is no other) may engage you to the least inconvenience, & wch may prejudice your health. You have already greatly oblig'd me by the hints you are pleas'd to send me, & by the notice y^u are pleas'd to take of that poore essay of mine on Lucretius, so long since escaping me. You may be sure I was very young, & therefore very rash, or ambitious, when I adventur'd upon that

---

[*] See Casaubon's Letter to Evelyn, under the date Jan. 24, 1669-70, in p. 216.

knotty piece. 'Tis very true, that when I committed it to a friend of mine (and one whom I am assur'd you intimately know) to inspect the printing of it, in my total absence from London, I fully resolv'd never to tamper more with that author; but when I saw it come forth so miserably deform'd, & (I may say) maliciously printed & mistaken, both in the Latine copy (which was a most correct and accurate one of Stephens's) & my version so inhumanly deprav'd, shame & indignation together incited me to resolve upon another edition; & I knew not how (to charme my anxious thoughts during those sad & calamitous times) to go thro' the five remaining bookes: but, when I had don, I repented of my folly, & that I had not taken the caution you since have given us in your excellent *Enthusiasme*, & which I might have foreseene. But, to commute for this, it still lies in the dust of my study, where 'tis like to be for ever buried.

Sir, I returne you a thousand thanks for the favour & honour you have don me, & which I should have sooner acknowledg'd, had I not ben from home when your letter came to my house: I shall now beg of God to restore y^r health, not for the satisfaction of my impertinent enquiries, but for the universal republiq of learning, & the benefit which all good men derive from the fruits of y^r worthy labour, who am,

S^r, y^r &c.

Sayes-Court, 15 July 1674.

To the Countess of Ossorie, &c.

Madame,

I cannot account my self to haue worthily discharg'd my duty to the memorie of my noble Lord, without deepely condoling the losse y{r} La{p} has sustain'd in the death of that illustrious person: never did a greate man go off this earthly stage with more regret & universal sorrow, never had Prince a more loyal subject, never nation a more publiq losse; & how greate my owne were in particular, the vn-interrupted obligations of above thirty yeares (joyn'd with a most condescending & peculiar friendship) may serve to declare, that nothing could haue happen'd to me more calamitous. But all this dos but accumulate to y{r} La{p}'s affliction, which were indeede deplorable, had you not, besides the greate & heroic actions of his life, the glorious name he has left behind, the hopefull branches that remaine to imitate his virtues, the consolation, above all, of his being safe, where he has receiv'd a crown brighter than any earthly Prince. It was my duty (as well as honor) to be with him night & day till I clos'd his eyes, & to joyne in those holy offices which were so devoutly perform'd by the Bishop of St. Asaph to the last article, & during all his Lord{p}'s sickness; which was pass'd thro' with such Christian patience & resignation, as that alone ought to giue y{r} La{p} exceeding comfort; I am sure it dos to me, & y^r La^p is to blesse Almighty God for it, who after so many honourable hazards in this wicked world, would haue him to a better, & that he is departed hence as a greate man & a true Christian should do, tho' for the present to our infinite losse. And now, Madame, I should beg pardon for entertaining you so long on this mournfull occasion, did I not assure myselfe that the testimony I giue y^r La^p of the religious & pious circumstances of his sickness, would afford you some consolation, as well as to shew how sincerely devoted I was to his L^{ps} service, how much obliged for his constant & generous friendship to me, & how much I am,

Madame, y^r, &c.

White Hall, 5 June 1680.

To Mr. PEPYS, &c. [after the Shipwreck in which the Duke of YORK escaped so narrowly, returning out of Scotland.]

Sir,

I have ben both very sorry, & very much concern'd for you, since your Northern voyage, as knowing nothing of it 'till you were embark'd (tho' I saw you so few daies before) and that the dismal and astonishing accident was ouer, which gaue me apprehensions & a mixture of passions not realy to be express'd 'til I was assur'd of your safety, and I gaue God thanks for it with as much sincerity as any friend you haue aliue. 'Tis sadly true there were a greate many poore creatures lost, & some gallant persons with them; but there are others worth hundreds saved, and Mr. Pepys was to me the second of those some, and if I could say more to expresse my joy for it, you should haue it vnder the band & from the heart of,

S^r, y^r, &c.

Sayes-Court, 5 June 1681.

To Dr. MORLEY, Bp. of Winchester.

1 June, 1681.

* * * * Father Maimbourg has had the impudence to publish at the end of his late *Histoire du Calvanisme*, a pretended letter of the late Dutchesse of York,* intimating the motives of her deserting the Church of England; amongst other things to attribute it to the indifference, to call it no worse, of those two Bishops, upon whose advice she wholly depended as to the direction of her conscience, and points of controversie. 'Tis the universal discourse that y^r L^p is one of those Bishops she mentions, if at least the letter be not supposititious, knowing

---

* This letter is printed in a small collection of Letters of Eminent Persons, in 2 vóls. 12mo.

you to have ben the most domestic in the family, and one whom her Highnesse resorted to in all her doubts and spiritual concernes, not only during her former circumstances, but all the time of her greatnesse to the very last. It is therefore humbly and earnestly desired (as well as indeede expected) amongst all that are concerned for our Religion and the great and worthy character which y^r L'p beares, that your L'p would do right to it, and publish to all the world how far you are concerned in this pretended charge, and to vindicate your selfe and our Church from what this bold man would make the world believe to the prejudice of both. I know your L'p will be curious to reade the passage your selfe, and do what becomes you upon this signal occasion, God having placed you in a station where you have no greate ones frownes to feare or flatter, and given you a zeale for the truth and for his glory. With this assurance I humbly beg your L'ps blessing.

A note added:—" This letter was soon followed with the Bishop's full vindication published in print."*

---

* Dr. Morley published an " Answer to a Letter written by a Romish Priest: together with the Letters themselves:" likewise a " Letter to Ann Duchess of York, a few months before her death."

To Mr. WILLIAM LONDON, at Barbados.

S^r,

I find my selfe so exceedingly oblig'd for the greate civilitie of y^r letter (abating onely for the encomiums you are pleas'd to bestow upon me, & which are in no sort my due), that having nothing to returne you but my thanks and acknowledgements, I was not to delay that small retribution, for so many usefull & excellent notices, as both your letter & the papers inclos'd haue com'unicated me. I haue indeede ben formerly more curious in ye culture of trees & plants, & blotted a greate deale of paper w^h my crude observations (& some of them I have had the vanitie to publish), but they do in no degree amount to ye accuratenesse of your designe, which I cannot but applaude, & wish you all the successe so excellent an undertaking deserves. I do not know that euer I saw a more pertinent & exact enumeration of particulars, & if it please God you liue to accomplish what you have drawn the scheme of, I shall not doubt to pronounce it the most absolute & perfect historie that we haue any where extant of either oure owne, or other plantations. So that I cannot but highly encourage & augure you all the prosperity imaginable: and I shall not faile, in order to it, to impart y^r papers to the Royall Society, who I am very confident will be ready to do you any service; although I do not see that your designe is any where defective. And I perswade my selfe that you will be curious to adorne y^r work with true & handsome draughts of the animals, plants, & other things that you describe in ye natural part. This I am bold to mention, because most of those authors (especialy English) who haue giuen us their relations, fill them with such lame & imperfect draughts & pictures, as are rather a disgrace than ornament to their books, they hauing no talent that way themselues, and taking no course to procure such as can designe; & if now & then you sprinkle here and there a prospect of the countries by ye true and naturall landskipe, it would be of infinite satisfaction, & imprint an idea of those places you passe thro', which are so strange to vs and so desirable. Gaspar Barlæus (in his elegant Historie of Brasile) has giuen an incomparable instance of this: in which work the landskips of divers parts of that country are accurately exhibited and grauen in copper, besides the chorographicall mapps, & other illustrations: but, S^r, I beg your pardon for mentioning a thing, which I am sure you haue well thought of, & will provide for. In your account of plants, trees, fruits, &c. there are abundance to which we are here utter strangers, & therefore cannot but be desirable to the curious. I am told there is newly planted in Barbados an orange of a most prodigious size; & such an improvement of the China as by far exceedes these we haue from Portugal, which are of late yeares much degenerated. As for flowers, I think I have heard that y^e *narcissus tuberosus* grow wild, & in plenty with you. I haue not the impudence to beg for my selfe any of those rarities you mention, but wish with all my heart I had any thing of my owne worthy y^r acceptance. I had at the beginning of last spring some forraine, & exotic seedes which I imparted to my friends, & some I sow'd & set, but with very little successe; & as rightly you complaine there is no trust in our mercenarie seedes men of London for any thing. In the meane time concerning nutmegs, cinnamon, cloues, & those other aromatics you so reasonably covet, I feare it will be a very difficult province to obtaine such of them from the East Indies, they being mostly in possession of the Hollanders, who are (you know) a jealous people, &, as I have ben informed, make it capital to transport so much as a single nutmeg (I meane such a one as being set would produce a tree) out of their countrie: the late Sr John Cox, who had often ben at Nova Batavia, told me he could not procure one handfull but such as were effoete and depriv'd of their sprouting principle, upon any tearmes: much lesse could he obtain a plant: & yet I haue ben told by a confident broaker about the Custome-house (whose name occurs not) & who has himselfe ben in the Indies more than once (pretending to curiosities), that he brought away 2 or 3 plants of the true nutmeg tree belonging to a certaine Dutch merchant; I suppose for the learned Dr Munting of that countrie, who has brought vp both nutmegs and cinnamon plants in his garden in Holland, but to what improvement I cannot tell. It were not to be despair'd but that some subtil & industrious person (who made it his buisinesse) might ouercome this difficultie among some of their plantations, & why not? as well as that a countrie man of ours, who some yeares since brought home the first heads of saffron out of Greece (whence it was death to transport it) in the hollow head or top of his pilgrime staff, if what our Hollingshed writes be true: some such contrivance or accident will doubtlesse at last inrich our western & propitious climate with those precious deficients; as it has don suggar, ginger, indigo, & other beneficial spices & drougs: & I know not whether the Jamaica peper be not already comparable to many of those we haue enumerated. I am sure it gratifies the tast & smell with most agreeable qualities, and little inferior to the oriental cinnamon. There is a wallnut in Virginia whose nuts prosper very well with us, but we want store of them. It is in the meane time deplorable that the Bermudas cedar, of all others the most excellent & odoriferous, is (as I am told) almost worne out for want of propagation: if it will thrive in other countries 'tis pitty but it should be vniversally cultivated. But, S^r, I tire you. The

Hortus Malabaricus * presents us with the most stupendious & vnheard-of plants in that elaborate work; the cutts being in copper are certainely (of any publish'd) the most accurately don, nor are their shapes & descriptions lesse surprizing. S^r, the Royal Society have lately put their Repositorie into an excellent method, & it euery day encreases, thro' the fauour & benevolence of sundry benefactors, whose names are gratefully recorded. If any thing incurr to you of curious (as certainely there daily do, innumerable,) you will greately oblige that assembly of virtuosi in communicating any productions of the places you trauell thro' vpon the occasion of the returne of vessells from those parts. The particulars they collect are animals and insects of all sorts, their skinnes and sceletons, fruits, stones, shells, swords, gunns, minerals, & whateuer nature produces in her vast & comprehensive bosome. S^r, your letter came to me from Mr. Harrwell, the 23^d of Sept. & by the same hand & fauour I returne you the hearty thanks & acknowledgments of,

S^r, y^r, &c.

Sayes-Court, 27 Sept. 1681.

---

* Published at Amsterdam in twelve volumes folio.

To Sam. Pepys, Esq. Secretary to the Admiralty.*

Sir,   Sayes-Court, Decr 6, 1681.

In compliance with y^r co'mands I have already transmitted to you the two large sea-charts, & now I send you the sheetes I have long since blotted with ye Dutch Warr, for which I should now make another apologie (besides its preface) were it not that you well understand the prejudices I lay under at that time, by the inspection of my Lord Treasurer Clifford, who could not endure I should lenifie my style, when a war with Holland was the subject; nor with much patience suffer that France should be suspected, tho' in justice to truth as evident as the day, I neither would, nor honestly could, conceale (what all the world might see) how subdolously they dealt & made us their propertie all along. The interception of De Lyonne's letters to his master, p. 266, is sufficient to make this good: and I am plainly astonished it should not long since have opened our statesmens eyes: unlesse it be, that we designe to truckle under France, and seeke industriously the ruine of our country. You will, Sir, pardon this severe reflection, since I cannot think

---

* The original letter, which varies from this copy, is in the possession of Samuel Pepys Cockerell, Esq. of Westbourn-green, Paddington, who kindly contributed it, with several other letters by Evelyn, which are printed in Pepys's Memoirs and Correspondence, recently published by Lord Braybrooke.

of it without perfect indignation. As to the compiler's part, 'tis not easy to imagine the infinite fardles of papers, treaties, declarations, relations, journals, original letters, & other volumes of print and writing, &c. which I was obliged to reade & peruse (furnish'd, and indeede imposed on me, from the Secretaries of State and others) for this small attempt, and that which was to follow; I am onely sorry that I was so hasty to returne some pieces to my Lord Treasurer, which I might honestly have kept, and with better conscience than his carrying them away into Devonshire, *vnde nulli retrorsum.*

I had drawn a scheme of the intire work down to the Treaty at Breda, and provided ye materials; but the late Lord Treasurer Danby* cutting me short as to some just pretensions of another nature I had to his more particular kindenesse, I cared not to oblige an ungratefull age; and perhaps the world is delivered by it from a fardle of impertinences.

Clifford (his predecessor) was, with all his other imperfections, a generous man, and, I very believe, of cleane hands; I am sure I was oblig'd to him;

---

* Thomas Viscount Dumblaine, afterwards Earl of Danby and Duke of Leeds. He married the Lady Bridget, second daughter of Montague Bertie, Earl of Lindsey, Lord Great Chamberlain of England, and died at Easton in Northamptonshire, the seat of his grandson, the Lord Lempster, on his journey to his house in Yorkshire, July 26, 1712, and in the 81st year of his age.

the other had ben sometimes so to me & mine, but that is all past. Clifford had greate failings, but was gratefull and firme to his friend.

As to y^r other queries, I have not any thing relating to the Prize Office; and for that Discourse wherein I did attempt to shew how far a Gentleman might become learned by the onely assistance of the modern languages (written at the request of Sir Saml Tuke for the Duke of Norfolk), to my griefe I feare I shall never recover it; for, sending it to the person I nam'd somctime since, he tells me he cannot find it; and so for ought I see it is lost. There is a List in it of Authors, and a method of reading them to advantage, besides something in ye discourse which would not have displeased you; nor was it without some purpose of one day publishing it, because 't was written with a virtnons designe of provoking our Court fopps, and for encouragement of illustrious persons who have leasure & inclinations to cultivate their minds beyond a farce, a horse, a whore, and a dog, which, with very little more, are the confines of the knowledge and discourse of most of our fine gentlemen and beaus. I will desire Sir James to make another search for it, when next I see him.

In the mean time the particulars wch here I send you are,

The battle of Lepanto : a description of the Armada in [15]88, I suppose authentiq.

A Paper written in French touching the severitie of their Marine Laws.

Trajan's Column with Alphonso Ciaconius's notes, referring to the bass-relieue by the figures. Such as concerne Ships and Gallies, &c. you will find by the figures 57. 243. 260. 153. 24. 236. 239. 152. 155. and especially 303. 235. where he speakes of copper or brass instead of iron-work; and the best season for the felling of timber; and there is, as to other notices, subject of a world of erudition beyond what Ciaconius has touched, which would deserve an ampler volume.

A Discourse concerning the Fishery, & Duty of the Flag.

A large volume of Sr R. Browne's Dispatches from 1641 to 1644, &c. during his publiq ministrie and character in the French Court. Besides which I have two folios more that continue it longer.

I also send you the Journal of Martin Frobisher and Captain Fenton.

That of Drake I cannot find as yet, so many papers and things there are to be removed and turned over in my confused study.

Item, a Map of an Harbour, whose name I find not to it.

Also an old Map of a Sea-fight.

Also a packet of original Letters belonging to the former of my L. of Leycesters, in number 14, which are all I have remaining.

With a Declaration of the old Prince of Orange, William of Nassau, who was assassinated at Delft.

The Earle of Leycester's Will.

Another packet of Letters & other matters, and Transactions of State relating to the late times, in number 88, and of which I have thousands more that you may command sight of, but these I think are most material.

A particular of wages due to the Deputy, Army, & other State Officers and affaires relating to Ireland, an° 1587—1588.

A packet of 38 papers containing Instructions and matters of State to severall public Ministers abroad, &c.

Item, another packet of 33 originall Lett[rs] to & from greate persons during the late Rebellion here.

A Scheme of the action of the Hollanders at Chatham, 1667, when they burnt our ships, and bloq'd up the Thames.*

Order of Council of State (then so called) for the apprehension of Charles Stewart, his present Majesty, so named by the regicides.

Lastly, a Relation of his Ma[tys] action & escape at Worcester, when he came out of Scotland with his

---

* This "Scheme" is a pen and ink sketch by Evelyn, preserved with Pepys' Official Correspondence in the Bodleian Library. An accurate fac-simile copy was made, and published in the second volume of Pepys' Memoirs, 4to. 1825.

army, being as far as Sr R. Browne wrote out of the then Queen Mother's lett^rs at Paris; that which he tooke from his Maties owne dictating (when he, after that escape, came into France at Paris) was sent to Monsr Renodaut, & was publish'd by him in the Weekly Extraordinarie A° 1651, where you'l find it in French among the volumes of his Gazettes. I am sorry the original was not retriev'd from him.

Thus, Sir, you see how diligent I have ben, since I came home, to answer yonr queries, as I shall in all other your com'ands as far as is in the power of,

Sir, y^r, &c.

These papers,* mapps, lett^rs, books and particulars, when you have don with, be pleas'd to take your owne time in returning.

Sayes-Court, 5 Dec. 1681.

To the Bishop of Oxford (Dr. FELL).

My Lord,

It cannot but be evident to your Reverend Lordship, to how greate danger & fatal consequences the Histoire Critique, not long since publish'd in French by Pere Simon, & now lately translated (tho' but ill translated) into English, exposes not onely the Protestant & whole Reformed Churches abroad, but

---

* *In the margin*—wch I afterwards never asked of him.

(what ought to be dearer to vs) the Church of England at home, which with them acknowledge the Holy Scriptures alone to be the canon & rule of faith; but which this bold man not onely labours to vnsettle, but destroy. From the operation I find it already begins to haue amongst diuers whom I converse with, especialy the young men, & some not so young neither, I euen tremble to consider what fatal mischiefe this piece is like to create, whilst they do not look vpon the booke as coming from some daring wit, or young Lord Rochester revived, but as the work of a learned author, who has the reputation also of a sober and judicious person. And it must be acknowledged that it is a masterpiece in its kind; that the man is well studied in the oriental tongues, & has carried on his project with a spirit and addresse not ordinarie amongst critics; tho' after all is don, whether he be really a Papist, Socinian, or meerely a Theist, or something of all three, is not easy to discouer; but this is evident—as for the Holy Scriptures, one may make what one will of them for him. He tells the world we can establish no doctrine or principles vpon them, and then, are not we of the Reform'd Religion in a blessed condition! For the loue of God, let our Vniversities, my Lord, no longer remaine thus silent: it is the cause of God, & of our Church! Let it not be said, your Chaires take no notice of a more pernicious plot than any that yet has alarm'd vs. Whilst euery body lets it alone, men think there's nothing to be said against it; & it hugely prevails already, & you will be sensible of its progresse when 'tis too late to take off the reproch. I most humbly therefore implore y^r Rev. L^p to consider of it seriously; that the penns and the Chaires may openly & on all occasions assert & defend the com'on cause, & that Oxford may haue the honor of appearing the first in the field. For from whom, my Lord, should we expect reliefe, if not from you the Fathers of the Church, & the Scholes of the Prophets? It is worthy the publiq concerne to ward the deadly blows which sap the rootes, & should by no meanes be abandon'd to hazard, or the feeble attempts of any single champion, who, if worsted, would but add to the triumph of our enemies, Papists & Atheists. My Lord, he who makes bold to transmitt this to y^r Lo^p, tho' he be no man of the Church, is yet a son of the Church, & greately concern'd for her; & tho' he be not learned, he converses much with books, & men that are as well at Court as in towne & the country; & thinks it his duty to giue y^r L^p an account of what he heares and sees, & is expected & call'd for from you, who are the snperintendents & watchmen that Christ has set ouer his Church, & appointed to take care of his flock. Sr John Marsham's booke* would likewise be consider'd farther than as yet it seemes to haue ben, & the obnoxious passages in it not put off to prefaces & accidental touches onely; whilst neither to that, nor yet to Spinosa, (made also vulgar) we haue had any thing publish'd of expresse, or equal force in a just volume, fitted either for domestic or forraine readers. I know that the late Bishop of Chester,† Dr. Stillingfleet, Huetius, & some few others, haue said aboundantly to confute our modern Atheists; but as these start new & later notions, or rally & reinforce the scatter'd enemie, we should, I think, march as often out to meete & encounter them. For the men of this curious & nicer age do not consider what has ben said or written formerly, but expect something fresh, that may tempt & invite them to consider, that for all the bold appearances

---

* "Chronicus Canon Ægyptiacus, Hebraicus, et Græcus, cum Disquisitionibus Historicis et Criticis," fol. Lond. 1672. He travelled into France, Italy, and part of Germany; studied the Law, and was one of the Six Clerks in Chancery. He suffered as a partizan of King Charles the First, but on the Restoration was restored to his situation, and soon after created a Baronet. He was one of the greatest antiquaries and most learned writers of his time. Father Simon calls him the Great Marsham of England. He wrote the Preface to the second volume of the Monasticon Anglicanum, besides the Diatriba above mentioned. Sir John was ancestor of the present Earl of Romney.   † Dr. Wilkins.

of the enemie, they are no stronger than heretofore, & can do vs no more hurt, vnlesse we abandon and betray ourselves and giue up the cause. 'Tis not (my Lord) sufficient to haue beaten doun the heade of the hydra once, but as often as they rise to vse the club, tho' the same weapon be vsed, the same thing repeated; it refreshes the faint, & resolves the doubtful, & stirrs-up the sloth-full, & is what our adversaries continualy do to keepe up & maintaine their owne party, when euer they receiue the least rebuke from vs :—*fas est et ab hoste doceri*. Nor, my Lord, whilst I am writing this, do I at all doubt of y^r L^{ps} greate wisdome, zeále, & religious care to obviate & prevent this and all other adversaries of our most holy faith, as built vpon the Sacred Scriptures of the Prophets & Apostles, Jesus Christ himselfe being the chiefe corner-stone. But if the excesse of my affection for the Vniversitie (which I haue sometimes heard perstring'd, as not taking the alarme so concernedly vpon these occasions) haue a little too far transported me, I most humbly supplicate y^r L^{ps} pardon for my presumption, & for my zeale & good-wishes to the prosperity of our Sion, your L^{ps} blessing,

Who am, my R^d Lord,
Y^r, &c.

Says-Court, 19 Mar. 1681-82.

To Sam. Pepys, Esq. late Secretary of the Admiralty.
Sʳ,

In answer to your queries, I will most ingenuously declare my thoughts upon second meditation since I publish'd my Treatise of Commerce, & what I have ben taught, but was not there to speake in publiq without offence. I will therefore reply in the method you seem to hint; and then say what I have concerning our pretence to dominion on the seas. To the first:

Boxhornius has written an historie of the Ansiatic Townes; where you'l find in what condition & credit Holland was for traffiq & com'erce, & in the Danish Annales. It would be enquir'd when the English staple was remov'd into Brabant, being 100 years since, & now fixed at Dort. How far forth Charles the Fift pursued or minded his interest at sea? As to Henry the 4th of France, 'tis evident he was not negligent of his interest there, by his many projects for trade, & performances at Marseilles; all that Richelieu and his successors in that ministrie produc'd was projected by their Greate Henry, as is plaine out of Claude B. Morisot his preface. And now

To our title of *Dominion* & the Fishery (which has made such a noise in this part of the world) I confesse I did lately seeke to magnifie & assert it as becomes me *pro hic & nunc* (to speake with logicians), and as the circumstances you know then requir'd. But betweene friends (and under the rose as they say), to tell you realy my thoughts, when such like topics were us'd sometimes in Parliament, 'tis plaine they were passed over there upon important reasons. To begin with the very first. Supposing the old Britains did prohibite forainers to come into their country, what inferrs that to any claime of dominion in the *Narrow,* but a jealosie rather over their proper coasts? Nor reade we that they euer practis'd it ouer the Gauls. The Chinezes we find forbad all to enter their countrie: are they therefore Lords of the Oriental seas? As for King Arthur (abating what is fabulous, *viz.* his legendarie dominion) the *Comes Litoris Saxonici,* &c. stretch'd to Denmark, Sweden, Norway, & Iceland, infers either to much or nothing. Haue we therefore any right of clayme to those realmes at present? Why then to the seas? Againe, admitt the most, may not dominion be lost or extinguish'd? Was not his rather a momentarie conquest or excursion, rather than an establish'd dominion? Was it not lost to the Danes? Had they not all the characters of domination imaginable—Lords of our seas, Lords of our shores too, & the tribute of *Danegelt* from England & Ireland both? If euer there were a real dominion in the world, the Danes must be yielded to haue had it: and if their title cannot be extinguish'd by subsequent revolutions, I greately question whether ours will euer be euinced. In short, the story of King Edgar is monstrously romantic, and the pretended deede I doubt will appeare but spurious. Truely, if forraine chronicles had ben as much stuff'd with the renowne of this prince as wth K. Arthur, I should giue more credit to it. In the mean time, what they report of Athelred is totaly against vs, since 'tis plaine he pay'd the *Danegelt* as a tribute to them, & settled it to ye end. One may querie whether the Scots seas, & Scotland to boote, be not a fee to England; for with as much reason we might challenge it, if the producing rolls, records, & Acts of Parliament, & of Statutes to that purpose were of any importance; because we can shew more to the purpose than in the other case : but how would then that nation take it, & what become of their laws about fishing? 'Ti^s declar'd in our laws that we are the Lords of the *Foure Seas,* & so adjudged in our courts, as to those born upon those seas ;- and yet the Parliament of Scotland can impose a tax on our fishermen, which is a shrewd argument against vs. Who euer read that the Kings of England prohibited any to fish on the coast of Scotland? Or charg'd them with vsurpation for taking toll and custome for the herring-fishery? The truth is, the licences (which I speak of in my book, from Scarbrough) were onely to fish on the Dogger-bank. Such English as were to fish in the Scottish seas about Orkney, & Shetland, Iceland,

and Fero, &c. did take licenses to fish from the Kings of Norway at Bergen & Northbarum; & this jurisdiction & sovereignty vndoubted of the Norwegian Kings is recognis'd by our own Parliament in a statute 8 Hen. 6. c. 2.; and by in'umerable treaties betwixt the two crownes, euen within a century of yeares; and if so, consider how feeble a proof is that famous roll *pro hominibus Hollandiæ*, & how it is to be limited in itselfe (by the historie & occasion that caused it) to the Narrow or Chanell onely. 'Tis also to be considered that the Danes protested at Breda, that the cession of the Scots fisherie about Orkney & Shetland was neuer made to our King James vpon his marriage of Q. Ann (as our tradition is), nor any time before to any Scotish king; and supposing that there were any such authentiq deede, it were better to fix ye fisherie (we contend about) euen in the Dutch, then either permit it to be regulated by the decrees of a Scotch Parliament, or transferr it to that nation. Now as to ye greate trade, & multitude of English vessels, by the historie of ye Haunse Townes, their privileges & power in England, one shall find, that for ye bulk our navies consisted most of hired ships of the Venetians, Genoezes, & Ansiatics, till Queene Elizabeth, tho' her father Henry the 8. had a flourishing fleete. The right of passes, and petitions thereupon, were formed vpon another part of the *Jus Gentium*, then our pretended dominion of the seas; which (to speake ingenuously) I could neuer find recognis'd expressly in any treaty wth forrainers. As to returne to the fishery, that of the Dutch fishing without licence, the *intercursus magnus* (so boasted) was a perpetual treaty, and made as well with all the people as the princes of Burgundy, & so as to be obligatorie, tho' they rejected their gouernors, as we see most of them did, & as perhaps they might according to the *lætus introitus*. And that the Dutch are still, & by Q. Eliz. were so declar'd to be, a *pars contrahens*, after their revolt and abjuration of Spaine, dos as much invalidate that proceeding of K. James, & Charles the First, who both sign'd that *intercursus*, & were in truth included thereby tho' they had not sign'd it.

But besides all this, the nature of prescription would be enqnir'd into as well when it makes against vs, as for vs; & therefore it should be demanded whether Queen Elizabeth did not first assert the *mare liberum* in opposition to ye Danes, and whether his present Matie has not don it at Jamaica against the Spaniard; pray consider the seale of that Admiralty. To speake plaine truth; when I writ that Treatise, rather as a *philological* exercise, & to gratifie the present circumstances, I could not clearly satisfie myselfe in sundry of those particulars, nor find ready that euer the Dutch did pay toll or tooke license to fish in Scotland after the contest, from any solid proofes. Indeede (as there I relate) they surpriz'd Brown who came to exact it, & detain'd him in Holland seuerall months; but I think they neuer payd peny for it, tho' the papers I haue pervs'd speake of an *assize herring;* nor did I find that any rent (whereoff in my 108 page I calculate the arreres) for permission to fish, was euer fixed by both parties; & so cannot properly be called a settl'd rent. This would therefore be exquisitely enquir'd into, and perhaps, both for these & many other particulars, a thro' search in his Ma^{tie's} Paper Office may afford clearer light, if there haue any due care been taken to collect & digest such important matters. As for the yeares 1635 and 1637, you cannot but espie an intreague in ye equipping those formidable fleetes; & that they were more to awe the French than terrifie Holland (see how the times & interests change! but no more of that, 'tis now a tender point) I fancy were no difficult matter to prove, and that any licenses were taken in those yeares, I could neuer be assur'd of: that of 1636 being but a single act of force on some particular men, the States neuer owning them in it; and you know the Admirall Dorp was casheer'd for not quarelling it with our Northumberland, & our conduct & licenses flatly rejected in 1637, when Capt. Field came. Lastly,

When K. James fixed his chamber, did he not either renounce ye English sovereignty of the seas, or violate therein his league with Spaine? (as that nation vrged, pleading that the British seas were *territorium domini regis)*; but he did not the latter, wherefore I am not single in this declaration. In a word, the intire argument of this fish'ry is too controvertable to be too peremptory decided by the penn, & vpon many other accounts (of which the plenty & wantoness of our full fed vnfrugal people, which deterrs them from hard labour, is not the least) a project wholy vselesse as circumstances be, and therefore might with much more benefit, ease, & facility, be supplied by increasing our fishery at New-found-land. Finaly,

As to the com'erce in generall of this nation: from all that I could observe during my short being of that noble and honourable Councip, & informing myselfe as I was able by books & discourses of experienc'd persons; I say, after all this, I considered it a very vaine thing to make any (the most probable, certaine, or necessarie) proposal about trade, &c. Not that it might not be infinitely improv'd, if princes & people did unanimously, & with a true publiq spirit, & as our naturall advantages prompt us, apply themselves honestly and industriously about it; but for that, as things now are & have hitherto ben manag'd since the renown'd Queene Elizabeth (for that *encomium* I must give her), the whole advantage this nation receives thereby is evidently carried on more by antient methods & the sedulitie of private men, than by any publiq encouragement; and as to the present, it certainely languishes vnder insupportable difficulties, And thus, Sir, I choose to convey you my second more digested thoughts, of a point which in your excellent designe and work cannot escape the ample handling as one of the most considerable, when you come to speake of the importance of our shipping & trade, or pretence of dominion, &c. And I do it, you see, with all *selfe denyall* imaginable (& not without some reproach) after what I have publish'd to the contrary, by which you may conclude how suspicious wise men should be of other histories and historians too, how confident & specious soever, vnlesse it were almost demonstration, that the authors had no interest of their own to serve, & were not influenc'd by their superiors, or the publiq cry. Let this ingenuous confession com'ute for my faults in that Treatise, and be put amongst the retractations of,

S^r, your, &c.

Sayes-Court, 19 Sept^r: 1682.

To Samuell Pepys, Esqr. Secretary of ye Admiralty.

S^r,

I were very unworthy of y^r late & former favours should I not render you some assurances, that I am often meditating on them; & that I shall ever (according to my small force & capacitie) obey your com'ands. Without more ceremonie then—I am in the first place to give you an account of Colours. But you will be better pleas'd to receive it from the learned Gisbertus Cuperus's *Apotheosis, vel consecratio Homeri,** in his curious conjectures upon an antique sculpture; where, speaking of the rhapsodists that were vs'd to sing the ballads of Vlysses' Errors & Maritime Voyages, they were wont to be clad in blew; when his Iliads & fighting Poems, in red; & were so superstitious, as allways to cover those bookes or rolls in parchment of those two colours. He pretends that one Oenomanus first invented distinctions of colours in the *Ludi Circenses*, where greene was ye ensigne of combatants by land, & blew at sea: so as when those who were clad in greene gain'd the prize, they look'd on it as presage of a fruitfull harvest; if the blew coates prevail'd, successful expeditions and exploits at sea: the first, it seemes, concern'd the husbandman, the other the mariner. He farther observes, that when there was any com'otion or rebellion in the parts of Italy or Gaule, the General of Horse carried a blew cornet, for as much as that generous creature was produc'd by Neptune's trident, & first manag'd by that sea god; & that whoever signaliz'd his courage on that element, was honor'd wth a flag of the same colour; which Suetonius gives a remarkable instance of, in the Life of Octavius Augustus: *M. Agrippam in*

---

* Printed at Amsterdam in 1683, 4to.

Siciliá, post navalem victoriam, cœruleo vexillo donavit, after the naval victory obtain'd against young Pompey. It were ostentation to cite more authors, Statius, Diodorus Siculus, Plutarch in Vit. Themist. &c. Enough to give you an impatient desire of that excellent entertainement Cuperus will afford you, not on this subject onely, but in a world of other choice & curious erudition.

S^r, I do not remember you charg'd me with any other particular of this sort: but as I am both dispos'd & esteeme myselfe very happy in seruing you, thô but as a pioneer to dig materials for a more skillfull hand to square & polish & set in work, so if in my desultory course of reading, & among the rubbish, I lite on any thing which is worthy your notice, & may contribute to it, reckon that you have in me a ready & faithfull servant: acqnir'd by many obligations, but (I assnre you) by none more than that singular love of virtue, & things worthy an excellent person, which I discover & highly honour in you.

In the notes of Isaac Vossius upon Catullus, *sive utrumque Jupiter simul secundus incidisset in pedem*, &c. he has many learned observations about Navigation, particularly that of sailing to several parts opposite to one another by the same wind, *ijsdem Ventis in contrarium navigatur prolatis pedibus,* as Pliny expresses it; & it was (you may remember) on this hint that I inform'd you Vossius had by him a treatise Περὶ Ταχυπλοία. I enquir'd of him (when last I was at Windsore) whether he would publish it; to which he gave me but an uncertaine answer. In the meane time you'l not be displeas'd at what he tells us of a certaine harmonie produc'd by the snapping of carters' whips, vs'd of old at the feasts of Bacchus & Cybele; & that the Tartars have to this day no other trumpets, & are so adroit, as at once to make the whip give three distinct clapps, & that so loude as to be heard very far off; and then speakes of a coachman at Maestricht, who plays severall tunes with his lash. To a lover of musiq & harmonie I could not omit this scrap, thô I know you'l laugh at me for it, & pay me with the tongues and gridiron. But ere I leave Dr. Vossius, I dare say you have perus'd what he writes in his late Opusculum, touching the reformation of Latitudes & Eclipses; and his asserting the Mediterranean & other places to be much larger than our Geographers report. He has something also of the North passage to the Indies, of the construction of gallies, the Pico Teneriffe, &c.; of all which you best are able to judge, & doubtlesse have form'd y^r remarkes thereon. Whilst I was running on, comes Mr. Dum'er to give me a visite; and I am so charm'd with his ingenuity, that I looke vpon it as a new obligation to you; & if you find I cultivate it for my owne sake a little, you will let him understand (by all that I am to speake to you of him vpon this short taste) how much I wish him the improvements of y^r favours, who am for so many myselfe,

S^r, y^r, &c.

Sayes-Court, 23 Sepr 1685.

From Mr. SAMUEL PEPYS.

S^r, Thursday night, 2 Oct. 1685.

Very sorry I am that I was not in ye way to enjoy you to-day, being gone (the only time I have beene able to doe it this summer) to make a visit to good Mrs. Ewer at Clapham. But I have 2 reasons to desire you will give mee yor company to-morrow noone, first because wee will bee alone, & next I have something to shew you, that I may not have another time,

Yo^r most obe^t serv^t, S. PEPYS.

To this letter Mr. Evelyn has subjoined the following curious note:

" That which was shew'd mee were *two papers** attested by his present Maties hand to be a true copie

---

* The following is extracted from the Life of King James II. published by the Rev. J. S. Clarke:

· " Some few days after the late King's death, his Majesty looking into the papers he had left behind him, found two relateing to Controversie, one in the strong box, the other in the closet, both writ in his own hand: they were short but sollid, and shewed that tho' his conversion was not perfected til a few of the originals which some day before he had shewed Mr. Pepys privately:—That his late brother,

---

houres before his death, his conviction was of a longer date. The King thought fit to shew them one day to the Archbishop of Canterburie in his closet, no body being by, who seem'd much surprised at the sight of them, and pawsed almost half a quarter of an houre before he said any thing; at last tould the King, he did not think his late Majesty had understood controversie so well, but that he thought they might be answer'd: 'If so,' sayd the King, 'I pray let it be done gentleman-like and sollidly, and then it may have the effect you so much desire of bringing me back to your Church;' to which the Archbishop reply'd, 'It would perhaps be counted a disrespect in him to contradict the late King;' but his Majesty reassured him in that point, by telling him the change it might produce in himself (if answer'd efectually) was of that consequence as to outbalance any other consideration; and therefore desired he might see a reply either from him or any other of his perswasion: but tho' he, my Lord Dartemouth and others, were several times reminded of this matter, and earnestly press'd to it, never any formal reply was produced during his Majesty's reign in England. It is true there was something of an answer published by an unknown hand, but the drift of it was rather to proue that the papers were not the late King's (which was a libel in reality upon the present) than any reply to the arguments of it, and it is probable the Archbishop dispair'd of answering it so efectually as to hring back his Majesty to their Communion, whereas the publishing a reply would have own'd and published the papers too: and he had reason to apprehend, that the authority and arguments of their dying Prince would influence more persons to that religion, than his answer would perswade to relinquish it." Vol. II. page 8. See also the Diary, vol. III. pp. 182, 183.

Charles ye Second, was of long time since a Roman Catholique. The papers contained ^severall *points* of religion, labouring to cast heresy, schism, &c. on the Church of England, but on my judgement without any force or reason, & a thousand times confuted."

To the Countesse of SUNDERLAND
(Lady ANNE SPENCER).

Madame,

I am not un-mindfull of the late com'and you lay'd vpon me, to give you a catalogue of such books as I believ'd might be fit to entertaine your more devout & serious hours: and I looke vpon it as a peculiar grace & fauour of God to y^r La^p, that, amidst so many temptations, and grandeur of Courts, the attendants, visites, diversions (& other circumstances of the palace, and the way you are ingag'd in) you are resolu'd that nothing of all this shall interrupt your duty to God, & the Religion you professe, when euer it comes in competition with the things of this world, how splendid soever they may appeare for a little & (God knows) uncertaine time: Madame, 'tis the best, & most gratefull returne you can make to Heaven for all the blessings you enjoy, amongst which there is none you are more happy in, then in the vertue, early & solid piety of my Lady Anne, and progresse of y^r little son. Madame, the foundation you haue layd in those two blessings, will not onely build, but establish y^r illustrious family, beyond all the provisions you can make of gallant and greate in estimation of the world; and will find the comfort of it, when all this noise & hurry shall vanish as a dreame, & leaue nothing to support vs in time of neede. I am persuaded you often make these reflections, from your owne greate judgment and experiences of the vicissitudes of things present, & prospect of future, which is onely worth our solicitude.

I am, &c.

Says-Court, 12 Sep. 1686.

To my Lord Lieutenant of Ireland, at Dublin Castle.
[HENRY Earl of CLARENDON.]

My Lord,

I had ere this giuen y^r Exc^y my most humble thanks for yours of the 7th past, but that I was expecting the event of some* extraordinary things then in suspence; and when I haue sayd this, I neede not tell y^r L^p what I am assur'd you have receiu'd from better hands, nor make any farther reflections on it, than to acquaint y^r Ex^y, that I know

---

* The Co'miss. of Ecclesiastical Affaires which suspended the Bp. of Lond. &c. and gaue greate offence to all the nation. J. E.

of no new com'issions, which y^r L^p desires to vnderstand ye meaning of, & that make (it seemes) no lesse noise with you than they do here. The character y^r Ex^y giues of the huffing greate man* is just: how the noyse he makes will operate I know little of; what it dos with you (and would euery where do else) is sufficiently evident: but God is above all, and your L^{ps} prudence, courage, & steady loyaltie, will, if it not surmount all malevolence, purchase you the estimation of all g^{ood} subjects, & I doubt not, but of his Matie also. I am plainely amaz'd at what y^r Ex^y tells me of Ireland, which country we haue seene giuen twice conquer'd into his Maties father's & brother's (our late Souraines) hands, at no small expense of blood & treasure; & therefore question not but his present Matie dos both see & well consider the infinite importance of cherishing its improvements and tranquillitie.

My Ld. Teviot, I think, has quite abandon'd vs; 'tis neere 4 moneths since we haue receiu'd any assistance from him at the Seale; so as I haue not ben able to make any excursion as yet this sum'er, & when I shall now make my flight to Swallowfield,† I am uncertaine. I haue agen ben to enquire

---

* Lord Tyrconnel.

† A seat belonging to Lord Clarendon, about six miles South-east of Reading, in Berkshire, which he possessed by marrying his second wife, Flower, widow of Sir William Backhouse, Bart.

out my Lord Cornbery: but his L^p is still so employ'd twixt the Court & his military charge, that I cannot expect the happinesse I promis'd my selfe of accompanying him thither, and to go without him would be a melancholy thing. The ladys are still at Tunbridge, tempted by the continuance of this Paradisian season; whilst we are here mightily in the dark, & curious (if lawfull) to vnderstand, whether a certaine new Countesse came lately ouer hither with his Maties knowledge & permission. I tell the inquisitiue, I know nothing of it, but that I am sure your Ex^y dos nothing saue what becomes you, & with g^{ood} advise. Now that Buda is taken, all our eyes are on Hambrow & Denmark :—I pray God giue peace to Christendome, and continue it in little England, with all prosperitie & blessing on y^r Ex^y & illustrious family: these are the assiduous prayers of, my L^d,

Y^r Ex^y, &c.

Says-Court, Sep. 1686.

To my Son, &c.

Son,

I just now receiv'd the narrative of the Princes march, and the political remarks you have made upon the occurrences where you have ben. My Lord Clarendon would gladly have conferred with you on several points seasonable at that juncture; but all have now it seemes submitted, and the bells and the bonefires proclaime as much joy & satisfaction as those are capable of, who have beheld so many changes & revolutions, without being able to divine how all this will conclude at last, & remembring that precept of the wisest of kings, (Proverbs, ch. xxiv. v. 21) which I neede not repeate to you. It will be no newes (I perceive) to you, to acquaint you wth his Majesty's late recesse, nor of his being stop't at Feversham, &c. But of his coming back to White-hall, and what has since intervened, you may not yet have heard. On Friday last there went thither my Lord Midleton, Earle of Alesbury, Ld Feversham, Sr Step: Fox, and Mr Grahame, where the rabble had detain'd the King (the vessel wherein he was embark'd with S^r Ed. Hales, & Ralph Sheldon, wch were all his attendance, coming in for want of balast), till the newes of it being brought to the L^{ds} of the Council, those Lords & Gent: I named were sent to perswade his Ma^{ty} to returne, or if not prevailing, to conduct and waite upon him wth two troopes of horse, to what other port or place he should please to go. The King, at last induced to come back to London, arrived at White-Hall on Sonday evening, went to masse at his Chapel on Monday, three priests officiating; the usual number of Roman Catholics, & a world more, filling the bedchamber and all the roomes with extraordinary acclamation. In this manner his Ma^ty went thence to dinner (a Jesuite saying grace), and all things seemed to passe in such order, as the eclipse the Court suffered, by his Ma^tys four dayes absence, was hardly discernable, all the clouds (as we thought) were vanishing, and a bright day againe appearing. So soone as he was retired, he sent my Ld Feversham with a letter under his owne hand to invite the P: of Orange to St: James's: the message was accepted, but the *messenger* arested & made prisoner at Windsor; upon which politicians make reflexions. But 'tis pretended that a *general* of an enemy ought not by the law of armes to come into the quarters of his antagonist without a trumpet & a passeport: others say, that his Hig^sse was much displeased at the Earle's disbanding his Ma^tys forces under his co'mand, without disarming them, and un-payed, as thereby leaving them in danger of seeking some desperate resolution, of disturbing the measures he had taken; and there are who believe upon some other account, which time will discover. Tuesday morning came the Marq: of Halifax (who with the Ld Godolphin had ben sent commissioner to the Prince) from Windsor, to let his Ma^ty know the Prince would be the next day at St. James's; but withall (foreseeing it might be dangerous to have his army quarter'd about the towne, so necessary to his safety, whilst the King's guards were so neere), he desires his Ma^ty that he would make choice of Hampton Court, or some other place about that distance, to repair to, for the avoiding jealousies & inconveniences which might happen betweene the guards of different interests. You will easily believe this was not very kindly taken, after so generous an invitation; & that it was the more surprizing for its coming to him at one o'clock in the morning, when he was weary & fast asleepe. The King upon this rises, & goes immediately to Council, where severall things being propos'd (but what I undertake not to say) & altogether rejected: and whilst by this time White-Hall and all its environs were crowded with Dutch souldiers, his Matie put himself into his barge, accompanied wth my Lord Ailesbery (now in waiting), the L^ds Dumbarton, Arran, & one or two more, follow'd wth three other barges & small boates, fill'd with a Dutch guard, & a troop of horse by land, steering their course towards Rochester againe, from whence he so lately had return'd. Thus have you the second recesse, or something more *dismaly boading;* which, whilst I my selfe, with Sr Chas: Cotterell & Sr Step: Fox, beheld from one of the windows of the new buildings—*vix tempero à lachrymis.*—I should have told you that the Prince being yesterday at Syon, sent Sr Rob: Howard & Hen: Powle with a letter to the Citty, acquainting them with his approach, with other complements of course. This was read before the Ld Mayor & Com: Council, and was answer'd with all submission & respect, & with an invitation that his Hig^{sse} would honour their Citty by vouchsafing to lodge in it, rather than at St: James's. On this there stood up an Alderman, & moved that an Addresse might first be made to congratulate his Ma^{tys} gracious returne to White-Hall. But the proposal was not approv'd of, one of them saying, *they had given a good pail of milke, & that this were to kick it downe againe.*

Thus, Son, I have given you as minute an account of the *Proteus* here as I am able for the present. The hero is now at St. James's, where I have seene him, and severall of my old acquaintance. I dined at the E: of Clarendons, whom I did not find altogether so well satisfied as I expected, considering that his son my Ld Cornebery tooke so considerable a stroke in his turne. I wish he do not πρὸς κέντρα λακτίζειν.—By what I collect, the ambitious & the covetous will be canvassing for places of honour, & rich employment; and that my Lord will withstand the mercat, and neglect, if not slight his applications, upon confidence of his neere relation, & the merites of my L^d his son, if not upon other principles. If none of this happen, and that successe do not quite alter the principles of men in power, we are to suspect *Astrea* upon earth againe : But as I have often told you, I looke for no mighty improvement of mankind in this declining age & catalysis. A Parliament (legaly cal'd) of brave & worthy patriots, not influenc'd by faction, nor terrified by power, or corrupted by selfe interest, would produce a kind of new creation amongst us. But it will grow old, and dissolve to chaos againe, unlesse the same stupendious Providence (which has put this opportunitie into mens hands to make us happy, dispose them to do just & righteous things, and to use their empire with moderation, justice, piety, & for the publiq good. Upon the whole matter, those who seeke employment, before the grandees are serv'd, may suspend their solicitation, the Queene having ('tis sayd) carried away the Greate Seale: most of the writs being burnt by his Ma^{ty}, it will cost time, & excogitation of expedients how legaly to supply them, if his Ma^{ty} should designe to travell againe, or the doore (which I feare most likely) be shut after him. These, and sundry other difficulties, will render things both uneasy and uncertaine. Onely I think Popery to be universaly declining, and you know I am one of those who despise not prophesying; nor, whilst I behold what is daily wrought in the world, believe miracles to be ceas'd.

S^r Ed: Hales & Obadiah (his old tutor) are both in gaole at Maidstone. C. Justice Herbert, Rob: Brent, & Peters above all, are not yet heard of. Poore Roger (for want of better observation) is carried to New-gate, & every houre is pregnant of wonders.

Anno Mirabil. Lond. 18 Dec. 1688.

To ye Countesse of SUNDERLAND.

Mad^{me},

The buisy and wond'rous age I have lived in, the not altogether confinement of my selfe to morose conversations in the world, the tincture I early receiv'd from generous and worthy parents, and the education they gave me, disposing (at least inciting) me to the love of letters, and a greate reguard to Religion, as the end and scope of all accomplishments, wisely and prudently consider'd (not that I have pursued this glorious and onely happy course, to my sorrow and reproach be it confess'd, but what I ought to have don,) dos now and has long since taken up my thoughts about that souvraine good which all the thinking part of mankind has in all ages and times ben searching after, to acquiesce and rest in; and in pursuance of this greate concerne, I have preferr'd the recesse of neere thirty yeares, during which, by meane complyances, and in a vicious age, one might probably have ariv'd to something which they call (tho' not very properly) a *figure*, (but I, an empty *cyfer*) in the world, to all other advantages whatsoever; and upon the foote and sum of all (for I do often cast it up), I have found nothing solid, nothing stable, and worth all this hurry, disquiet, & expense of time; but the pursuite of moderate things for this life, with due and modest reguard to qualitie, and the decent circumstances of that maintain'd and procurable by worthy, open, and honorable wages, in a vertuous, but to be neglected and despis'd as base and ignoble, in a false and vicious age. For, besides acquisitions so obtain'd, are ever procured by low and servile arts, they are of no longer durance than the favorite prostitute his conscience: and sacrifices all sentiments of genuine and real greatenesse, which will recurr some time or other vpon generous minds, seduc'd, if once they euer come to recollect themselues. It were a most happy thing if young persons (and next to a miracle 'tis they should not) did believe the experience of that almost 7000 yeares forefathers, who once were young, haue told their children, and the wisest bookes recorded, and the perpetual events of things declar'd it; that piety, sincerity, justice, temperance, and all that series and chaine of moral vertue, recom'ended to vs, as well by the wiser heathen as by God himselfe, and the very dictates of nature, are the onely meanes of obtaining that tranquill and happy state a prudent man would choose, euen in this life onely, a religious and truely wise in that to come; and he was both greate and wise, and well experienced, who pronounced it: I haue seene an end of all perfection, but thy com'andments are exceeding broade; ample in all dimensions, in a word, im'ortal.

Madame, this topic is as large as the world. This book I say of all the philosophers, the precepts of all the divines, the histories and records of all ages. The experience of all mankind, every day's vicissiude proclaims it alowd, and neuer was it more articulate and conspicuous than in this conjuncture, present, and approaching revolution. And it is an eternal truth, and can neuer be otherwise, that true honor and happinesse and the things which we seeke (would consum'ate our felicity and bound our farther pursuits) is not to be found in the things which passe away like a dreame when we awake; but in a brave and generous soule, that hauing those advantages by birth or laudable acquisition, can cultivate them to the production of things beneficial to mankind, the government, and eminent station in which God has placed him. This is greate indeede, and truely noble. The fruit of it is a present good, the memorie and contemplation of it a lasting pleasure and a glorious recompense. But what's all this to y^r La^p, who knows all I can say in this, or any other subject? It is then nothing to informe and teach y^r L^p. But an account of my most retired thoughts, and an idea of the passion I haue, that you may, from the yet remaining hopes of y^r illustrious family (in whome there already appeares such faire impressions and noble characters of virtue) I find allways something to aleviate y^r past sufferings and unexpected trauerses in your present circumstances. Do not therefore with much anxiety afflict y^r selfe at what is past, farther than to improve y^r experience and exercise y^r virtue by its documents. But looke forward at present and allways upwards for the time to come, and to things possible and permanent, which will bring peace at the last, and those will God keepe in perfect place whose minds are staied in him. Suffer nothing then to abate of y^r courage and Christian fortitude; you know who is a present help in trouble, and you will do nothing without consulting him, and you'l neede no other in this world to bring you safe out of them all. Remember that One (who yet suffer'd much greater) found by experience (as so will y^r La^p I am perswaded wth joy) how good it was that he had been afflicted. And verily, this is the best vse we should make of all God's methods and dispensations of this sort; and it is by the suffrage and observation of all holy persons, a greater indication of God's paternal care and fauour, than a continual current and succession of temporal prosperity. This y^r La^p will find to be the tenor of those divine oracles you so assiduously reade and meditate on, and which will fill your heart with more real joy and inward consolation than you could ever have derived from all other helps and friends, princes and greate men in this wretched, perishing world.

The tiresome mortifications I haue gon thro' for aboue 15 yeares past, being intangled in a trust: besides that of the late V. Countesse Mordaunt (of which I am but newly deliver'd) my owne tedious suite in Chancery, with the burden of no few yeares upon me, and domestic cares (requiring some indulgence) consider'd y^r La^p is pleas'd to accept of my son, who is disposed to serve you, if you com-'and it, and that my Ld Godolphin be one in the trust: because, tho' his L^p should not be so active in the industrious part, he will be of greate advantage to the safe and prudential; which is, I assure your La^p, of greate moment in confidences of this nature.

I am, Mad^m, y^r, &c.

Says-Court, 22 Dec. 1688.

To my Lord Spencer.

My Lord,

Having now tempted and sufficiently provoked your L^p in Plautus, Cicero, Pliny, Seneca, Lipsius, &c. (for y^r L^p is master of all styles) I give it over. On my word, your L^p has tam'd the shrew, and 'tis more than time for me to leave off the pedant, and write henceforth in my mother tongue.

And now I think on't, I cannot a little wonder that whilst there are extant so many volumes of letters, and familiar epistles in the politer modern languages, Italian, Spanish, & French, we should have so few tolerable ones of our owne country now extant, who have adorned ye part of elegancy, so proper and so becoming persons of the nobility, quality, and men of businesse, and education too, as well as lovers and courters of the faire sex. Sir Fr: Bacon, Dr Donne, and I hardly remember any else who haue publish'd any thing of considerable, and they but gleanings of, or cabbal men, who have put many things in a heape, without much choice or fruits, especially as to the culture of the style or language. The genius of the nation being almost another thing than it was at that time. James Howell published his "Ho-Elianæ," for which he indeede was laught at; not for his letters, which acquaint us with a number of passages worthy to be known, and had never else ben preferred, but which, were the language enlightened with that sort of exercise and conversation, I should not question its being equal to any of the most celebrated abroade. When, therefore, your L^p shall think fit to descend so low as to believe it not unworthy your reflexions (you who are so perfect a master in the learned tongues), how would you embellish your native language, and set an emulous example to others; revive the dire and mournful age, and put it out of debt by the product of a native flock of our owne, and, as I said, the most usefull.

I am, Dr Sir, &c.

To Mr. Pepys.

Sir,

I was on Wednesday last (afternoone) to kisse your hands; but finding you abroad, and my selfe obliged to returne that evening, that I might receive the Countess of Sunderland, who sent me word she would call at my house the next morning early, before her embarkment for Holland, I do now write, what I should have said to you, if time had permitted; and that is to let you know, that upon your late communicating to me your desire of adorning your choice library with the pictures of men illustrious for their parts and erudition, I did not in the least suspect your intention of placing my shallow head amongst those heroes, who, knowing my unworthynesse of that honour, will in spight of your good opinion of Mr. Kneller for his skill of drawing to the life, either condemne his colouring, that he made me not blush; or me for impudence that I did not. But this is not all: for men will question your judgment, or suspect you of flattery, if you take it not downe; for in good earnest, when I seriously consider how unfit I am to appear in the classe of those learned gentlemen, I am perfectly asham'd, & should say with much more reason than Marullu[s] (after a recension of the famous poets)

> Nos, si quis inter cæteros locat Vates,
> Onerat, quam honorat verius.

'Tis pitty and a diminution, so elegant a place & precious collection should have any thing in it of vulgar, but such as Paulus Jovius has celebrated, and such as you told me you were procuring; the Boyles, the Gales, & the Newtons of our nation: what, in God's name, should a planter of colewort do amongst such worthies? Setting him aside, I confesse to you I was not displeas'd with the fancy of the late Lord Chancellor Hyde, when to adorne his stately palace (since demolished) he collected the pictures of as many of our famous countrymen as he could purchase or procure, instead of the heads and busts of forreiners, whose names, thro' the unpardonable mistake or (shall I call it) pride of painters, they scorne to put to their pieces, imagining it would dishonour their art, should they transmit every thing valuable to posterity besides faces, which signifie nothing to the possessor (vnlesse their relations were to live for ever, & allways in being), so as one cannot tell whether they were drawn from any of their friends or ancestors, or the picture of some porter or squalid chimney sweeper, whose prolix beard and wrinkled forehead might passe him for a philosopher. I am in perfect indignation at this folly, as oft as I consider what extravagant sums are given for a dry scalp of some (forsooth) Italian painting, be it of Raphael or Titian himselfe; which would be infinitely more estimable, were we assured it was the picture of the learned Count of Mirandula, Politian, Guicciardini, Machiavel, Petrarch, Ariosto, or Tasso; or some famous pope, prince, poet, or other hero of those times. Give me Carolus Magnus, a Tamerlaine, a Scanderbeg, Solyman the Magnificent, Matt: Corvinus, Lorenzo, Cosimo Medicis, Andrea Doria, Ferdinando Cortez, Columbus, Americus Vesputius, Castracani Castruccio, and a Sforza; the effigies of Cardan, and both the Scaligers, Tycho Brahe, Copernicus, and Galileo. I say give me the portraits of an Isabella of Arragon or Castile, and her foure daughters; Lucretia d'Este (to whom our Queene is related), Victoria Colonna, Hippolita Strozzi, Petrarch's Laura, Anna Maria Schurman, and above all Hellen Cornaro, daughter of a procurator of St. Marco (one of the most illustrious families of Venice) who received the degree of Doctoresse at Padua for her universal knowledge & erudition, upon the importunity of that famous University prevailing on her modesty. She had ben often sought in honorable marriage by many greate persons, but prefering the Muses before all other considerations, she preserved herselfe a virgin, and being not long since deceased, had her obsequies celebrated at Rome by a solemn procession, & elogie of all the witts of that renowned citty. Nor may I forget the illustrious of our owne nation of both sexes: the Westons, Moores, Seymours, Sir J. Cheke, Ann Countess of Oxon (whose monument is in Westminster Abbey), the late Mrs. Philips, & Princesse Elizabeth, eldest daughter to the unfortunate Queen of Bohemia, to whom the greate Des Cartes dedicates his bookes, with a world of more renowned characters, famous for armes & arts; rather than the most beautiful courtezan or prostitute of them all, who has nothing to commend her but her impudence & that she was a painted strumpet. Did it ever prejudice the glory of the inimitable Holbein, for putting the names of our greate Duke of Norfolk, Henry the Eighth when lesse corpulent, Edward the Sixth & Treasurer Cromwell, Jane Seymour, Anne Bulleyn, Charles Brandon, Althea Talbot, Countesse of Arundel, Card. Wolsey, Sʳ Thomas More & his learned daughters, Sʳ Brian Tuke, Dr. Nowel, Erasmus, Melancthon, and even honest Frobenius, among innumerable other illustrious of that age for learning & other vertues? I aske if this were the least diminution to the fame of one who realy painted to the life beyond any man this day living? But, in truth, they seeme from the beginning jealous of their owne honour, & afraid of being forgotten: hence we find ΓΑΥΚΩΝ ΑΘΗΝΑΙΟC ЄΠΟΙЄΙ insculpt on the Farnesian Hercules, and *Michael Angelo fecit*, *P. P. Rubens pinxit*, *Marc. Antonio cœlavit*, &c. There is not that wretched print but weares the name of no-artist, whilst our painters take no care to transmitt to posterity the names of the persons whom they represent; through which negligence so many excellent pieces come after a while to be dispers'd amongst brokers & up-holsters, who expose them to the streetes in every dirty and infamous corner. 'Tis amongst their dusty lumber we frequently meete with Queene Elizabeth, Mary Q. of Scots, the Countesse of Pembroke, Earles of Leycester and Essex, Sir Walter Raleigh, Sr Philip Sidney, Cecil, Buckhurst, Walsingham, Sir Francis Bacon, King James & his favourite Buckingham, and others, (who made the greate figure in this nation), of John Husse, Zisca, Luther, Calvine, Beza, Socinus, William & Maurice Princes of Orange, Charles the Fifth, Philip the Second, Francis the First; the Dukes of Alba, Parma, Don John of Austria, and Count Egmont; authors of sects, greate captaines and politicians (famous in our historie in other countries), flung many times behind the hangings, covered with dust and cobwebs. Upon this account it is, men curious of books & antiquities have ever had medals in such estimation, & rendered them a most necessary furniture to their libraries, because by them we are not onely inform'd whose real image & superscription they beare, but have discovered to us, in their reverses, what heroical exploits they perform'd;—their famous temples, bazilicæ, thermæ, amphitheaters, aquæducts, circuses, naumachias, bridges, triumphal arches, columns, historical & other pompous structures & erections by them; and which have ben greately assistant to ye recovery of the antient & magnificent architecture, whose real monuments had ben so barbarously defac'd by the Goths & other truculent invaders, that without this light (& some few ruines yet extant justifie those types) that so vsefull order and ornament of columns & their concomitant members were hardly to be known by the text of Vitruvius, and all his learned Commentators: and till Daniel Barbaro, Leon Alberto, Raphael, M. Angelo & others raised it out of the dust, & restor'd that noble art, by their owne and other learned men consulting & comparing the reverses of medals & medalions: besides what they farther contribute to the elucidation of many passages in historie, chronologie, & geography. So as I do not see how Mr. Pepys's library can be long without this necessary adjunct. It is amongst the medals we meete the ancient legislators, Lycurgus, Solon, Numa, &c. There we find Orpheus, Linus, & the old bards, and there is mention of Numus Homericus by Strabo, & (if I well remember) by Aristotle himselfe too; as there is stil extant those of the brave Hector & Achilles: so as among them we may see what kind of persons were Aristides, Themistocles, Epaminondas, Miltiades, Alexander, & Cyrus, Darius, &c. The grave philosophers Socrates, Pythagoras, Plato, Aristotle, Epicurus, Zeno, and Demosthenes, shew their faces to this day revered in our medals. Those of the Hebrew represent to us the rod of Aaron & pot of manna, & shew how Juda was led captive. We come by medals to understand the antient weight & measures, and the value of monies: you will see there when it was that princes assum'd the radiant crownes, and what the diademe was. I might proceede to ye Punic Hanibal, Juba, &c. to the Consular & Imperial of the Romans from Romulus, the Scipios, Catos, down to this age of ours, if after Pertinax, and decline of that empire, sculpture & all good arts had not fall'n with it. You will therefore be curious of having the first Cæsars, the greate Julius (after his Pharsalian victorie) being the first honour'd with having his effigies, old, leane & bald as he was, in medal, or rather in monie, which are rare to procure in gold or small copper. There are of these and the other Emperors with Greeke inscriptions also. Who is not delighted to behold the true effigies of the famous Augustus, cruel Nero, & his master Seneca? Vespasian, Titus, Nerva, Trajan, Antoninus, Severus, the greate Constantine & his devout mother Helena? For we have in medals the beautiful Cleopatra & her paramour; Drusilla, Livia, Julia, Agrippina, Antonia, Valeria, Me^{ss}alina, Octavia, Poppæa Sabina, all of them Augustas; and sundry more of the faire sex, who rul'd the world. I have seene a series of the Popes from St. Peter, & amongst the reputed Heresiarcs, that medalion of John Huss & Hierome of Prague's martyrdome, with the memorable inscription *Post centum annos vos Cito,* which fell out at the appearing of Martin Luther exactly at that period. But, Sir, I am sensible I have quite tir'd you by this time with medals, & therefore I will say nothing concerning those observations in the filing, sharpnes, & due extanic vernish, & other markes, necessary to be critically skill'd in to prevent the being cheated & impos'd upon by copies & counterfeits for antique & original: (tho' yet all copies, if well dissembled, stamp'd, or cast, are not to be rejected), because you will both for this and all the rest, consult Fulvius Ursinus, Goltzius, Monsr St. Amant, Otto, Dr Spon, Vaillant, Dr. Patin, and *(instar omnium)* the most learned Spanhemius in that treatise *de præstantia et usu Numismatum Antiquorum.* You will likewise make vse of your friends Dr Gale, M[r]. Henshaw, Hill, and Mr Justell, vpon whose skill & judgment you may relie; tho' even the most skillful may now & then be mistaken: but you shall be sure not to be paied with trash, such as I do not (as I say'd) call the Antiquo Moderno if well imitated. These persons y[r] friends whom I mention'd, will I am sure be ready to assist you in this laudable curiositie. And if they can be purchas'd together, as accidentaly they sometimes may, it will save you a greate deale of paines, & enrich you at once. But otherwise, they are likeliest met withall amongst the goldsmiths, & casualy as one walkes the streetes on foot, & passes by the stalls. Mr. Ashmole, our common friend, had collected all the antient & modern coines of this kingdome, which were very rare, together with seuerall medalls of our British, Saxon, & other Kings vpon occasion of births, coronations, marriages, & other solemnities. I know not whether they escap'd the burning of his study at the Middle Temple. But for the most accurate ordering & disposing of medals, so as one may more commodiously take them out of their repositories, Mr. Charleton * of that Society, has a peculiar method, as he is the most elegant & rarely furnish'd in all his other collections. In the meane time, the curious of this sort of erudition (I meane of medalls) were formerly, & I believe at present, very few in England. For besides Sr Robert Cotton, Mr Selden, Sr Simon D'Ewes, Sr Tho. Hanmer of Hanmer, Sr Willm Paston, and the late Mr Hervey, I find hardly any. That greate lover of antiquity Thomas Earle of Arundel had a very rich collection as well of medalls as other intaglias, belonging to the cabinet he purchas'd of Daniel Nice at the cost of ten thousand pounds, which with innumerable other rarities, haue ben scatter'd & squander'd away by his Countesse when she got that treasure to Amsterdam, whilst my Lord was in Italy, where he died. Aboundance of them she be-

---

* See vol. III. p. 219.

stow'd also on the late vnhappy Viscount Stafford, her beloved son; & such as remained, Lely, Wright, & the rest of the painters, panders and misses, haue cheated the late Duke of Norfolk of. The same fate befell a noble collection of medals belonging to the then curious Sr Simon Fanshaw of Ware-park; they were after his decease thrown about the house (as that worthy gent: his son Sr Richard, Ld Ambass^r in Spain, from whom I had the relation, has told me,) for children to play at counter with: as were those elegant types of Sr Henry Savills at Eaton, which that learned Knight procur'd with greate cost for his edition of St. Chrysostome, & as it com'only fares with such curiosities where the next heire is not a virtuoso. So vaine a thing it is to set ones heart vpon any thing of this nature with that passion & mania, that unsatiable Earle whom I mention'd did, to the detriment of his estate and family;—*mediocria firma.* The medals in our Universitie Libraries are not yet at all considerable, tho' Obadiah Walker were an industrious promoter of it, & not vnskillfull in them. Mr. Ralph Sheldon, of Weston in Warwickshire, left a very handsome collection both of gold, siluer, & copper, antient & moderne, part of which were bequeathed to a sister of my Lady Tuke's, who not long since offer'd to haue sold them. I brought Monsr Justell to see them, but they were much ouer-valued, & whether she haue since dispos'd of them I neuer inquir'd. At present I know of none who can show a better chosen set of medals than the Earle of Clarendon, to whose late father (after all this tedious parenthesis) I returne, & haue a mind to entertaine you a while longer with what I had begun, where I spake of his purpose to furnish all the roomes of state and other apartments with the pictures of the most illustrious of our nation, especialy of his Lo^{ps} time & acquaintance, & of diuers before it. There were at full length, and as I doubt not but you well remember to haue seene, the greate Duke of Buckingham, the brave Sr Horace & Francis Vere, Sr Walt. Raleigh, Sr Phil. Sidney, the greate Earle of Leicester, Treasurer Buckhurst, Burleigh, Walsingham, Cecil, Ld Chan^r Bacon, Elsmere, & I think all the late Chancelors & graue Judges in the reignes of Q. Elizabeth, & her successors James & Charles the First. For there was Treas^r Weston, Cottington, Duke Hamilton, the magnificent Earle of Carlisle, Earles of Carnarvon, Bristol, Holland, Lindsey, Northumberland, Kingston, and Southampton: Lords Falkland and Digby (I name them promiscuously as they come into my memorie), & of Charles the Second, besides the Royal Family, the Dukes of Albemarle and Newcastle, Earles of Derby, Shrewsbery, St. Alban's, the brave Montrosse, Sandwich, Ma^{h}che^{s}ter, &c.: and of the coife, S^r Ed. Coke, Judge Berkeley, Bramston, Sr Orlando Bridgman, Jeofry Palmer, Selden, Vaughan, S^r

Rob. Cotton, Dugdale, Mr. Camden, Mr. Hales of Eton. The Archbishops Abbot & Laud, Bishops Juxon, Sheldon, Morley, and Duppa: Dr. Sanderson, Brownrig, Dr. Donne, Chillingworth, & seuerall of the Cleargie & others of the former & present age. For there were the pictures of Fisher, Fox, Sr Tho. More, tho. Lord Cromwell, Dr. Nowel, &c. And what was most agreeable to his L^{ps} general humor, old Chaucer, Shakspere, Beaumont & Fletcher, who were both in one piece, Spencer, Mr. Waller, Cowley, Hudibras, which last he plac'd in the roome where he vs'd to eate & dine in publiq, most of which, if not all, are at the present at Cornebery in Oxfordshire; together with the library, which ye present Earle has considerably improv'd, besides what bookes he has at Swalowfield not contemptible, & the manuscript copies of what concernes the Parliamentary Records, Journals, & Transactions which I haue heard hoth himself & the late vnfortunate Earle of Essex (who had also the same curiosity) affirme cost them £500 transcribing & binding, & indeede furnish a prety large roome. To compleate & encourage this noble and singular collection, I sent his L^p a list of the names following: Cardinals Pole and Wolsey; Gardner Bp. of Winchester, Cranmer, Ridley, old Latimer, Bp. Usher, Mr. Hooker, Occham, Ripley, John Duns, Roger Bacon, Suisset, Tunstal Bp. of Duresme (correspondent with Erasmus), Tompson, Ven: Bede, if at least to be met with in some ancient office or masse booke, where I haue seene some of those old famous persons accurately painted either from the life or from copies: Sr John Cheke, Sr Tho. Bodley, Smith, Jo. Berkeley, Mr. Ascham, Sr Fulk Greuil, Buchannan, Dr. Harvey, Gilbert, Mr. Oughtred, Sr Hen. Wotton (I still recite them promiscuously & not like an herauld), Sr Fra. Drake, Sr Rich. Hawkins, Mr. Cavendish, Martine Frobisher, &c.; some of which his Lo^p procured, but was you know interrupted, and after all this apparatus and grandeure, died an exile, & in the displeasure of his Majesty & others who envied his rise & fortune — *tam breves Populi Romani amores!* But I shall say no more of his ministrie, and what was the pretence of his fall, than that we haue liued to see greate revolutions. The buffoons, parasites, pimps, & concubines, who supplanted him at Court, came to nothing not long after, and were as little pitied. 'Tis something yet too early to publish the names of his delators, for fear of one's teeth. But time will speake truth, and sure I am the event has made it good. Things were infinitely worse manag'd since his disgrace, & both their late Maties fell into as pernicious counsels as euer Princes did: whilst what euer my Ld Chancel^{rs} skill, whether in law or politics, the offices of State & Justice were filled with men of old English honor & probitie; lesse open bribery & ostentation; there was at least something of more grauity and forme kept up (things, howeuer railled at, necessary in Courts): magnificence & antient hospitalitie in his Maties houses, more agreeable to the genius of this nation than the open & avowed luxurie & prophaneness which succeeded, *à la mode de France*, to which this favorite was a declared enemy vpon my certaine knowledge. There were indeede heinous matters laied to his charge, which I could neuer see prov'd; & you & I can tell of many that haue fall'n and yet suffer under that calamitie.

But what's all this, you'll say, to our subject? Yes, he was a greate lover at least of books, & furnish'd a very ample library, writ himselfe an elegant style, fauour'd & promoted the designe of the Royal Society; and it was for this, and in particular for his being very kind to me both abroad & at home, that I sent Naudæus to him in a dedicatory Addresse, of which I am not so much asham'd as of the Translation. There be some, who not displeas'd with the style of that Epistle, are angrie at the application. But they do not consider that greate persons, & such as are in place to doe greate & noble things, whateuer their other defects may be, are to be panegyrized into the culture of those vertues, without which 'tis to be suppos'd they had neuer ariv'd to a power of being able to encourage them. *Qui monet vt facias*—you remember the sequel. And 'tis a justifiable figure; nor is it properly adulation, but a civilitie due to their characters. As for the Translation, it has ben so insufferably abus'd at the presse, that the shame any uncorrected copy should come abroad has made me suppresse as many as I could light on, not without purpose of publishing a new edition, and which now perhaps might be more seasonable, since the humor of exposing books *sub hastâ* is become so epidemical, that it may possibly afford some direction to gentlemen who are making collections out of them. Besides, the first impression is I heare prety well worne out, and I should be very unfortunate if it should miscarry twice, or meete with such another accident as happen'd, it seemes, to the blotted manuscript at Oxford: the circumstances whereof I will not now trouble you withall.

And so I haue don with my Ld Chancelor. But not so soone with my worthy friend Mr. Pepys, to whose learned & laudable curiosity of still improving his choice collection I should not aduise a solicitous expense of hauing the pictures of so many greate persons paynted in oyle, which were a vast & unnecessary charge; tho' not so extraordinary a one to my Ld Chancel^r as one may imagine, because when his designe was once made known, euery body who either had them of their owne or could purchase them at any price, strove to make their court by these presents; by which meanes he got many excellent pieces of Vandyke, and other originals of

Lely, & the best of our modern masters hands. But if, insteade of these, you think fit to add to your title-pages, in a distinct volume, the heads & effigies of such as I haue enumerated, and of as many other as either in this or any other age have ben famous for armes or arts, in *taille douce*, and with very tollerable expense to be procur'd amongst the print-sellers, I should not reprove it; I am sure you would be infinitely delighted with the assembly, and some are so very well don to the life, that they may stand in competition wth the best paintings. This were a cheape and so much a more vsefull curiosity, as they seldome are without their names, ages, and elogies of the persons whose portraits they represent: I say you will be exceedingly pleas'd to contemplate the effigies of those who haue made such a noise & bustle in the world, either by their madnesse & folly, or a more conspicuous figure by their wit & learning. Nor would I yet confine you to stop here, but to be continualy gathering as you happen to meete wth other instructive types. For vnder this classe may come in batails, sieges, triumphs, justes & tournaments, coronations, cavalcads, & entries of ambassadors, processions, funebral & other pomps, tombs, tryals & executions: stately edifices, machines, antique vases, spoiles, basse relievos, intaglios, & cameos taken from achates, onyxes, cornelians, & other precious stones; ruines, landskips, if from real subjects, not fancies which are innumerable & not necessary, but such as relate to historie, and for reasons specified more at large in my Treatise on Chalcographie. Your library being by this accession made suitable to your generous mind & steady virtue, I know none liuing master of more happinesse, since besides the possession of soe many curiosities, you vnderstand to vse & improue them likewise, & haue declar'd that you will endeauour to secure * what with so much cost & industrie you haue collected, from the sad dispersions many noble libraries & cabinets haue suffer'd in these late times: one auction, I may call it diminution, of a day or two, hauing scatter'd what has ben gathering many yeares. Hence it is that we are in England so defectiue of good libraries among the gentlemen & in our greatest townes: Paris alone, I am persuaded, being able to shew more than all the three nations of Greate Britaine: those of Mem'ius, Puteane, Thuanus, Cordesius, Seguire, Colbert, Condé, & others innumerable of bishops, abbots, advocates, antiquaries, & a world of learned persons of the long robe; besides the publiq libraries at St. Victoire, the Sorbonne, & aboue all, that of Mazarin (now, with Richelieu's & sundry others, swallow'd vp in the present King's), far exceeding any thing

---

* This Mr. Pepys did, by giving his books and collection of prints to Magdalen College, Cambridge, where they now are under the name of the Pepysian Library, in the original bookcases and presses, placed in a room which they exactly fit.

we can shew at home, tho' we have as much (if not greater) plenty & variety of the best books as any country in the learned world. But, as I said, they are in private cabinets, & seldome well chosen, vnlesse in the Vniversities, where, if one may judge by the few productions of so many learned men as are there at leasure, they signifie so very little to the learned world. This greate & august citty of London, abounding with so many wits and letter'd persons, has scarce one library furnish'd and indow'd for the publiq. Sr John Cotton's, collected by his noble vncle, is without dispute the most valuable in MSS. especialy of British and Saxon antiquities; but he refuses to impart to vs the catalogue of this treasure, for feare, he tells me, of being disturb'd. That of Westminster is not much considerable: still lesse that of Syon Colledge. But there is hope his Maties at St. James's may emerge & be in some measure restor'd againe, now that it comes vnder the inspection of the learned Mons. Justell, who you know was owner of a very considerable one at Paris. There are in it a greate many noble manuscripts yet remaining, besides the Tecla; and more would be, did some royal or generous hand cause those to be brought back to it, which still are lying in mercenary hands for want of two or three hundred pounds to pay for their binding; many of which being of the oriental tongues, will soone else find Jewes & chapmen that will purchase & transport them, from whence we shall neuer retreiue them againe. For thus has a cabinet of ten thousand medals, not inferior to most abroad, & far superior to any at home, which were collected by that hopefull cherisher of greate and noble things Prince Henry, been imbezil'd and carried away during our late barbarous rebellion, by whom & whither none can or is like to discouer. What that collection was, not onely of bookes and medals, but of statues & other elegant furniture, let the learned librarykeeper Patritius Junius tell you in his notes ad Epist. S^{ti} Clementis ad Corinthos: "quem locum," (speaking of St. James's) "si vicinam pinacothecam bibliothecæ celeberrimæ conjunctam, si numismata antiqua Græca ac Romana, si statuas & signa ex ære et marmore consideres, non im'erito thesaurum antiquitatis et $ταμιεῖον$ instructissimum nominare potes," &c.

Were not this losse enough to break a lover's heart? The Royal Society at Gresham Colledge has a mixture, tho' little apposite to the institution & designe of that worthy assembly, yet of many excellent books & some few MSS. given them at my instance by the late Duke of Norfolck, w^h is but a part of that rare collection of good authors which by the industrie & direction of Francis Junius, the learned son of the learned Patrick, Mr. Selden, & the purchase of what was brought at once out of Germanie, was left neglected at Arundel

House before it was demolished & converted into tenements. I now mention Mr. Selden. There is a fragment of that great antiquarie's librarie at the Middle Temple; but his manuscripts & best collections were bequeath'd to the Bodleian at Oxford, to which both himselfe & especialy Archbishop Laude were the most munificent benefactors: tho' with all these, so poore in manuscripts that they were ashamed to publish their catalogue with that of the *impressorum*, but which might yet have ben equaly inriched with any perhaps in Europe, had they purchas'd what was lately offer'd them by the executors of Isaac Vossius, tho' indeede at a great price, who have since carried them back into Holland, where they expect a quicker mercate. I wish'd with all my heart some brave and noble Mæcenas would have made a present of them to Trinity Colledge in Cambridge, where that sumptuous structure (design'd for a library) would have ben the fittest repository for such a treasure. Where are our Suissets, Bodleys, Lauds, Sheldons, bishops & opulent chancelors? Will the *Nepotismo* neuer be satisfied.— *Sed præstat motus componere.* The next to that of the Bodleian are the librarys of Magdalen Coll., Christ Church, University, & Baliol, which last is furnish'd with diuers considerable MSS. & lately (thro' the bounty of Sir Tho. Wendie) with a number of other curious books. But to returne againe neerer this Citty: That at Lambeth, replenish'd at present with excellent books, ebbs & flows like the Thames running by it, at euery prelat's succession or translation: there's at present a good assembly of manuscripts in a roome by themselues. The Bishop of Ely has a very well stor'd library; but the very best is what Dr. Stillingfleet, Deane of St. Paule's, has at Twicknam, ten miles out of towne. Onely that good & learned man (Dr. Tennison) of St. Martine's, neere you, has begun a charity, for so I reckon it as well as that of his two scholes, &c. worthy his publiq & generous spirit, and the esteeme of all who know him. Our famous lawyer Sr Edw. Coke purchas'd a very choice library of Greeke & other MSS. which were sold him by Dr. Meric Casaubon, son of the learned Isaac; & these, together wth his delicious villa, Durdens, came to ye possession of ye present Earle of Berkley from his unkle Sr Robert Cook. He has sometimes told me he would build a convenient repository for them, which should be publiq for the use of the cleargie of Surrey; but what he has don, or thinks to do herein, I know not. Why is not such provision made by a publiq law & contribution in euery county of England. But this genius dos not allways preside in our representatiues. I haue heard that Sr Henry Sauill was master of many precious MSS. & he is frequently celebrated for it by the learned Valesius, almost in euery page of that learned man's annotations on Eusebius & the ecclesiastical historians publish'd by him. The late Mr. Hales of Eton, whom I mention'd, had likewise a very good library; and so had Dr. Cosin (late Bishop of Duresme), a considerable part of which I had agreed with him for my selfe during his exile abroad, as I can shew under his owne hand;* but

---

* The following letter from Dr. Cosin, afterwards Bishop of Durham, to Mr. Evelyn, is probably here alluded to:

Sir,

I haue here set y^e prices (wch I paid) to y^e bookes wch you have a_{dd}e_d. but there be 4 or 5 of them (marked wth -+-) which I desire to keepe, because I haue written some notes in y^m of my owne. The remaynder of y^e whole summe (as you will see at y^e foote of y^e inclosed paper) wilbe 105^l. And truly, S^r, I thought I had p^evented any further motion of abatem^t, by the large offer y^t I made to you, of putting yor wives confident [friend] (for it concernes her only) to lose the third part of what her fr^d paid: specially considering that she is now forced to pay very neere 200^l. for ye library, besides what it cost at first. I doe not conceive that it wilbe any great charge to you to have y^m brought to London, where they wilbe subject to lesse hazard then in other places, & to no more there then all other worldly things are in all other places besides. If you consider their number, I desire you would be pleased to consider likewise, that they are a choice-number, & a company of ye best selected books among y^m all. When these & others of the like sort are gone, I haue good hope, y^t those who come to buy the remaynder & ye worst of y^m all, will not desire to have above a third part of the price abated them: & therefore the better sort (such as you haue chosen) might in reason goe at a better rate; & indeed I haue advised her, not to abate above a 4th part for most of them, & for some to hold y^m at ye same or

his late daughter, since my Lady Garret, thought I had not offer'd enough, & made difficulty in deliuering them to me 'till neere the time of his Maties restauration, & after that, the Deane her father, becoming Bishop of that opulent see, bestow'd them on the library there. But the Ld Primate Usher was inferior to none I haue named among the cleargie for rare MSS. a greate part of which being brought out of Ireland, & left his son-in-law Sr Timothy Tirrill, was dispos'd of to giue bread to that incomparable prelate during the late fanatic war; such as remain'd yet at Dublin were preserv'd, and by a publiq purse restored & placed in the colledge library of that citty. I haue already mention'd what Isaac Vossius brought ouer, that had been his learned father's, & many other manuscripts which Isaac had himselfe brought from Queene Christina out of Sweden in recompense of his honorarie,

---

a greater price then they cost; as for example, there is in yor note Plinie's Naturall Historie in Engl^sh priced at 36^s wch is worth 3^l.; Camden's Errors pric'd at 5^s 6^d for wch I have seen 20^s given; Paulus Jovius at 20^s, wch sells now in Paris at 4. pistols, & Pol. Vergil at 10^s, wch sells here for 10^l.; Will'm Malmesbury at 15^s fo^l. wch they demand here 30^l.; & Asser. Menev. &c. at 14^s, wch they will not part with here nor elsewhere abroade for 20^l. In regard whereof I made accompt, that you would rather have said ye abatem^t had ben too large then too little, wch was made & offered so freely by

This 18th of July,   Yo^r humble serv^t.
1651.   TC.

whilst he was invited thither with Salmasius, Des Cartes, Blundel, & others, by the heroic and royal errant. But those birds, as I sayd, haue taken their flight, & are gon. I forbear to name the late Earle of Bristol's & his kinsman Sr Kenelm Digby's libraries, of more pomp than intrinsic value, as chiefly consisting of modern poets, romances, chymical, & astrological bookes, for I had the Catalogue in my possession before they were disposed of, put into my hands by my Lord Danby, then Treasurer, who desir'd me to giue my opinion of them, which I faithfully did. As for those of Sr Kenelm's, the Catalogue was printed, & most of them sold in Paris, as many better haue lately ben in London. The Duke of Lauderdaile's is yet intire, choicely bound, & to be sold by a friend of mine, to whom they are pawn'd: but it comes far short of his relation's, the Lord Maitland's, which was certainely the noblest, most substantial, & accomplished library that euer pass'd vnder the speare, and it heartily grieu'd me to behold its limbs, like those of the chaste Hippolytus, separated & torne from that so well chosen & compacted body. The Earle of Anglesey's, & severall others since, by I know not what invidious fate, pass'd the same fortune, to what euer influence & constellation now reigning malevolent to books & libraries, which can portend no good to the future age.

And now I haue in good earnest don with libraries; but yet not quite with Mr. Pepys. For I mention none of all these as if I thought it necessary euery private gentleman's study should be made common, but wish we had some more communicatiue & better furnish'd with good books, in one of the greatest citties of the universe (London); & for that end that a stately portico were so contriu'd at the west end of St. Paule's, as might support a palatine, capable of such a designe; & that every company and corporation of the Citty, euery apprentise at his freedom, assisted at first by a general collection thro-out the nation, a copy of euery booke printed within the Citty & Vniversities, did cast in their symbals for a present stock & a future ample funde. But this we are to expect when kings are philosophers, or philosophers kings; which I think may happen not in this but in Plato's revolution. All that I shall add concerning gentlemen being furnish'd with competent libraries & for most part residing in towne is, how obliging a thing it were, & of infinite effect to the promoting a noble and vsefull conversation of learned gentlemen, if, as there is a Society for the Improvement of Natural Knowledge, and which was fit should be first, since things were before words, so there was an Academie for that of Art & Improvement of speaking & writing well; of which sort there are (you know) some in Paris, & almost in euery considerable citty of Italy, which go under the devises of *La Crusca*, sadors as well as bishops, abbots, presidents, and other learned men & trauellers, this brought together into conversation the most humane & obliging in the world; & how exceedingly to be wish'd some noble & worthy gent. would giue a diuersion so becoming & usefully entertaining as it would be. We should not then haue so many crude and fulsome rhapsodies impos'd upon the English world for genuine witt, language, & the stage, as well as on the auditors & spectators, which would be purg'd from things intollerable. It would inflame, inspire, & kindle another genius and tone of writing, with nervous, natural strength & beauty, genuine and of our owne growth, without allways borrowing & filching from our neighbours. And indeede such was once design'd since the restauration of Charles the Second (1665), and in order to it three or fowre meetings were begun at Gray's Inn, by Mr. Cowley, Dr. Sprat, Mr. Waller, the D. of Buckingham, Matt. Clifford, Mr. Dryden, & some other promoters of it. But by the death of the incomparable Mr. Cowley, distance & inconvenience of the place, the contagion, & other circumstances intervening, it crumbled away & came to nothing: what straw I had gather'd towards the bricks for that intended pyramid (having the honour to be admitted an inferior labourer) you may command & dispose of, if you can suffer my impertinences: and that which I haue not shew'd you, the plan I drew & was laying before them for that designe, which was, I said, the polishing of the English tongue, & to be one of the first intentions & chiefest subjects of the Academicians.

And now for shame haue don! Methinks I heare you cry out, "What a ramble has Mr. Evelyn made! what a deale of ground for so little game!" Well, you see what the setting up an empty noddle has produc'd, what a deale of inke is run to waste. And indeede I had ben criminaly vnanswerable of detriment to the publique as well as to your owne repose, should I haue dar'd to debauch you with so tedious & intemperate a scribble, whilst you were not *(tuo jure)* your owne man. But if for all that, this prove an affliction also, as I haue cause to apprehend it may, the only expedient to rid yourselfe of such impertinents will be, to assume your late buisy & honourable charge againe; when no man can be so impudently uncivil as to expect you should reade his long letters, when he considers how many you will then be obliged to write.

Says-Court, 12 Aug. 1689.

SAM. PEPYS's reply to the preceding Letter.
Printed from a MS. Copy, preserved in the Bodleian Library.

Hon[re]d Sir,   Aug. 30, 1689.

I shall never be anxious about pardon for not doing what I ought, where what I ought, is what I can't. And such is y\ue giving a due answer to y\ue inestimable honour and favour of your letter of this day: and so much the less estimable, by that alone for which you would censure it, its length: as containing in less than five pages, what would cost me five volumes reading, from any other hand but Mr. Evelyn's. And yet some answer you shall (in time) have to it, and y\ue best I can give you, namely, by my endeavouring to leave no one syllable unpractis'd of what you have had the goodnesse to teach me in it, and lyes within y\ue reach of my pate and purse to execute.

Let this, I beg you, suffice to be sayd upon it at the first view. For though I could hardly find time to take breath 'till I had gone through it, yet I wont promise to haue done reading it this month. One word only I would now say to you upon your first words, about y\ue place I have been bold in dooming your picture to, namely, that besides forty other reasons I had (founded upon gratitude, affection, and esteeme,) to covet that in effigie which I most truly value in the original, I had this one more, that I take it for y\ue only head living I can hope to invite most by after it, of those few whose memories (when dead) I find myself wishing I could do aught to perpetuate. Among which fills a principal place y\ue most excellent Mr. Boyle, concerning whom I lately bespoke your favour, and dare now be y\ue bolder in doing it againe, from my having heard,

that he has newly been prevail'd with by Dr King, to have his head taken by one of much less name than Mr. Kneller, and a stranger, one Causabon.
I am ever,
Your most obedient servant and honourer,
S. Pepys.

Mr. Evelyn's second Letter to Mr. Pepys, in prosecution of his former one of 26th August, 1689.

Sir, Deptford, 4 October, 1689.

I had newly been reading Aristotle's book περὶ τῆς μαντικῆς, &c. or Divination by Dreams (wch followes his other Treatises "De Animâ, Memoriâ, & Reminiscentiâ"), when ye very night after, methought Mr. Pepys and I were, among other things, discoursing in his library about ye ceremonious part of conversation and visites of forme between well-bred persons: and I distinctly remember, that I told him (what is true and no dream) that ye late E. of St. Alban's (I meane uncle to H. Germaine, ye present E. of Dover) took extraordinary care at Paris, that his young nephew should learne by heart all ye formes of encounter, and Court-addresses; such as the Latines would express by *verba honestatis;* and ye French (if I mistake not, who are masters in these civilities to excess) *l'entregent:* as upon occasion of giving or taking ye wall, sitting downe, entering in or going out of ye doore, taking leave at parting; *l'entretien de la ruelle,* and other encounters; *à la cavaliere* among ye ladys, &c. In all which never was person more adroit than my late neighbour the Marquis de Ruvigny. And indeed the Italians and Spaniards exceed us infinitely in this point of good breeding. Nay, I observe generally that our women of quality often put us to " O Lord, Madam !" when we have nothing to fill up and reply; but, *quorsum hæc?* (a little patience).—I was never in my life subject to night visions 'till of late, that I seldom pass without some reverie, wch verifies that of St: Peter (cited from the prophet), " That your old men shall dream dreams ;" and so you will shortly give me over for a dotard, should I continue to interrupt you thus with my impertinencies. I will only tell you, that my wife, who is of a much sedater temper, and yet often dreaming, has now and then diverted me with stories that hung as orderly together as if they had been studied narratives, some of which I had formerly made her write down for ye prettiness of them, very seldom broken, or inconsistent (such as commonly are mine), but such as the Peripatetick meanes, where he says *Quieto sanguine fiunt pura somnia ;* comparing those other extravagant and confused dreames to ye resemblances which ye circles of disturbed and agitated waters reflect, that blend and confound ye species, and present us with centaures and terrible specters, whilst ye calmer fountaine gives ye entire image (as it did with Narcissus's in ye fable), and entertaine us with our waking thoughts. What could be more explicit of ye cause of this variety of dreames which he, as well as Hippocrates, and others from them, attribute to the crasis and constitution of ye body and complections domineering, with other perturbations affecting the phancy. But leaving these to the Oneirocriticks, I shall make use of it no further, than to let you see, how often you are in my best and serenest thoughts. *Amici de amicis certa sæpè somniant,* ἐρωτικὸς ἐν Ἔρωτι. And if ye subject of my wild phantasme (which was a dialogue with you about forme of speaking upon ceremonious occasions) naturally leading me to something which I lately mention'd, where I spake of academies and ye refining of our language, have not already quite worne out your patience, I would entertaine you here with a copy of what I sent our Chairemain * some years since, as an Appendix to my former Letter, and as you injoyned me.

* * * * * * * * * * * * * * *

---

* The observations referred to by Evelyn, will be found already printed in this volume, pages 145—149, having been written 24 years earlier than the present letter. They are inserted in a copy of the very communication to which he alludes, addressed to Sir Peter Wyche, Chairman of a Committee appointed by the Royal Society to consider of the improvement of the English Tongue.

So much for this, and I fear too much, now I see how I have blurr'd: but 'tis not worth the writing fairer.

Sir, I stay'd at Lambeth with his Grace 'till past 4, being to returne with ye Bishops, and go home, as I was engag'd that evening: I called at your house, but you were gone forth, they told me, in your coach, which made me conclude it was not to Lambeth, when I should have been sorry not to have waited on you.

I have now gotten me a paire of new horses; but they are very young, and hardly broken to ye coach as yet: so soone as I may trust them, and that ye weather be a little settled, I shall not faile of waiting on you to Mr. Charleton's, and those other virtuosos.

To the Countess of SUNDERLAND.

Madame,

I had prepar'd a lett^r, to congratulate my young Lorde & y^r Ladys^p, & all y^r illustrious families happy arival & returne to Althorp, when just as I was writing came the sad tidings of the death of that excellent lady y^r daughter the Countesse of Arran, which struck such a damp in me that I was forc'd to breake off from a gratefull subject, to condole with y^r La^p, and those whom I thought it my obligation to endeavour the comforting: and this was the more afflicting, that after such assurances of her Lap^s perfect recovery, vpon which I was meditating to write to you, this fatal newes should dash our hopes againe without any reserue. But so is the will of God, & this the constitution of all things here : no true satisfaction, no permanent felicity to be found on this side heaven : whateuer other circumstances of happinesse, as far as we can reckon any such thing in the power of this world to giue us, may seeme to promise of more lastingnesse & stabilitie, 'tis all but a seeming, a meere shew & false appearance; for either the things which we hope to enjoy are taken from vs &˙perish in the fruition, or we are taken from them when we think ourselues most secure. Surely if in this life any thing were desirable, the hauing & the leauing virtuous & gracious children behind us (such as might be examples of virtue, adorne & improue the age,) were to be esteemed the most valuable of blessings. But as such blessings are rare, so when God bestows them they are soonest taken from vs againe. They can no more liue in so corrupt an age than a healthfull body in a vitiated aire. What then are we to do when we loose them? Not consider them as lost, but happily absent. Madame, you know how easy 'twere to say aboundance of fine things on this subject—no topiq more fruitefull; but what's all this? The wound is deepe and in a sensible part, and tho' time and reason mitigate. the present smart, I cannot say it has healed what I often times suffer when the losse of some deare children &

friends come into my thoughts. One onely consideration remaines, that as I said they are so far from being lost or dead, that they liue & are now immortal, & would not for all the world be with us againe. Why then grieue we for them? Why, plainely for ourselues, whom we loue more than God, whose will it is we should part with them, and whateuer he pleases to take from vs heare, & depend on Him alone, who alone will neuer faile, neuer forsake vs, but give us that which shall neuer be taken from vs. Live we then, Mad^me, in this religious indifference & resignation. But still God has not left y^r La^p without those blessings. He has but in part eclips'd, & rather borrowed for a while than taken them away. Besides my Lord y^r husband, whom you haue seene restored, & which to see so, you esteemed so greate a mercy; you haue a daughter & a son, who are & ought to be all that you can wish or desire in children. And him will Almighty God preserue: in both you will see the fruites of y^r pious care & reward of your submission to the will of God, and receiue all the discipline you haue past thro' as a greater mark of his favour & loue than if you had neuer suffer'd ye least checq or diminution of y^r former prosperity. This I am so well perswaded of you feele already, howeuer now by this lugubrous accident as by others sometimes interrupted, that you would not exchange y^r inward consolation, for the returne of all those external fugitives you once injoy'd to be depriv'd of this. Mad^me, this is a seacret knowne onely to those who feele it, which, since I am sure you do, I leaue y^u to that God who giues it, who is y^r stay, y^r refuge, and may He be all that you can want & desire to supply this losse, & more than you can wish.

Says-Court, 25 July, 1690.

To Lady Sunderland.

Deptford, 4 Aug. 1690.

As for the "Kalendar" y^r L^p mentions, what ever assistance it may be to some novice gardiner, sure I am his Lo^p will find nothing in it worth his notice but an old inclination to an innocent diversion, & the acceptance it found with my deare (and while he liv'd) worthy friend Mr. Cowley, upon whose reputation only it has survived seaven impressions, & is now entering on the eighth with some considerable improvements, more agreeable to the present curiosity. 'Tis now, Mad^me, almost fourty yeares since first I writ it, when horticulture was not much advanc'd in England, and neere thirty since first 'twas publish'd, which consideration will I hope excuse its many defects. If in the meane time it deserve the name of no un-usefull trifle, 'tis all it is capable of.

When many yeares ago I came from rambling

abroad, observ'd a little there, & a greate deale more since I came home than gave me much satisfaction, & (as events have prov'd) scarce worth one's pursuite, I cast about how I should employ the time which hangs on most young men's hands, to the best advantage; and when books & severer studies grew tedious, & other impertinence would be pressing, by what innocent diversions I might sometime relieve my selfe without complyance to recreations I took no felicity in, because they did not contribute to any improvement of the mind. This set me upon planting of trees, and brought forth my "Sylva," which booke, infinitely beyond my expectation, is now also calling for a fourth impression, and has ben the occasion of propagating many millions of usefull timber-trees thro'out this nation, as I may justifie (without im'odesty) from ye many letters of acknowledgement receiv'd from gentlemen of the first quality, and others altogether strangers to me. His late Ma^{ty} Cha. the 2d. was sometimes graciously pleas'd to take notice of it to me, & that I had by that booke alone incited a world of planters to repaire their broken estates & woodes, which the greedy rebells had wasted & made such havock of. Upon this encouragement I was once speaking to a mighty man, then in despotic power, to mention the greate inclination I had to serve his Ma^{ty} in a little office then newly vacant (the salary I think hardly £300) whose province was to inspect the timber trees in his Maties Forests, &c. and take care of their culture & improvement; but this was conferr'd upon another, who, I believe, had seldom ben out of the smoke of London, where tho' there was a greate deale of timber, there were not many trees. I confesse I had an inclination to the imployment upon a publique account as well as its being suitable to my rural genius, borne as I was at Wotton, among the woods.

Soon after this, happen'd the direfull conflagration of this Citty, when taking notice of our want of bookes of architecture in the English tongue, I published those most usefull directions of Ten of the best Authors on that subject, whose works were very rarely to be had, all of them written in French, Latine, or Italian, & so not intelligible to our mechanics. What the fruite of that labour & cost has ben (for the sculptures, which are elegant were very chargeable) the greate improvement of our workmen, & several impressions of ye copy since, will best testifie.

In this method I thought properly to begin with planting trees, because they would require time for growth, and would be advancing to delight & shade at least, & were therefore by no means to be neglected & deferr'd, while building might be raised and finish'd in a sum'er or two if the owner pleas'd.

Thus, Madame, I endeavour'd to do my countrymen some little service, in as natural an order as I could for the improving & adorning their estates & dwellings, &, if possible, make them in love with these usefull & innocent pleasures, in exchange of a wastfull & ignoble sloth which I had observ'd had so universally corrupted an ingenuous education.

To these I likewise added my little History of Chalcography, a treatise of the perfection of Paynting, and of erecting Libraries, ... Medals, with some other intermesses which might divert within dores, as well as altogether without.

To Mr. Anthony a Wood.

S^r,

Having lately received an account from Mr. Aubrey (as formerly by the Specimen & Proposals you have publish'd) of the progresse of y^r intended Historie (Athenæ Oxonienses), and that you desire to be inform'd who one Mr. Welles (sometime since of Deptford) was: the best light I can give you will be from the inscription vpon his wife's monument in that parish-church. Of what county, or family of that name, he originally was, I cannot say; but it might happly be conjectur'd by the armes, had not the cleark (whom I order'd to send me the inclos'd note) forgotten that circumstance. Thus much onely I can add, that Mr. Welles the husband married into a very antient & worthy family of the

Wallengers & Gonstones, of which the last (namely Benjamine) had ben Treasurer of the Navy Royal during the reignes of Hen. VIII. K. Edw. VI. Q. Mary & Eliz. a place of greatest trust & honour. And to these two families my wife has a neere relation.—But to returne to Mr. Welles. He was the author of a booke of Shadows or Dialing, an excellent mathematician, well acquainted with Mr. Gunter, Gelibrand, Doc[r] Gilbert, Mr. Oughtred, & other famous mathematicians of his time : I have several horoscopes, & other schemes of his, among my papers. He had two sons (whom I well knew), whereof the eldest succeeded in his father's office of Store-keeper in the Naval Arsenal, a place of good credit, and requiring extraordinary application: His second son, Ben. Welles, physitian, formerly fellow of All Soules in Oxon, a very good scholar, lately deceas'd at Greenewich, leaving onely two daughters.

This, S[r], being all I can at present learne of Mr. Welles, I take opportunity to superadd something which more immediately concernes my-selfe : 'Tis some time since that Dr. Plot, communicating to me your noble designe, required me (as from y[r] selfe) to give him some account of my owne family, &c.: what then I writ I do not now so well approve of : & divers circumstances since that intervening, both as to my fortune (which may possibly transfer my hitherto abode here at Sayes-Court in Kent to the seate of my ancestors in Surry) and an honorable charge, which his late Majestie conferr'd on me, of one of the Commissioners of the Privie Seale, seemes to require some other account from me than that which Dr. Plot exacted of me, which I desired he would intreate you to manage, not as written by me in my owne person (which were a vanitie insupportable), but that you would vse the sponge, as you thought fit, & as becomes the modestie of one who has no other ambition in this, than that (if needes you will take notice of an inconsiderable man) thô I can contribute little to your worthy labour, I may yet endeavor, that the honour you intend me, and the glorious Vniversitie who is pleas'd to owne me, may not suffer thrô your too greate civilitie, or reproch me of presumption, or ingratitude. I am,

S^r, y^{rs}, &c.

Sayes-Court, May 29, 1691.

S^r,

If I may be so bold I should esteeme it a greate favour, if at least y^u have prepar'd any thing concerning me, that you would transmitt me a copy thereoff before you print it.

To my Ld Bishop of LINCOLN.   (Dr. THOMAS TENNISON.)

My Lord,

Whatsoever my opinion had been concerning the cause of earthquakes, I am sure it had become me to haue submitted to y^r Lo^ps better judgement. But, indeede, I haue long had no other sentiments of it than what I find confirm'd by y^r L'p with so greate reason, by so many experiments, & pregnant instances of the irresistible effects of niter, which no chaines can bind. An experiment which was long since made at Gressham Colledge, were enough to convince one. They prepar'd a ball of solid yron about the thicknesse of a pretty cannon bullet, which was hammer'd both hot and cold, to render it as hard & tough as possible. In this they drill'd a small hole to the center, and after having dropp'd in a few graines of gunpowder, and stopping them up by forcing in a screw, exceedingly well riveted at the top, they set it on a pan of charcoale, in a large quadrangle of the Colledge, which no sooner thereby heated, but with a terrible explosion it brake the ball into a thousand pieces. Now tho' this was com'on gunpowder, yet 'tis not the sulphur, but the niter which operates with this pernicity, & breakes all bands whatsoever. The sulphur and coale which enter into the composition and blacken the cornes, are onely (y^r L^p knows) in order to its speedy kindling, adding little else to its force. The consideration whereof frees me from all questionings of the being and power of spirits (I meane intellectual ones), & of creatures & beings invisible. The dire effects of compressed and incarcerated aer, when the turn-key fire [sulphur] unlocks the prison-doors are not to be express'd but with astonishment; nor passe I by a wind-mill without wonder, to see a stone of that magnitude, & so ponderous, & of so many tuns weight, whirl'd about with that swiftnesse by something which we do not see, & sometimes hardly feele, for a very little breath will set it going. Indeede it was to this pent-up vapour, which the antient meteorologists attributed those coliques & convulsions of the earth; but they did not dreame of niter, which tho' no more than aer contracted, has so much the more violent operation when expanded, as inclines me to think it has raised all the famous fires we meete with, & not onely the vulcanos at present burning (such as Hecla, Vesuvius, Ætna, Stromboli, &c.) but perhaps most of the mountaines of the world, which I fancy might have been thrust up by the force of subterranean fires. Powder'd alabaster, chalke & sand being put into a vessell, & set on the fire, will (when hot) boile, & bubble up to some pretty & odd resemblances of such protuberances. Nor is it unlikely that where the hills are highest, the caves are as profound underneath them; & that there are vast ones under those Alpes & Sierras from whence our rivers derive their plentifull streames, and haue their supplies from some such capacious cisternes & *hydrophylatia* as Kircher mentions. Besides these, may there not also be many dry & empty *cryptas*, sometimes above, & sometimes beneath these water receptacles, where

Vulcan and the Cyclops are perpetualy at work? And that in processe of time, the fire arriving at a bed of niter & sulphure blowing up all incumbences, not onely cause these concussions, but frequently spew oute greate quantities of water? 'Tis evident that the very glebe & soile all about Naples is natural fuel, where I have in many places taken up *sulphur vivum,* both under and above the surface. All the ground both under that noble citty & country about it, sounds hollow like a tub. The hot bathes, natural stoves, & other extraordinary things of this kind thro' all that territorie, are the effects of subterranean fires, which feeding on the bituminous & other unctuous & inflammable matter (which it copiously finds) when it comes once to meete with a stratum of niter, it forces up all above & about it, & makes that prodigious havock, however thick, deepe, & heavy be the incumbent weight or matter. Thus did Vesuvius A° 1630, and now since (more terrible) at Catanea, ejecting stones and huge rocks of monstrous bulk; belching out flames & scattering ashes some hundred leagues distance from the eruption. Now when this niter has don its execution, and one thinks it quite at rest (for so it seem'd to be for about a thousand years, nay I think ever since the elder Plinie perish'd there[*]) emitting only a little smoke, it was all this while, it

---

[*] For in this confidence they built citties and palaces, & planted viniards and places of pleasure. J. E.

seemes, lurking 'till it came to another stratum, and then up went all againe, and thus 'tis evident haue ben made those deep and dreadful *calderras* both of Vesuvius & Ætna. Whither at first these fires were kindled by lightnings from without (as y^r L^p well conjectures) or from coruscations within, or by the collision of pyrites & other stones of the arched caverns, the prepar'd matter soone conceives a kindling, which breaking into a flame, rarifies the stagnant aer, that bursts those rocky barrs, which 'till it breaks out puts oftentimes a country in those paroxisms and ague fitts which we call earthquakes. The noise, explosion, & inconceivable swiftnesse of its motion, affecting so distant places in the same moment almost of time, shewes thro' what recesses, long extended channels & hollow passages (as in so many mines) this sulphrous niter lies in traine, ready for the *lin-stock*. These furnaces are doubtlesse the laboratories where minerals are concocted into metals; *fluors* sublimated, salts and juices condens'd, & precious stones, the several ferments imparting various qualities to earths and waters, & promoting vegetation; nay who knows (& I pray God we may never know) whether local Hell be not the central fire; or whether this vast terraqueous globe may not one day breake like a granado about our eares, & cast itselfe into another figure than the deluge did according to the ingenious Doctor's[*] theorie?

---

[*] Dr. Burnet of the Charter-House.

But, my Lord, from philosophising and conjecture I am rambling I know not whither, when all that I would signifie is my full assent to your L^{ps} reasoning; very believing the cause of earthquakes to proceede from the ingredient mention'd, mutually inkindled, & then, in searching vent, teares all up, where it finds the obstacle, & shaking all about it. 'Tis observable that Ægypt and the lower regions seldome feel these concussions, whilst the mountainous countries are most obnoxious, as most cavernous; especialy in hot climats. Sad instances of this are the yet ruines of Old Antioch, Smyrna, &c. and in our days Ragusa, Benevento, Smyrna againe, & that terrible one of Jamaica, which had its operation & was felt as far as England but a few days since. All the mountainous countries of Sicily & Greece & along Dalmatia's side are hollow, perhaps for thousands of miles, even under the very sea itselfe; as I believe from Vesuvius to Ætna, and thence to other further remote mountaines & vulcanos, perhaps as far as Iseland, China, & the Andes of Peru, which are full of *picos*, whereof Potosi (that inexhaustible magazine of silver and other metalls) seemes to be no other. Those furious ravages may also probably have made so many rugged rocks, cliffs, hiatus's & peloponesus's, & have seperated those many ilands, & scatter'd, nay, as it were sow'd about the ocean, & divided from the continent; & what if raised in the very sea itselfe, as the

Terceras were & Teneriffe in the Grand Canaries, not to insist on the new mountaine neere the Baiæ: So that (my L^d) I am in no distresse at all to solve this phænomenon, at least to my ownè satisfaction. But when all is said, tho' all proceede from natural causes, yet doubt I not their being inflicted & directed, by the Supreme Cause of causes, as judgements upon a sinfull world, and for signes of greate calamities, if they work no reformation: if they do, of chastisements. Upon these accounts I looke on them as portentous & of evil præsage, and to shew us that there is no stabilitie under heaven, where we can be safe & happy, but in Him alone who laied the foundations of the earth, the rock of ages that shall never be removed, when heaven & earth shall passe away.

As to our late earthquake here, I do not find it has left any considerable marks; but at Mons 'tis said it has made some demolitions. I happen'd to be at my Brother's at Wotton in Surry when the shaking was, & at dinner with much companie; none of us yet at table sensible of any motion. But the mayd who was then making my bed, & another servant in a garret above her, felt it plainely, and so did my Wife's laundry mayd here at Deptford; and generaly wherever they were above in the upper floores they felt the trembling most sensibly, for a reason I neede not explaine to y^r Lo^p. In London, & particularly in Dover street (where my Son's house is) they were greatly affrighted. But the stories that go about in this neighbourhood, by many who are lately return'd from Jamaica, are many, & very tragical. I doubt not at the next meeting of Gressham Coll. (which will now shortly be after their usual recesse during summer) we shall have ample & authentic histories & discourses on this subject from several places of their correspondents. I cannot in the meane time omitt acquainting of y^r Lo^p with one very remarkable, which we have received here from credible hands: that during this astonishing & terrible paroxysme, multitudes of people running distractedly out of their tottering houses, & seeing so many swallow'd up & perishing; divers of them espying the minister of the towne at some distance, ran and compass'd him all about, desiring him to pray for them, as im'ediately he did, all falling on their knees, when all the ground about them suddenly sinking, the spot onely upon which they were at prayer remained a firm & steady iland, all the rest of the contiguous ground turning into a lake, other places into gulphs, which drown'd & buried all that stood upon them, & which were very many. And now, my Lord, 'tis time to implore your pardon for this tedious paper, together with your blessing.

Sayes-Court, 15th Octr 1692.

To Doctor Plot.

Worthy D^r,

Our common and excellent friend Mr Pepys acquaints me, that you would be glad to know upon what I am at present engaged relating to *Coines,* there being (it seemes) a designe of publishing something about that subject as they concerne the monye of this nation. It is true indeede (& as I remember to have told you) that I had blotted some sheetes upon an argument of that nature, but without the least reference to current money antient or modern, but on such *Medals* as relate purely to something historical, which does not at all interfere with other coines, unlesse it be such as our *Spur-royal* as they call it, being a single stamp of gold, and, as you know, suggesting something of our storie here in England, besides its intrinsic value, upon which account I may have occasion to mention it. For the rest, I meddle not with them. But this prompts me to send my request to you, for the assistance you promis'd, by imparting to me what you had of this kind, which might contribute to what I am now preparing, & by which you will very much oblige,

S^r, y^r, &c.

Sayes-Court, 27th Aug. 1693.

To John Evelyn, Esq.

Hond Sr,
Thredneedle Street, London,
Octob. 2nd, 1693.

According to yr desire I have look't out all the Historicall Medalls I have in my possession, which I have laid aside for your use, whenever you please to call for them. In the mean time I must begg a favour of you in behalf of the University of Oxford, who are now publishing a Tract of Plutarch's concerning Education, & would gladly add another of St. Chrysostom publish't in France by Combefis in Greek, could they meet with the book. Pauls Church yard and Little Britain have been search't for it without success, nor is there now any hopes left but in you, who it seems have translated it into English, wherefore they presume you must have the Greek copy, which they promise themselves (upon my importunity) you will be pleased to accommodate them with. Wherein you are also desired to be very speedy, because they designe to have both tracts out before Christmas. Our common and most excellent friend Mr. Pepys told me this day he hoped to see you this week, wth whom, should I be out of towne (as I guess I may on Wensday & Thursday in quest of some Roman antiquities now under my consideration), I desire you would leave the book, wherein you will very much oblige the whole University, and amongst them more particularly, Yr most humble and oblig'd servt,

Rob. Plot.

To my Lord Spencer.

My Lord,

Tho' I have not the opportunitie of waiting on y^r L^p so often as I ought and should do, was I perfectly at my owne disposure (which by reason of many impediments in my circumstances of late I neither have ben, nor as yet am); yet my worthiest thoughts & inclinations are never absent from you; and I often revive my selfe with the meditation of y^r virtues, & some very few noble young persons more, when that of the sad decadence of the age we live & converse in interposes its melancholy prospect.

I was with greate appetite coming to take a repast in the noble library which I heare you have lately purchas'd (& by the catalogue I have seene, must needes be a very chosen collection), when at the same time I understand you are taking a journey with resolution of making a toure about England, thereby joyning to books and paper-descriptions, experience; and to speculation, the seeing of the things themselues. It has certainly ben a greate mistake & very preposterous in our education, the usualy sending our young gent: to travell abroad, & see forraine countries, before they have seene or known any thing of their owne. Your L^p remembers who says it, *Ne sis peregrinus domi;* & therefore worthily don & memorable in my Ld Tress^r Burleigh, to hinder the Council, who in those days it seemes us'd to give passes to trauel, from granting them to any who had not first seene and could giue a good account of their owne countrie. Your L^p therefore has taken the best & most natural method; & I know not what can now be added to the rest of y^r accomplishments, but the continuance of your health, which I shall pray may attend all your motions, who am,

My L^d, y^r, &c.

Deptford, 4 Septr 1693.

To Mr. GIBSON,* &c. (afterwards Bishop of London.)

S^r,

To the notes & papers you desired of me, I have since endeavour'd to informe my selfe in those particulars you mention'd, & which I presume are come to you; & now by this let^r from a friend of mine, well acquainted with the trustees of Dog Smith (as he is call'd), I send you the particulars of that extraordinary benefactor to this County. You may please to take notice, that besides what I writ to you of Geo: Abbot Ab^p: of Canterbury, & his bro: Robert Bishop of Salisbury, he had at the same

---

* The learned person who published the Saxon Chronicle, and was now setting forth a new edition of Camden's Britannia, with additions. J. E.

time Moris another bro: who was L^d: Mayor of London; all sons of the same cloathier, & natives of Guildford. Also that Hammond whom I mention'd, was not onely a benefactor to the schole there, but founder of a felowship at Balliol Coll. Oxon. Io. de la Haye died about 300 years since, about whom & other particulars expect in my next, for I would not retard the printer longer than is necersary, who remain,

Y^r, &c.

Wotton, 31 May, 1694.

To the Bishop of LINCOLNE (Dr. TENNISON).

My L^d,

It is none of the least mortifications, that besides other circumstances obliging me to be at this distance from my old abode, I cannot haue the opportunitie of waiting on y^r L^p, & receiving those advantages & improvements, which I allways return'd with whenever I came from my L^d of Lincolne. We are here in no unpleasant solitude: some good books which I find here, with a cart load which I brought along with me, serve to aleviate the tediousnesse of sitting still; but we know nothing of new, but what our friends from your side impart to us. Mr. Pepys sent me last week the Journal of

S^r Jo. Narbrough & Capt. Wood;* together with Mr. Wharton's preface to his intended History of the Life of A: Bishop Laude.† I do not know whether I might do the learned editor (for it seemes he onely publishes a Mss: written by that greate prelate of his owne life) any service, by acquainting him with a passage relating to that person, namely, the Jubilee which the sacrifice of the Bishop caus'd among some at Rome; it being my hap to be in that citty, and in company of divers of the English fathers (as they call them) when the newes of his suffering & the sermon he made upon the scaffold ariv'd there; which I well remember they read & com'ented on, with no small satisfaction, & (as I thought) contempt, as of one taken off who was an enemy to them, and stood in their way; whilst one of the blackest crimes imputed to him was (we may well calle to mind) his being popishly affected. I know not, I say, whether the Memoirs may be of any import to Mr. Wharton, with whom I haue no acquaintance; I therefore acquaint y^r L^p wth it, and in the formes almost that I haue mention'd & subjoin'd it to my Discourse of Medals under that of this Arch-Bishop's figure, which toge-

---

* Entitled, "An Account of several late Voyages and Discoveries to the South and North, towards the Straits of Magellan, the South Seas," &c. 8vo. 1694.

† Printed in two folio volumes in 1695—1700.

ther with my copy, I haue now sent Ben: Tooke to print (as he desires) if it be worth his while. I add nothing more but that of my Wife's humble service to you & my lady, & that there is still a part of our small family at Says-Court, where my Daughter Draper & husband are the young œconomists, & all of us concern'd to beg y^r L^{ps} blessing and prayer, especialy   Y^r, &c.

I should rejoice to heare how Mr. Bentley proceedes with ye Library at Whitehall. I hope y^r L^p will mind him of the sermons he owes us & the publiq; I heare nothing of the Bish: of Chichester, who is likewise in our debt.

Wotton, 29 May, 1694.

To Mr. BENJAMIN TOOKE (Printer).

Mr. Tooke,

Tarde, sed tandem. At last I send you the copy you have so long expected; never the worse, I hope, for coming no sooner. I wish it may answer the paines I have taken in compiling: for it would amount to the value of many Medals. I was indeede unwilling it should scape from me without something more than an ordinary treatise. It will therefore require a more than ordinary supervisor. You tell me, such a one you have; if not, pray make use of the poore man I directed to you, who is also acquainted wth my hand, & will be ready to assist you. There being aboundance of writers on this subject in all other polite European languages, & but one very short & partial one in ours, will I hope render this the more acceptable, & give ferment to the curious. I expect attaques from some peevish quarter, in this angry age, but so it make for y^r interest, & satisfy equitable judges, I shall not be much concern'd.

The Medals which are here sent you, pray take care of, & deliver but one by one to y^r graver, nor supply him with any other till he returnes you that he is graving with the plate. You'l find I have mark'd the paper, wherein you must keepe the plates, and apply to the pages as directed, by which you'l avoid mistakes, easily fallen into without some such method. Such as you are to have from the Earle of Clarendon, Dr. Plot, &c. I will take care to procure you by the time these are dispatch'd. As for the graving, so the contours and outlines be well design'd, I am not solicitous for the hatching (as they call it), since we have laudable examples of the other in Gruter, Spanheim, & other excellent authors. Mr White, if he have leisure, will be y^r best man; & for the volume, I should think a thin moderat folio, with a faire letter, most desireable. As for the title, epistle, & preface, I shall provide you in good time, & as I see cause; onely I pray take special care of the insertions & paragraphs which I have marked [:

when all this is finish'd, I purpose a very accurate index. This being all at present, I wish you good successe, and am,

Y^r, &c.

Wotton, 2 June, 1694.

To Mr. Wotton.

S^r,

I most heartily beg y^r pardon for detaining your books so unreasonably long after I had read them, which I did with greate satisfaction, especialy the Life of Descartes. The truth is, I had some hopes of seeing you here againe, for methought (or at least I flatter'd myselfe with it) you said at parting you would do us that favour before my going to London, whither I am, God willing, setting out tomorrow or next day for some time; not without regret, unlesse I receive y^r commands, if I may be any ways serviceable to you, in order to that noble undertaking you lately mention'd to me, I meane your generous offer & inclination to write the Life of our illustrious philosopher Mr. Boyle, and to honor the memory of a gentleman of that singular worth & vertue. I am sure if you persist in that designe, England shall never envy France, or neede a Gassendus or a Baillet to perpetuate & transmit the memory of one not onely equaling but in many things transcending either of those excellent & indeede extraordinary persons, whom their pens have render'd im'ortal. I wish my selfe was furnish'd to afford you any considerable supplys (as you desir'd) after my so long acquaintance with Mr. Boyle, who had honor'd me with his particular esteeme, now very neere fourty yeares, as I might have don, by more duly cultivating frequent opportunities he was pleas'd to allow me. But so it is, that his life & virtues have ben so conspicuous, as you'll neede no other light to direct you, or subject-matter to work on, than what is so universaly knowne, and by what he has don & publish'd in his books. You may perhaps neede some particulars as to his birth, family, education, & other lesse necessarie circumstances for introduction; and such other passages of his life as are not so distinctly knowne but by his owne relations. In this if I can serve you, I shall do it with greate readinese, & I hope successe; having some pretence by my Wife, in whose grandfather's house (which is now mine at Deptford) the father of this gentleman was so conversant, that contracting an affinity there, he left his (then) eldest son with him whilst himselfe went into Ireland, who in his absence dying, lies buried in our parish church, under a remarkable monument.* I mention this because my Wife's relation to that fa-

---

* A Tent and Map of Ireland in relievo.

mily giving me accesse to divers of his neerest kindred; the Countesse Dowager of Clancartie (living now in an house of my Son's in Dover-streete) and ye Countesse of Thanet, both his nieces, will I question not be able to informe what they cannot but know of those & other circumstances of their uncle, which may not be unworthy of your notice; especialy my Lady Thanet, who is a greate virtuosa, and uses to speake much of her uncle. You know she lives in one of my L^d of Nottingham's houses at St. James's, and therefore will neede no introductor there. I will waite upon my Lord Burlington if there be occasion, provided in the meane time (and after all this officiousness of mine) it be not the proffer of a very uselesse service; since my Lord B^p of Salisbury, who made us expect what he is now devolving on you, cannot but be fully instructed in all particulars.

It is now, as I said, almost fourty yeares since first I had the honor of being acquainted with Mr. Boyle; both of us newly return'd from abroad, tho' I know not how, never meeting there. Whether he travell'd more in France than Italy, I cannot say, but he had so universal an esteeme in forrain parts, that not any stranger of note or quality, learn'd or curious, coming into England, but us'd to visit him with the greatest respect and satisfaction imaginable.

Now as he had an early inclination to learning

(so especialy to that part of philosophy he so hapily succeeded in), he often honor'd Oxford, and those gentlemen there, with his company, who more peculiarly applied themselves to the examination of the so long domineering methods & jargon of the scholes. You have the names of this learned junto, most of them since deservedly dignified in that elegant History of the Royal Society, which must ever owne its rise from that assembly, as dos the preservation of that famous University from the phanatic rage & avarice of those melancholy times. These, with some others (whereof Mr. Boyle, the Ld. Viscount Brouncker, Sr Robert Morray, were the most active,) spirited with the same zeale, and under a more propitious influence, were ye persons to whom the world stands oblig'd for the promoting of that generous and real knowledge, which gave the ferment that has ever since obtain'd, and surmounted all those many discouragements which it at first incounter'd. But by no man more have the territories of the most usefull philosophy ben inlarg'd, than by our *hero*, to whom there are many trophys due. And accordingly his fame was quickly spread, not onely among us here in England, but thro' all the learned world besides. It must be confess'd that he had a mervailous sagacity in finding out many usefull and noble experiments. Never did stubborn matter come under his inquisition but he extorted a confession of all that lay in her most intimate recesses; and what he discover'd he as faithfully register'd, and frankly com'unicated; in this, exceeding my Ld Verulam, who (tho' never to be mention'd without honor and admiration) was us'd to tell all that came to hand without much examination. His was probability; Mr. Boyle suspicion of successe. S^r, you will here find ample field, and infinitely gratifie the curious with a glorious and fresh survey of the progresse he has made in these discoveries. Freed from those incumbrances which now & then render the way a little tedious, 'tis aboundantly recompensing the pursuite; especialy those noble atchievements of his, made in the spring and weight of the two most necessary elements of life, aer & water, and their effects. The origin of formes, qualities, and principles of matter: histories of cold, light, colours, gems, effluvias, & other his workes so firmely established on experiments, polychrests, & of universal use to real philosophy; besides other beneficial inventions peculiarly his; such as the dulcifying sea-water with that ease & plenty, together with many medicinal remedys, cautions, directions, curiosities & arcana, which owe their birth or illustration to his indefatigable recherches. He brought the phosphorus & anteluca to the clearest light that ever any did, after inumerable attempts. It were needlesse to insist on particulars to one who knows them better than my selfe. You will not, however, omitt those many other treatises relating to religion, which indeede runs thro' all his writings upon occasion, and shew how unjustly that aspersion has ben cast on philosophy, that it disposes men to Atheisme. Neither did his severer studys yet soure his conversation in the least. He was the furthest from it in the world, and I question whether ever any man has produc'd more experiments to establish his opinions without dogmatising. He was a *Corpuscularian* without Epieurus; a greate & happy analyzer, addicted to no particular sect, but as became a generous & free philosopher, preferring truth above all; in a word, a person of that singular candor & worth, that to draw a just character of him, one must run thro' all the vertues, as well as thro' all the sciences.* And tho' he tooke the greatest care imaginable to conceale the most illustrious of 'em, his charities & the many good works he continualy did could not be hid. It is well known how large his bounty was upon all occasions: —witness the Irish, Indian, Lithuanian Bibles, to the translations, printing & publishing of which he layd out considerable summs; the Catechisme, & Principles of the Christian Faith, which I think he caus'd to be put into Turkish, & dispers'd amongst those infidels. And here you will take notice of the Lecture he has endow'd and so seasonably provided for.

---

* See Bishop Sanderson, " De Juramenti promissorii obligatione," 2d edit. dedicated to him.

As to his relations (so far as I have heard) his father Richd Boyle was *faber fortunæ;* a person of wonderfull sagacity in affaires, & no lesse probity, by which he compass'd a vast estate & greate honors to his posterity, which was very numerous, & so prosperous, as has given to the publiq both divines & philosophers, souldiers, politicians, & statesmen, and spread its branches among the most illustrious and opulent of our nobility. Mr. Robert Boyle, born I think in Ireland, was the youngest, to whom he left a faire estate; to which was added an honorary pay of a troop of horse, if I mistake not. And now, tho' amongst all his experiments he never made that of the married life, yet I have ben told he courted a beautifull & ingenious daughter of Carew, Earle of Monmouth; to which is owing the birth of his "Seraphic Love," and the first of his productions. Descartes * was not so innocent. In the meane time he was the most facetious & agreeable conversation in the world among the ladys, whenever he happen'd to be so engag'd; and yet so very serious, compos'd, & contemplative at all other times; tho' far from moroseness, for indeede he was affable & civil rather to excesse, yet without formality.

As to his opinion in religious matters and discipline, I could not but discover in him the same free

---

* Who confesses he had a bastard daughter. See M. Baillet in Vita Descartes. J. E.

thoughts which he had of philosophy; not in notion onely, but strictly as to practise an excellent Christian and the greate duties of that profession, without noise, dispute, or determining; owning no master but the Divine Author of it; no religion but primitive, no rule but scripture, no law but right reason. For the rest, allways conformable to the present settlement, withont any sort of singularity. The mornings, after his private devotions, he usualy spent in philosophic studys & in his laboratory, sometimes extending them to night; but he told me he had quite given over reading by candle-light, as injurious to his eyes. This was supply'd by his amanuensis, who sometimes read to him, and wrote out such passages as he noted, and that so often in loose papers, pack'd up without method, as made him sometimes to seeke upon occasion, as himselfe confesses in divers of his works. Glasses, potts, chymical & mathematical instruments, books & bundles of papers, did so fill & crowd his bed-chamber, that there was but just roome for a few chaires; so as his whole equipage was very philosophical without formality. There were yet other roomes, and a small library (and so you know had Descartes),* as learning more from men, real experiments, & in his laboratory (which was ample & well furnish'd), than from books.

---

* One at Egmond desiring to see his library, he brought him to a roome where he was dissecting a calfe. J. E.

I have said nothing of his style, which those who are better judges think he was not altogether so happy in, as in his experiments. I do not call it affected, but doubtlesse not answerable to the rest of his greate & shining parts; and yet, to do him right, it was much improv'd in his "Theodora" and later writings.

In his diet (as in habit) he was extreamely temperate & plaine; nor could I ever discern in him the least passion, transport, or censoriousnesse, whatever discourse or the times suggested. All was tranquil, easy, serious, discreete, and profitable; so as besides Mr. Hobbes, whose hand was against every body, & admir'd nothing but his owne, Francis Linus excepted (who yet with much civility wrote* against him), I do not remember he had the least antagonist.

In the afternoones he was seldom without company, which was sometimes so incom'odious that he now & then repair'd to a private lodging in another quarter of the towne, and at other times (as the season invited) diverted him selfe in the country among his noble relations.

He was rather tall & slender of stature, for most part valetudinary, pale & much emaciated: nor unlike his picture in Gressham Colledge; which, with an almost impudent importunity, was, at the request

---

* Viz Tract. de Corporum Inseparabilitate, &c. 8vo. Lond. 1661. J. E.

of the Society, hardly extorted or rather stolen from this modest gentleman by Sr Edmund King, after he had refus'd it to his neerest relations.

In his first addresses, being to speake or answer, he did sometimes a little hesitate, rather than stam'er, or repeate the same word; imputable to an infirmity, which, since my remembrance, he had exceedingly overcome. This, as it made him somewhat slow and deliberate, so after the first effort he proceeded without the least interruption in his discourse. And I impute this impediment much to the frequent attaques of palsys, contracted I feare not a little by his often attendance on chymical operations. It has plainely astonish'd me to have seene him so often recover when he has not been able to move, or bring his hand to his mouth: & indeede the contexture of his body, during the best of his health, appear'd to me so delicate, that I have frequently compar'd him to a chrystal or Venice glasse; which tho' wrought never so thin and fine, being carefully set up, would outlast the hardier metals of daily use; and he was withall as clear & candid; not a blemish or spot to tarnish his reputation; & he lasted accordingly, tho' not to a greate, yet to a competent age; threescore yeares I think; & to many more he might, I am persuaded, have ariv'd, had not his beloved sister, the Lady Viscountesse Ranalagh, with whom he liv'd, a person of extraordinary talent & suitable to his religious

& philosophical temper, dyed before him. But it was then that he began evidently to droope apace; nor did he, I thinke, survive her above a fortnight. But of this last scene I can say little, being unfortunately absent, & not knowing of the danger 'til it was past recovery.

His funeral (at wch I was present) was decent, and tho' without the least pomp, yet accompanied with a greate appearance of persons of ye best & noble quality, besides his owne relations.

He lies interr'd (neere his sister) in the chancell of St. Martin's Church; the Ld Bishop of Salisbury preaching the funeral sermon, with that eloquence natural to him on such & all other occasions. The sermon, you know, is printed, with the panegyric so justly due to his memory. Whether there have ben since any other monument erected on him, I do not know, nor is it material. His name, (like that of Joseph Scaliger) were alone a glorious epitaph.

And now, S^r, I am againe to implore y^r pardon for giving you this interruption with things so confusedly huddl'd up this afternoone, as they crowded into my thoughts. The subject you see is fruitfull, & almost inexhaustible. Argument fit for no man's pen but Mr. Wotton's. Oblige then all the world, and with it, S^r, y^r, &c.

Wotton, 30 Mar. 1696.

To Mr. Evelyn.

Honored S^r, Apr. 7, 1696.

I was unfortunately out of the way when you did me the honor to send me that admirable & obliging letter concerning Mr. Boyle, & was so fatigued on my return, by my coming home upon a lame horse, that I could not wait upon you a Sunday at Wooton as I intended to do. I cannot sufficiently express my thanks to you for your excellent hints; if my Ld Archbishop of Canterbury encourages me, & I can get those materials out of Mr. Warre's hands, wch I was speaking of, I will set about it. I suppose you will receive by the penny-post 2 Philos. Transactions, N° 219, in which is my abridgement of Sig^r Scilla's book of Shells. I had brought more down for that purpose, but not being able to compass my designe of waiting upon you at Wooton, I have sent to the bookseller to convey y^m to you that way. One of y^m with my humblest thanks I would entreat you to present to Sr Cyril Wyche, when you see him. I wish I knew how to express the joy I feel in having my poor projects approved by so great a judge and patron of learning, & its welwishers. I am, hon^d S^r,

Your most obliged servant,

W. Wotton.

Ind^d: Mr. Wotton, &c.
Of a present made me of a book.

To Mr. Evelyn.

Honored S^r,   Albury, May 24, 1696.

Your last obliging letter has put me into greater fears than any thing that ever befell me in my whole life. How I shall possibly answer Mr. Evelyn's expectation I can'ot conceive, & without the highest vanity I can as little bring myself to think that I shall not fall extreamly short of it. Your naming me at my Lord of Canterbury's upon such an occasion was the highest honour could have ben done a young writer. Next to that was the trustees approving your nomination. I say next to that, for they were ashamed to seem backward to comply with what Mr. Evelyn should think fit to propose. I am now therefore onely to wait for the B^p of Salisbury's fiat, which, if it is granted, it will be too late for me to recede, tho' I know very well I shall be *impar operi* in every respect. I will study, however, to preserve Mr. Evelyn's reputation as much as ever I can, & I do hereby faithfully assure him, that care & industry shall not be wanting to carry on a work, in which he has generously been pleased to have so distinguishing a share.

As soon as I shall hear of your return to Wotton where your freinds in this countrey ardently expect you, I shall do my self the honour to tell you more at large, how very much I am, as well as ought to be,   Honored S^r,
Your most obliged & most faithfull humble serv^t,
W. Wotton.

To my Lord GODOLPHIN, one of the L^ds Justices,
  and first Commiss^r of the Treasury.

My Lord,

There are now almost foure yeares elaps'd, since looking over some papers of mine, I found among other things divers notes which I had taken relating to Medals; when reflecting upon the usefullnesse of the historical part of that noble study, and considering that there had been little, or indeede rather nothing at all written of it among us here in England (whilst other countryes abounded in many excellent books & authors of greate name on this subject), I began to divert my solitary thoughts by reducing & putting my scatter'd collection into such method as grew at last to a formal treatise. Among other particulars (after I had more at large dispatch'd what concern'd the Greeke & Roman, and those of the Lower Empire) I endeavor'd the gath'ring up all such Medals as I could any where find had ben struck before and since the Conquest (if any such there where) relating to any part of good history. Now tho mony and coines during the severall reignes of almost all our kings, from the British to this present time (as may be seene in what Mr. Walker has added to the late edition of Cambden) be forraine to my subject; and that I could meet with none which deserved the name of Medal 'til the two last centuries; yet I could not well avoyd speaking something of the Mint, where medals were coin'd as well as mony. The copy being thus prepar'd for the presse, I two yeares since deliver'd to a bookseller, who after he had wrought off almost 80 pages in folio (emulating what had ben don and publish'd by Jaques de Bie & Mons. Bizot, in their Histoire Metaliq of France & Holland) would needes be at the charge of ingraving an hundred stamps to adorne a chapter relating to our English Medals. This requiring time (& far better artists than any I perceive he is like to find) retarding the publication of his book, I thought it might not be either unseasonable or unagreeable to y^r L^p, if on this conjuncture of affaires (and when every body is discoursing of these matters) I did present y^r L^p with a part of that chapter concerning Mony which (tho' passing thro' the same mechanisme) I distinguish from Medal at the beginning of my first chapter, proceeding in the VIIth to that of the Mint. It is there that I show (after all the expedients offer'd and pretended, for the recovery & security of this nation from the greate danger it is in by the wicked practices of those who of late have so impudently ruin'd the publiq credit & faith of all mankind among us by clipping, debasing, & all other unrighteous ways of perverting the species) what is it which can possibly put a stop to the evil & mischiefe, that it go no farther; if at least it have not ben so long neglected as to be irremediable.

But, my L^d, this is not all. There are severall other things of exceeding greate importance, which had neede be taken care of, & to be set on foote effectualy, for the obviating the growing mischiefs, destructive to the flourishing state of this mercantile nation. Amongst the rest:

There is certainely wanting a Council of Trade, that should not be so call'd onely, but realy be in truth what it is call'd; compos'd of a wise, publiq-spirited, active & noble President, a select number of Assessors, sober, industrious & dextrous men, & of consum'ate experience *in rebus agendis;* who should be arm'd with competent force at sea, to protect the greater com'erce & general trade ; if not independent of the Admiralty, not without an almost co-ordinate authority, as far as concernes the protection of trade; and to be maintained chiefely by those who, as they adventure most, receive the greatest benefit.

To these should likewise be com'itted the care of the Manufactures of the kingdome, with stock for employment of the poore; by which might be moderated that unreasonable statute for their relief (as now in force) occasioning more idle persons, who charge the publiq without all reamedy, than otherwise there would be, insufferably burdening the parishes, by being made to earne their bread honestly, who now eate it in idleness, & take it out of the mouthes of the truely indigent, much inferior in number, & worthy objects of charity.

It is by such a Council that the swarmes of private traders, who, tho' not appearing in mighty torrents & streames, yet like a confluence of silent, almost indiscernable, but in'umerable riveletts, do evidently draine & exhaust the greater *hydrophylacia* & magazines, nay the very vital blood of trade, where there is no follower to supply those many issues, without which the constitution of the body politic, like the natural, needes must fail for want of nourishment & recruits. But whom this article affects I have spoken in my discourse of Mony.

'Tis likewise to this Assembly, that all proposals of new inventions (pretended for the publiq benefit) should first be brought, & examin'd, incouraged or rejected, without reproch as projectures, or turning the unsuccessful proposer to ridicule, by a barbarity without example, no where countenanc'd but in this nation.

Another no lesse exhauster, & waster of the publiq treasure, is the progresse & increase of buildings about this already monstrous Citty, wherein one yeare with another are erected about 800 houses, as I am credibly inform'd; which carrys away such prodigious summs of our best and weightiest mony by the Norway trade for deale-timber onely, but exports nothing hence of moment to balance it, besides sand & gravell to balance their empty ships;

whilst doubtlesse those other more necessary com'odities (were it well incourag'd) might in a short time be brought us in greate measure, and much preferable to their goodnesse, from our owne plantations, which now we fetch from others, for our naval stores.

Truely, my L^d, I cannot but wonder, & even stand amaz'd, that Parliaments should have sate from time to time, so many hundred yeares, & value their constitution to that degree, as the most sovraine remedy for the redresse of publiq grievances; whilst the greatest still remaine unreform'd & untaken away. Witnesse the confus'd, debauch'd, & riotous manner of electing members qualified to become the representatives of a nation, wth legislative power to dispose of the fate of kingdomes; which should & would be compos'd of worthy persons, of known integritie & ability in their respective countries, and still would serve them generously, & as their ancestors have don, but are not able to fling away a son or daughter's portion to bribe the votes of a multitude, more resembling a pagan bacchanalia, than an assembly of Christians & sober men met upon the most solemn occasion that can concerne a people, and stand in competition with some rich scrivener, brewer, banker, or one in some gainfull office, whose face or name, perhaps, they never saw or knew before. How, my L^d, must this sound abroad! With what dishonor & shame a home!

To this add the disproportion of the Buroughs capable of electing members, by which the major part of the whole kingdom are frequently out-voted, be the cause never so unjust, if it concerne a party interest.

Will ever those swarmes of *locusts*, lawyers & attorneys, who fill so many seats, vote for a publiq *Register*, by which men may be secur'd of their titles & possessions, & an infinity of suits & frauds prevented?

Im'oderate fees, tedious & ruinous delays, & tossings from court to court before an easy cause, which might be determin'd by honest gentlemen & understanding neighbours, can come to any final issue, may be number'd amongst the most vexatious oppressions that call aloud for redresse.

The want of bodys (slaves) for publiq & laborious works, to which many sorts of animals might be usefully condemn'd, and some reform'd instead of sending them to the gallows, deserves to be consider'd.

These, & the like are the greate desiderata (as well as the reformation of the coine), which are plainely wanting to the consum'ate felicity of this nation; and divers of them of absolute necessitie to its recovery from the atrophy & consumption it labours under.

The King himselfe should (my L^d) be acquainted with these particulars, & of the greate importance of them, by such as from their wisdome & integrity, deserve the nearest accesse, and would purchase him the hearts of a free & emancipated people, & a blessing on the government; were he pleas'd uncessantly to recommend them to those, who, from time to time, are call'd together for these ends, & healing of the nation.

And now your Ex^y will doubtlesse smile at this politiq excursion, & perhaps of the *biscoctum* of the rest; whilst the yeares to which I am by God's greate goodnesse ariv'd, your L^p's com'ands in a former letter to me, some conversation with men & the world, as well as books, in so large a tract & variety of events & wonders as this period has brought forth, might justifie one, among such crowds of pretenders to *ragioni di stato,* some of which I daily meete to come abroad with the shell still on their heads, who talke as confidently of these matters as if they were counsellors of state & first ministers, with their sapient & expecting lookes, & whom none must contradict; and no doubt but (as Job said) "they are the people, and wisedome is to die with them." To such I have no more to say, whilst I appeale to y^r L^p, whose real & consum'ate experience, greate prudence & dexterity *in rebus agendis* without noise, were enough to silence a thousand such as I am. I therefore implore y^r pardon againe, for what I may have written weakely or rashly. In such a tempest & overgrown a sea, every body is concern'd, and whose head is not ready to turne? I am sure, I should myselfe almost despaire of the vessel, if any, save y^r L^p, were at the helme. But, whilst your hand is on the staff, & your eye upon the star, I compose myselfe & rest secure.

Surrey Street, 16 June 1696.

To Mr. PLACE (Bookseller).

Mr. Place,

I have seriously consider'd y^r Letter concerning y^r resolution of sparing no cost whereby you may benefit the publiq, as well as recompence your owne charge & industry (which truely is a generous inclination, not so frequently met with amongst most book-sellers), by inquiring how you might possibly supply what is wanting to our Country (now beginning to be somewhat pollish'd in their manner of building, and indeede in the accomplishment of the English language also) by the publication of whatever may be thought conducible to either. In order to this, you have sometime since acquainted me with y^r intention of reprinting the "Parallel;" desireing that I would revise it, and consider what improvements may decently be added in relation to y^r general designe. As for the Parallel, I take it to be so very usefull & perfect in its kind & as far as it pretends to (namely, all that was material in those Ten Masters upon the Orders), that I cannot think of any thing it further needes to render it more intelligible. As for what I have annex'd to it concerning statues, my good friend Mr. Gibbons would be consulted; and for the latter, so much as I conceive is necessary, I will take care to send you wth y^r interfoliated copy. In the meane time, touching that universal work, or cycle, which you would have comprehend and imbrace the intire art of building, together with all its accessories for magnificence & use, without obliging you to the paines in gleaning, when a whole harvest is before you, or the trouble of calling many to y^r assistance (which would be tedious), I cannot think of a better, more instructive, & judicious an expedient, than by your procuring a good & faithfull translation of that excellent piece which has lately been published by Monsieur D'Aviler; were he made to speak English in the proper termes of that art, by some person conversant in the French, and if neede be, adding to him some assistant, such as you would have recommended to me, if my leasure & present circumstances could have comply'd with my inclinations of promoting so beneficial a designe.

I should here enumerate the particulars he runs thro', in my opinion sufficiently copious, & in as polish'd, & yet as easy & familiar a style as the subject is capable of; in nothing exceeding the capacity of our ordinary workmen, or unworthy the study & application of the noblest persons who employ them, and to whom a more than ordinary & superficial knowledge in architecture is no small accomplishment. I say I should add the contents of his chapters, and the excellent notes he has subjoyn'd to a better version of Vignole, Mic. Angelo, & the rest of our most celebrated modern architects and their works; together with all that is extant of antique, & yet in being, apply'd to use, & worthy knowing, if I thought you had not already heard of the book, since it has now ben 4 or 5 yeares extant, and since reprinted in Holland, as all the best & most vendible books are, to the greate prejudice of the authors, by their not only printing them without any errata, by which the reader might reform them, or (as if they had none at all) correcting the faults themselves: which indeede, that of the Paris edition (faire as it seemes, & is in the elegancy of the character) exceedingly will neede, before it be translated, by whomsoever taken in hand.

But as the letter and its other beauties exceede the Dutch edition, so do likewise the plates, which are don with that accuratnesse & care, as may almost com'ute for the oversights of the presse. I do not say the Holland Sculps are ill perform'd; but tho' they seeme to be pretty well copied, they will yet require a strict examination, and then I think they might be made use of, & a competent number of plates (provided not overmuch worn) procured at a far easier rate out of Holland, than by having them perhaps not so well graven here; for 'tis not the talent of every artist, tho' skill'd in heads & figures (of which we have very few), to trace the architect as he ought. But if they could be obtain'd from Paris, as happly with permission they might, it were much to be preferr'd. I forget to tell you, that there is a most accurate, learned, & critical Dictionary by the same author, explaining (in a 2^d part) not onely the termes of architecture, but of all those other arts that waite upon, & are subservient to her, which is very curious.

And now, if what I have said in recommending this work for the full accomplishment of your laudable designe (& which in truth, I think, were aboundantly sufficient) induce you to proceede in it, and that you would with it present the publiq with a much more elegant letter than I believe England has ever seene among all our printers; perhaps it were worth your while to render it one of the first productions of that noble presse which my worthy & most learned friend Dr Bentley (his Ma^{tys} Library-keeper at St. James's) is with greate charge & industrie erecting now at Cambridge.

There is another piece of mechanics, and some other very rare & usefull arts agreeable to this of architecture, & incomparably curious, which, if translated & joyn'd to ye rest, would (without contradiction) render it a most desireable & perfect work. If when you passe this way, you will visite a lame man (who is oblig'd to stay within at present) I shall endeavour to satisfie you in any thing I may have omitted here, but the teazing you & myselfe with a tedious scribble (upon y^r late importunity before my leaving this town) which you may wish I had omitted.

Surrey-street, 17 Aug. 1696.

To Mr. Wotton.

Worthy Sir,

I should exceedingly mistake the person, and my owne discernment, could I believe Mr Wotton stood in the least neede of my assistance; but such an expression of your's to one who so well knows his own imperfections as I do mine, ought to be taken for a reproche; since I am sure it cannot proceede from y^r judgment. But forgiving this fault, I most heartily thank you for y^r animadversion on *Sylva*; which, tho' I frequently find it so written for ξυλεια & υλη, wood, timber, wild & forest trees, yet indeede I think it more properly belongs to a promiscuous casting of severall things together, & as I think my Ld Bacon has us'd it in his "Natural History," without much reguard to method. *Deleatur*, therefore, wherever you meete it.

Concerning the gardning and husbandry of the Antients, which is ye inquirie (especialy of the first), that it had certainely nothing approching ye elegancy of the present age, Rapinus (whom I send you) will abundantly satisfie you. The discourse you will find at the end of Hortorum, lib. 4º. capp. 6. 7. What they cal'd their gardens were onely spacious plots of ground planted with platans & other shady trees in walks, & built about with porticos, xisti, & noble ranges of pillars, adorn'd with statues, fountaines, piscariæ, aviaries, &c. But for the flowry parterre, beds of tulips, carnations, auricula, tuberose, jonquills, ranunculas, & other of our rare coronaries, we heare nothing of, nor that they had such store & variety of exotics, orangeries, myrtils, & other curious greenes; nor do I believe they had their orchards in such perfection, nor by far our furniture for the kitchen. Pliny indeede enumerates a world of vulgar plants & olitories, but they fall infinitely short of our physic gardens, books, and herbals, every day augmented by our sedulous botanists, & brought to us from all the quarters of the world. And as for their husbandry & more rural skill, of which the same author has written so many books in his Nat. History, especial lib. 17. 18. &c. you'l soone be judge what it was. They tooke great care indeede of their vines and olives, stercorations, ingraftings, & were dilligent in observing seasons, the course of ye stars, &c. and doubtlesse were very industrious; but when you shall have read over Cato, Varro, Columella, Palladio, with the Greek Geoponics, I do not think you will have cause to prefer them before the modern agriculture, so exceedingly of late improv'd, for which you may consult & compare our old Tusser, Markham, y^e *Maison Rustic*, Hartlib, Walter Blith, the Philosophical Transactions, & other books, which you know better than my selfe.

I have turn'd down the page, where poore Pulissy begins his persisting search. If you can suffer his prolix style, you will now & then light on things not to be despised. With him I send you a short Treatise concerning *Metals*, of Sr Hugh Platts, which perhaps you have not seene. I am sorry I have no more of those subjects here, having left the rest in my library at Deptford, & know not how to get them hither till I get thither.

S^r, I am in no hast for the returne of these, if they may be serviceable to you, but in no little paine for the trouble y^r civility to mine puts one, who knows so much better how to employ his time, than to mind the impertinence of, S^r, y^r, &c.

Wotton, 28 Oct. 1696.

To Dr. Richard Bentley.

Worthy D^r:

You have under your hands something of Mr. Wotton, whilst he has ben so kind as to offer me his help in looking over the typographical and other faults escaped in the last impression of the "Silva," which I am most earnestly call'd upon to reprint. The copy which I frankly gave about 30 years since to Allestry, is now in, the hands of Chiswell and your namesake Mr. Bentley (Booksellers), who have sold off three impressions, & are now impatient for the fourth: and it having ben no vnprofitable copy to them, I had promised some considerable improvements to it, vpon condition of letting Ben: Tooke (for whom I have a particular kindnesse) into a share. This, tho' with reluctancy, they at last consented to. I will endeavour to render it with ad vantage, and have ambition enough to wish, that since it is a folio, & of so popular and usefull a subject as has procured it some reputation, it might have the honor to beare the character of Dr. Bentley's new Imprimerie, which, I presume, the proprietors will be as prowd of as my selfe. To the reproch of Place, who made so many difficulties about my booke of architecture as you well know, I have however made very considerable additions to that treatise, as far as concernes my part, & meane to dedicate it to Sr Christopher Wren, his M^aties Surveyor & Intendent of his Buildings, as I did the other part to Sr J. Denham his predecessor, but infinitely inferior to his successor. I confesse I am foolishly fond of these & other rustications, which had ben my swete diuersions during the dayes of destruction and devastation both of woods and buildings, whilst the rebellion lasted so long in this nation: and the kind receptions my bookes have found makes me the more willing to give them my last hand: sorry in the meane time for all my other aberrations in pretending to meddle with things beyond my talent *et extra oleo :* but enough of this.

Wotton, 20 Jany 1696-7.

To Dr. BENTLEY.

Worthy D^r:

Tho' I made hast out of town, and had so little time to spend after we parted, I was yet resolv'd not to neglect the province which I undertook, as far as I had any interest in S^r Ed: Seymour, whom I found at his house, & had full scope of discourse with. I told him I came not to petition the revival of an old title, or the unsettlement of an estate, so often of late interrupting our late Parliaments, but to fix and settle a publiq benefit* that would be of

---

* The new library to be built in St. James's Park. J. E.

greate & universal good & glory to the whole nation. This (with y^r paper) he very kindly and obligingly receiv'd, & that he would contribute all the assistance that lay in his power, whenever it should come to the House. To send you notice of this, I thought might be much more acceptable to you than to acquaint you that we are full of company, & already enter'd into a most dissolute course of eating & indulging, according to the mode of antient English hospitality; by which meanes I shall now & then have opportunity of recom'ending the noble designe you are intent upon, & therefore wish I had some more of the printed proposals to disperse. Sr Cyril Wyche, who accompanied me hither, is altogether transported with it, & thinks the project so discreetly contriv'd, that it cannot miscarry. Here is Dr Fuller with his spouse. The D^r gave us a sermon this morning, in an elegant and trim discourse on the 39. Psalm, which I find had ben prepar'd for the court, & fitter for that audience than our poore country churches. After this you will not expect much intelligence from hence, tho' I shall every day long to heare of ye progresse you make in this glorious enterprize, to which I augure all successe & prosperity, & am,

        Worthy D^r, y^r &c.

Wotton, 25 Dec. 1697.

To Dr. Godolphin, Provost of Eton.

Wotton, 8 Feb. 1697-8.

Had you ben in towne when my copys [on Medals] were distributed among my friends, the small present which I presum'd to send you, had ben brought by y^r most humble servant with an apology for my boldnesse in obtruding upon the Provost of Eton (who is himselfe so greate a judge of that and all other learned subjects) my meane performance. It were quite to tire you out, should I relate on what occasion I came to be ingaged on a topic on which I could advance so little of my owne to extenuate my presumption: yet give me leave to take hold of this opportunity to discharge a debt owing to yourselfe, and those of your learned relations who condescend to reade my book. 'Tis now neere fifty yeares past since Gabr. Naudæus publish'd directions concerning librarys and their furniture, which I had translated, minding to reprint it, as what I conceiv'd might not be unseasonable whilst auctions were become so frequent among us, and gentlemen every where storing themselves with bookes at those learned marts; & because it was so very thinn a volume, I thought of annexing a sheete or two of Medals, as an appendant not improper. But being persuaded to say something of our modern Medals relating to our country (as France and Holland had of theirs) I found it swell to so incompetent a bulk, as would by no meanes suit with that treatise. Whilst I was about this (and indeed often and long before) I had ben importun'd to make a second edition of my Chalcography (now grown very scarce) and to bring it from 1662, where I left off, to this time, there having since that ben so greate an improvement of Sculpture. This being a task I had no inclination for (having of a long time given over collections of that sort) I thought yet of gratifying them in some manner with an ex-chapter in my Discourse of Medals, where I speake of the effigies of famous persons, and the use which may be deriv'd of such a collection, and that which follows it.—'Tis now a good while ago since first I put it into the hands of a book-seller, with strict injunction not to work off a sheete 'til it had ben revis'd by abler judgments than my owne; and so remain'd whilst the Medals could be collected that were to be grav'n, which tho' hardly amounting to an hundred, were with difficulty enough procur'd in two yeares time. This slow proceeding, together with my long & frequent excursions att this distance from towne, made me absolutely resolv'd to abandon and think of it no further, but give it up to the book-seller to dispose of it for wast paper, when he would needes perswade me that he had such an accomplish'd superviser of the presse he imploy'd, as would do me all the right I could expect from an able & learned man; and that now he had ben at such charges for the sculptures, I should extreamly injure him to withdraw my copy, & what I had to annex, as certainly I should [have done] but for that consideration only. So as I had now no remedy left me but by imbarquing the errata to my greater reproch, & it was very slender comfort to me the being told that even the most incomparably learned Spanheim, whose glorious work of medals was not long since reprinted, scap'd not the presse without remarkable and cruel scarrs.

But now I mention'd the noble Spanheim (to whose judgment all deferr) I may haply be censur'd for what I have said concerning *Etiminius*, after what he has objected against that Medal (de præst. Numis: Rep: 647); but if I was, and still am, unwilling to degrade our renowned Citty of her so Metropolitan dignity, whilst I had any to stand by me, I cannot be so deepely concern'd, and indeed asham'd, should any think me so ignorant as not long-since to know that *obryzum* signifys gold of the most exalted purity & test, or, as the ancients express'd, *ad obrussam exactum*, which yet, I know not how, escap'd me when I was gathering out the errata. [As for CONOB, tho' I ever read it *Constantinople*, the extreame rudenesse of a reverse and metal I had shew'd me of that coine, so perfectly resembling that of *Cuno,* might favour my conjecture.*]

There is in margine, p. 207, a mistake of *Richborow* for *Regulbium,* which also escap'd me.

But, Sir, there are so many more & greater faults as put me out of countenance, for which & this tedious scribble I heartily beg your pardon, who am, &c.

Mr. W. Wotton to J. Evelyn.

Hond Sr,

Milton, near Newport Pagnell,
Bucks, Jan. 2, 1697-8.

When I was in town last moneth I did myself the honour to call at your lodgings, but was not so happy as to find you at home. I intended to acquaint you what progress I had made in a design wch owes its birth wholly to your encouragement. After a positive promise from ye executors that I should have ye use of Mr. Boyle's papers, my Lord Burlington at last insisted upon my giving a bond that I demanded no gratification. I had voluntarily given a note to ye same purpose, wch Dr. Bentley sufficiently blamed me for: but I gave no bond, &

---

* In the following letter to Mr. Henshaw, the latter part of which is almost a transcript of the above, this sentence is thus expressed: "I found the period omitted, p. 22. wch shod have been read, mixt & obrize sort also, which has on it a horse rudely design'd with the letters *CON-OB. Constantinopoli obrizatum,* wch some will have to signify *Cōnstantinople* only — others, some Prince of ours."

so left the town (tho' I had come up on purpose about this business) doubtfull what further I should doe. But since I came home, my Lord Burlington is come over, so far that he has delivered up my note, & has ordered all ye papers to be delivered to my order, with a promise to me of all manner of assistance & encouragement. So that now I intend to dedicate all my spare howrs to this business; & then, S^r, as you have hitherto prevented my desires, so again I fear I must be importunate in troubling you with new doubts & queries w^{ch}, in the progress of the work, will infallibly arise. I am glad to find that we may so soon expect your long-desired work about Medals, from which I propose no small entertainment to myself, as soon as it appeares.

I am, hon^d S^r,
Your most obliged & most humble $serv^t$,
W. WOTTON.

Shall I not wish you & your excellent lady many happy new yeares? No body, I am sure, do's it more cordially.

Mr. W. WOTTON to J. EVELYN.

Honored S^r,   Milton, Bucks, Jan. 20, 1697-8.

Duty & gratitude requiring me to give you a second interruption in a short time, I think I ought to make no apology. Not long since I did myself the honour to acquaint you with ye success of my affaire about Mr. Boyle's life. I knew you would be pleased to hear that I had weathered that difficulty, since you had been my first .... to that work. I had just got a box of papers, & was going to digest matters for the forge, when I was agreeably stopp'd by your admirable Numismata, wch the last return of the carrier brought me. I needed no spur to read it; ye author, ye subject, added wings to my diligence. Dr. Bentley had raised my thirst by the essay he had given me before in conversation. Yet these three incitements, & I know not three more powerful, all gave place to a fourth, which was ye book itself. I was so truly charmed, so pleasingly taught thro' the whole work, that ye grief of being so soon at an end, wrought as violently at last as the joy I felt as I went along. The printer, indeed, raised my indignation; I was angry with him, & troubled to see my pen so often disfigure so elegant a book. However, I took care to have no remotas for the future, when upon a second & third reading (wch yet will scarce suffice) I hope every thing shall be rivetted in my head, wch a first reading in so vast a copia could not carry along with it. My head is so very full of what I have learned & am to learn by your instructions, that I had almost forgotten to thank you for your honourable mention of my poor performances in so standing a work. This was more than I ought to have promised myself. The field I chose was vast & uncultivated, nobler & learneder .... will hereafter arise who will till it to more advantage, & reap a richer harvest. I proposed but to outdoe Glanvill, & to set Mons[r] Perrault & S[r] William Temple right, w[ch] now, Sir, I ought for your sake to believe I have performed. I am pleased likewise with your quoting of me, even when in all probability you knew nothing of the matter. My first essay at loading the world with my scribbles, was in the Philos. Trans. (a place since fatal to me for a reason you are not ignorant of), and it was in *re metallica*. My most honoured friend y[e] late S[r] Philip Skippon, who had a noble cabinet of Medals, w[ch] he thoroughly understood, sent me an account of some Saxon coyns found in Suffolke, which I printed with some remarks of my own in y[e] Transact. N[o] 187, with the initial letters of both our names. The new editor of Camden took no notice of these coyns, tho I gave them warning, & tho there are some there w[ch] are not in their collection. You have been pleased to referr to them, for w[ch], Sir, I am bound to express my thanks. But this is not all. I have been censured heavily for blaming Sr W. T.'s Delphos, & substituting Delphi in its place. Your authority will now (if I am publickly a . . . .) decide ye controversy. I am opposed with an authority of a Medal in F. Hardoüin's Num'i Urbium, with this inscription, ΔΕΛΦΟΥ, ye genitive, say they, of Delphos, ye nominative of the name of the city. I use to reply that it was the genitive of

Delphus, Apollo's son, mentioned by severall of ye ancients; wch explication you confirm, p. 189, where you inform these cavallers, that Εἰκὼν or Νομισμα, is understood. 'Tis time to release you; onely pray, Sir, do me the favor at your leisure to inform me, whether there is ever another Coyne published with the Bipennis Tenedia upon it, besides that wch John Graves printed in his Roman Denarius. I could say abundance more, but my paper tells me what I have farther to say, that

I am, your most obliged serv^t,
W. WOTTON.

For the Honored John Evelyn, Senr, Esq.
at Wotton, near Dorkinge, in Surrey.

To Mr. HENSHAW.
Wotton, 1 Mar. 1697-8.

The bearer hereof, Dr. Hoy, a very learned, curious, and ingenious person (& our neighbour in Surrey), acquainted (as who is not?) with the name & greate worth of Mr. Henshaw, hearing that I had the honor to be known to you, desires me to introduce him; I neede say no more how worthy he is to be let into your esteeme, than to acquaint you how deservedly we value him here in this country, not only for his profession & successe, but for those other excellent talents wch were ever incourag'd by your free & generous communications. And in this I serve myselfe also, by taking the occasion to present the most humble service of a now old acquaintance, begun long since abroad, & cultivated ever since by the continuance of your friendship thro' many revolutions. I frequently call to mind the many bright & happy moments we have pass'd together at Rome and other places, in viewing & contemplating the entertainments of travellers who go not abroad to count steeples, but to improve themselves. I wish I could say of myself so as you did; but whenever I thinke of the agreeable toile we tooke among the ruines & antiquitys, to admire the superb buildings, visite the cabinets & curiositys of the virtuosi, the sweete walkes by the banks of the Tiber, the Via Flaminia, the gardens & villas of that glorious citty, I call back the time, & methinks growing yonge againe, the opera we saw at Venice comes into my fansy, and I am ready to sing, *Gioconda Gioretri—memoria sola tù—con ramento mi"l fu—spesso spessò vien a rapir mi, e qual che si sia ancor ringiovenir mi.* You remember, Sir, the rest, and we are both neere the conclusion, *hai che non torni, non torni piu—mo—ri—bondo.*

Forgive me, Sir, this transport, & when this gent: takes his leave of you, permit me to beg your pardon also for the presumption I am guilty of, in obtruding a Discourse of Medals on one who is so greate a master & so knowing, and from whose example I sometimes diverted to that study. 'Tis now neere fifty yeares, &c.

[The rest of the letter is nearly the same as the preceding, see p. 385.]

To Archdeacon NICOLSON, Dean of Carlisle.

10 Nov. 1699.

After thanking him for the tendernese and civility with which he had mentioned his book on Medals, Mr. Evelyn says:—

"You recommend the study of our own municipal lawes & home antiquitys, most becoming an Englishman & lover of his country, which you have skilfully deriv'd from the fountaine, & trackt thro' all those windings & meanders wch rendered the study generally deserted as dull & impolite, unlesse by those who, attrackted by more sordid considerations, submitted to a fatigue which fill'd indeede their purses for the noyse they made at Westmin^r Hall, whilst their heads were empty, even of that to which they seem'd to devote themselves. Did our Inns of Court Students come a little better grounded in ethics & with some entrance into the civil law, such an History as you are meditating would leade them on with delight, & inable them to discover & penetrate into the grounds of natural justice & human prudence, & furnish them with matter to adorn their pleadings, before they wholly gave themselves up to learn to wrangle & the arts of illaqueation, & not make such haste to precedents, costomes, & common-places. By reading good history they would come to understand how governments have ben settl'd, by conquest, transplantations, colonys or garrisons thro' all vicissitudes & revolutions, from east to west, from the first monarchy to the last; how laws have ben establish'd, & for what reasons chang'd & alter'd; whence our holding by knight's service, & whether feudal laws have ben deriv'd from Saxon or Norman. 'Tis pity young gentlemen should meete with so little of this in the course of their academic studys, at least if it continue as in my time, when they were brought up to dispute on dry questions which nauceat generous spirits, & to discourse of things before they are furnish'd with mediums, & so returne home rather with the learning of a Benedietine Monk (full of schole cant) than of such usefull knowledge as would inable them to a dexterity in solving cases, how intricate soever, by analytics & so much of algebra as teaches to draw consequences & detect paralogisms & falacies, which were the true use of logic, & which you give hopes our Universitys are now designing. To this I would add the improvement of the more ornate & gracefull manner of speaking upon occasion. The fruit of such an education would not onely grace & furnish the bar with excellent lawyers, but the nation with able persons fit for any honorable imployment, to serve & speake in Parliaments & in Councils: give us good magistrates & justices for reference at home in the country: able ambassadors & orators abroad; in a word, qualified patriots & pillars of state, in which this age does not I feare abound. In the meane time what preference may be given to our constitutions I dare not determine, but as I believe ethics & the civile law were the natural mother of all good laws, so I have ben told that the best lawyers of England were heretofore wont to mix their studys together with them, but which are at present so rarely cultivated, that those who passe forsooth for greate sages & oracles therein were not onely shamefully defective, but even in the feudal & our owne.

You are speaking, Sir, of records, but who are they among this multitude even of the coife, who either study or vouchsafe to defile their fingers with any dust, save what is yellow? or know any thing of records save what, upon occasion, they lap out of Sr Edw. Coke's basin, & some few others? The thirst of gaine takes up their whole man; like our English paynters, who, greedy of getting present money for their work, seldom arive to any farther excellency in the art than face-painting, & have no skill in perspective, sym'etry, the principles of designe, or dare undertake to paint history.

Upon all these considerations then, I cannot but presage the greate advantage your excellent book, and such an history, may produce, when our young gentlemen shall ripen their studys by those excellent methods. At least there will not likely appeare such swarms & legions of obstreperous lawyers as yearly emerge out of our London seminarys, *omnium doctorum indoctissimum genus* (for the most part) as Erasmus truly styles them.

Concerning the Paper Office, I wish those instruments and state arcana had ben as faithfully & constantly transmitted to that usefull magazin as they ought; but tho' Sr Jos: Williamson tooke paines to reduce things into some order, so miserably had they ben neglected and rifled during the Rebellion, that at the Restoration of Char. II. such were the defects, that they were as far to seeke for precedents, authentiq & original treatys, negotiations, & other transactions formerly made with Foraine States & Princes, dispatches & instructions to Ambassadors, as if there had never before ben any correspondence abroad. How that office stands at present I know not; but this I do know, that aboundance of those dispatches & papers you mention, & which ought to centre there, have ben carried away both by the Secretarys of State themselves (when either dismiss'd or dying, & by Ambass^{rs} & other Ministers when recall'd,) into the country, & left to their heires as honorable marks of their ancestors imployments. Of this sort I had formerly divers considerable bundles concerning transactions of state during the ministry of the greate Earle of Leycester, all the reigne of Q. Elizth, containing divers original letters from the Q. herselfe, from Mary Q. of Scots, Cha. IX. and Hen. IV. of France, Maximilian the 2d Emp., Duke of Norfolk, Ja: Stewart Regent of Scotland, Marq. of Montrose, Sr Wm Throckmorton, Randolfe, Sr Fra: Walsingham (whom you mention), Sec. Cecill, Mr. Barnaby, Sir J. Hawkins, Drake, Fenton, Matt. Parker Archb. of Cant^y, Edwyn Bp. of London, the Bp. of Winchester, Bp. Hooper, &c. From abroad: Tremelius and other Protestant Divines, Parquiou, Spinola, Ubaldino, and other com'anders, with divers Italian Princes; and of ladys, the Lady Mary Grey, Cecilia Princesse of Sweden, Ann Countesse of Oldenburgh, the Dutchesse of Somerset, & a world more. But what most of all, & still afflicts me, those letters & papers of the Q. of Scots, originals & written wth her own hand to Q. Eliz. & Earle of Leycester, before & during her imprisonment, which I furnish'd to Dr. Burnet (now Bp. of Salisb.), some of which being printed in his History of the Reformation, those, & others with them, are pretended to have ben lost at the presse, which has bin a quarrell betweene me & his L^p, who lays the fault on Chiswell,* but so as between them I have lost the

---

* Printer or publisher.

originals, which had now ben safe records as you will find in that History. The rest I have named I lent to his countryman the late Duke of Lauderdale, who honouring me with his presence in ye country, and after dinner discoursing of a Maitland (ancestor of his) of whom I had several letters impaqueted with many others, desired I would trust him with them for a few days; it is now more than a few years past, that being put off from time to time, til the death of his Grace, when his library was selling, my letters & papers could no where be found or recover'd, so as by this tretchery my collection being broken, I bestowed the remainder on a worthy and curious friend * of mine, who is not likely to trust a S—— with any thing he values.

But, S^r, I quite tire you with a rhapsody of impertinences, beg your pardon, and remain," &c.

Among the errata of the Numismata, but of wch I immediately gave an account in the Philos. Transactions, the following were thus to have been read: p. 22. l. n. 22—*mixt* as well as *obrizd* † sort in the margin, for such a metal is mention'd by Aldus (of Valentinian) with *CONOB:* which he reads,— *Constantinopoli Obrizatum*, belonging, he says, to Count Landus: v: Aldus Manut. Notar: Exp'ta, p. 802. Venet. cIɔ.Iɔ.xcI. & p. 51. l. q. r. *Etiminius:*

---

* Qu. Mr. Pepys?
† *Obryzum* signifies gold of the most exalted purity. J. E.

Spanheime indeed is suspicious of this medal, but I was unwilling to degrade our metropolis of the honor. P. 202 in margin r. *Regulbium* (with in- numerable more).

Sir,

I know not whether Sir Jo: Hoskins, Sir R. Southwell, Mr. Waller, and Dr. Harwood (who is concern'd in what I have said of *Taille Douce)* and the rest (on whom I have obtruded books) would have the patience of Mr. Hill, to read my lett^r, when you meete at ye learned Coffee-Club, after they are gon from Gressham.

W. WOTTON to J. EVELYN.

Honored S^r, Jan. 22, 1701-2.

The kind notice you have been pleased to take of my poor performances gives me a satisfaction wch few things in the world could have equalled. Few authors, I believe, are so entirely disengaged from the world, as to be proof against applause even from com'on readers: but ye approbation of great mas- ters is ye highest reward any writer ought to look for. I am sure my time has not been mispent since Mr. Evelyn has past so favorable a judgment upon what I have been doing. It encourages me also to go on with Mr. Boyle's Life, for wch I have been so long indebted to ye public. I have now all the materials I am to expect, and intend with all convenient speed to digest them into such an order as may make them at hand when I shall use them.

His works having been epitomated by Mr. Bolton after a sort, I am at a losse whether I shall interweave a kind of a system of his philosophy into ye Life as I at first designed, or only relate matters of fact. In that matter I shall be guided by my friends; especially your judgment I shall long for, if you will do me the honor to give it me; and then I am sure to make no mistake. The work, I am sure, will please me; if I fall not short of my subject I shall be glad

I am extreamly sorry y^t the greediness of some people hath driven you to cutt any part of those charming groves that made Wotton so delicious a seat. What, are those woods behind ye house towards Leith-Hill cut down? If they are, the greatest ornament of ye finest county in England is gone. But I hope better; and do not know if God spares my life, but I may wait upon you this sum'er at Wotton, and then I shall inform myself.

That God Almighty may long preserve you to your family, and continue to make young Mr. Evelyn what he promises, and you desire, is the hearty praier of,

Honored S^r,
Your most obliged and most faith^l serv^t,
W. WOTTON.

I beg leave to present my humblest service to your lady. I have the same intelligence concerning Mr. Hare that you have.

Mr. W. Wotton to J. Evelyn.

Honored S^r, Jan. 23, 1703.

When I see two letters of your's before me, and both unanswered, it fills me with confusion. I ought not to be so insensible of ye honor you do me by your correspondence; an honor wch I shall never be able sufficiently to acknowledge; tho' I confess it is with the extremest pleasure that I think I shall ere long tell ye world that I have had the happiness to be known to so great an ornament of our age and nation as Mr. Evelyn.

Your last papers have cleared some doubts wch I was in concerning Mr. Boyle's family, and some still remain. I want to know whether Sr Geoffry Fenton was not Secretary of State; I think he was. Sr Wm Petty's will I have got a copy of. I have many other things to ask you, of wch you will in a short time have a list. You encourage me, Sir, to come to you; I will labour that you sha'nt repent.

I received last post two letters out of Surrey, one from Dr Duncombe, of Shere, ye other from Mr. Randyll, of Chilworth, in behalf of one Mr. Banister, Vicar of Wonersh, a small vicarage just by

Albury. It seems one Steer, of Nudigate, has left an exhibition for a poor scholar of Trinity College, Cambridge. Now Mr. Banister has with great difficulty bred up a son whom he desygns for ye University, and hopes he shall procure this exhibition. But that will be a slender support. I am solicited therefore to desire Dr Bentley to look favorably upon him if he shall deserve it. There are very many ways by wch a master of such a house may assist a promising lad whose fortune is narrow. I intend to send a letter to the master by the lad when he goes up, and I take the boldness to say all this to you, because I have reason to think it will be esteemed by Mr. Randyll and Dr. Duncomb (whose family are patrons of that vicarage) as an exceeding great obligation, if you will vouchsafe to interpose with our friend in this lad's behalf. Many a boy who struggles at his first entry into ye world proves afterwards a very considerable man. Dr. Duncomb says the child is qualified to go to Cambridge. My wife desires to have her most humble service presented to Mrs. Evelyn. I am,

  Honored S^r,
  Your most obed^t and faithfull serv^t,
     W. WOTTON.

For John Evelyn, Esq. at his house in Dover Street, near St. James's Street, Westminster.

W. Wotton to J. Evelyn.

Hon^d S^r, Milton, Aug. 13, 1703.

It is now so long time since I first mentioned to you my design of giving some account to ye world of ye life and writings of Mr. Boyle, that I question not but you have long since looked upon it as a vain brag of an impertinent fellow, who when he had once appeared in public, thought he might be always trespassing upon their patience. The discouragements I met with since I undertook it were so many, that I have often wished that I had let it alone or never thought of it. And I was ordered to pursue another scent by ye Bishop of Salisbury, wch it pleased God to make unsuccessful. However my design has long been resumed, and every day I do something to it. Next spring I hope to wait upon you in Dover Street, and shew you what I have done. I am sensible I am a slow and a lazy writer, and since y^e public can well spare me and what I shall ever do, it is no great harm if I am dilatory. But since you, Sir, were the first $\epsilon\rho\gamma o\delta\iota\omega\kappa\tau\eta s$ to me in this affair, and were pleased so far to flatter me, as to make me hope y^e world would (upon Mr. Boyle's account) pardon what I should say, I must take y^e freedom to be yet farther troublesome to you. By your letter of March 29, 1696, I am encouraged to trouble you, and for that letter I again must thank you, since notwithstanding the notices w^{ch}

Mr. Boyle's own papers and ye Bp. of Sarum's hints have given me, I found your informations so usefull, that without them my work would be very lame. I beg therefore of you farther,

1. An account of Mr. Hartlib: what countryman: what his employment? in short, a short Eloge of him, and his writings and designs, with an account of the time of his death.

2. The like of ye beginnings of Sr Wm Petty. Those two were very great with Mr. Boyle before ye Restorac'on.

3. Do you know any thing of one Clodius * a chymist? Was he (or who was) Mr. Boyle's first master in that art?

4. What was the affinity between your Lady's family and Mr. Boyle? What son of that family was it that lies buried in Deptford Church? and particularly all you can gather of the old Earl of Cork's orginal. Was Sr Geoffry Fenton Secretary of State in Ireland; if not, what was his employment? Did not he translate Guicciardini into English?

5. In what year began your acquaintance with Mr. Boyle? I find l^res of your's to him in 1657. Have you any letters of his; and would you spare me the use of them? they should be returned to you with thousands of thanks.

---

* Claudius.

I think, Sir, you will look upon these as queries enough for one time. It is in your power to make my work perfect, and ye obligations I shall have thereby, tho' they can't well add to those you have conferr'd already, yet they will give me a new title to subscribe myself,

Honored S^r,

Your most obedient & most obliged servant,

W. WOTTON.

My wife and I desire our services to be most humbly offered to Mad^m Evelyn.

Pray was Sr Maurice Fenton * (whose widow Sr W. Petty married) a descendant of Sr Geofry's? or what else do you know of him?

In one of your l^res to Mr. B. you mention a Chymico-Mathematico-Mechanical Schole designed by Dr. Wilkins: what farther do you know about it?

Copy to Mr. WOTTON, in answer to one of his in order to the History of the Life of Mr. BOYLE, &c. which I first put him upon.

Worthy Sir,   Wotton, 12 Sept. 1703.

I had long ere this given you an account of y^rs of the 13th past (which yet came not to me 'til the

---

* A question partly founded on a mistake of names, Evelyn having added, " Felton it should be."

20th), if a copy of the inscription you mention, and which I had long since among my papers, could it have ben found, upon diligent search; but lost I believe (with other book-notes) upon my remove hither, *cum pannis.* To supply which, it is now above ten days past that I sent to Dr. Stanhope (Vicar of Deptford) to send me a fresh transcript: but hearing nothing from him hitherto, I believe my letter might not come to his hands, and now a servant of mine (who lookes after my little concernes in that place) tells me the D^r is at Tunbridge drinking the waters; and perhaps my letter may lie dormant at his house, expecting his returne: upon this accident and interruption, unwilling you should remain any longer in suspense, or think me negligent or indifferent in promoting so desirable a work, I send you this in the meane time.

To the first of your quæries, Mr. Hartlib was, I think, a Lithuanian, who coming for refuge hither to avoid the persecution in his country, with much industry recommended himselfe to many charitable persons, and among the rest to Mr. Boyle, by communicating to them many secrets in chymistry, and improvements of agriculture, and other useful novelties by his general correspondence abroad, of which he has published several Treatises: besides this, he was not unlearned; zealous, and religious, with so much latitude as easily recommended him to the godly party then governing, among whom (as well as Mr. Boyle and others, who us'd to pity and cherish strangers,) he found no small subsistance during his exile. I had very many letters from him, and often relieved him. Claudius, whom you next inquire after, was his son in law, a profess'd adeptus, who by the same *methodus mendichandi* and pretence of extraordinary arcana, insinuated himselfe into acquaintance of his father-in-law: but when or where either of them died (though I think poor Hartlib's was of the stone), or what became of them I cannot tell; no more than I can who innitiated Mr. Boyle among the Spagyrists, before I had the honour to know him; though I conjecture it was whilst he resided at Oxford after his return from travel, where there was then a famous assemblage of virtuosi: Dr. Bathurst of Trinity, Dickinson of Merton, Wren, now Sir Christopher, Dr. Scarburgh, Seth Ward (afterwards Bishop of Sarum), and especially Dr. Wilkins (since Bishop of Chester): the head of Wadham Coll: where these and other ingenious persons used to meete to promote the study of the new philosophy, which has since obtained. It was in that Colledge where I think there was an elaboratory, and other instruments mathematical, mechanical, &c. which perhaps might be that you speake of as a schole: and so lasted till the Revolution following. This, Sir, is the best account I can at present render you, having since lost so many of my worthy friends, who might possibly have informed me better.

As to the date of my first acquaintance with this honourable gentleman, it sprung from a courteous visit he made me at my house in Deptford, which as I constantly repayed, so it grew reciprocal and familiar; divers letters passing between us at first in civilities and the style peculiar to him upon the least sense of obligation: but these compliments lasted no longer than till we became perfectly acquainted, and had discovered our inclination of cultivating the same studies and designes, especially in ye search of natural and usefull things; my selfe then intent on collections of notes in order to an History of Trades and other mechanical furniture, which he earnestly incouraged me to proceed with: so that our intercourse of letter was now only upon y^t account, and were rather so many receipts and processes, than letters. What I gathered of this nature (and especially for the improvement of planting and gardening; my Sylva and what else I published on that subject, being but part of that worke, (a plan whereof is mentioned in my late Acetaria,) would astonish you, did you see the bundles and packets, amongst other things in my *chartaphylacia* here, promiscuously ranged among multitudes of papers, letters, and other matters, divine, political papers, poetry, &c. some as old as the reign of

Henry VIII. (my Wife's ancestors having ben Treasurers of ye Navy to the reigne of Q. Eliz:) and exceedingly encreased by my late Father in law, Sr R. Brown's grandfather, who had the first employment under the greate Earl of Leycester, Governor of the Low Countries in the same Queen's reign, and of Sr Richard Brown's dispatches during his 19 years' residence in the Court of France, whither he was sent by Charles the I. and continued by his successor. But to return from this digression: this design and apparatus on severall other subjects and extravagances growing beyond my forces, was left imperfect upon the Restoration of the banished King, when every body expected a new world, and had other things in view, than what the melancholy dayes of his eclipse suggested to passe away anxious thoughts, by those innocent imployments I have mentioned. So as this Revolution and my Father in law's attendance at Court (being eldest Cleark of the Counsel) obliging me to be almost perpetually in London, the intercourse of formal letters (frequent visits, and constant meetings at Gressham Colledge succeeding,) was very seldom necessary; some I have yet by me, but such as can be of no importance to your noble work, one of which excepted, in answer to my returning him my thanks for sending me his Seraphic Love; which is long and full of civility, and so may passe for compliment with the rest, long since mingled among my other packets.

I can never give you so accurate an account of Sir Wm Petty (which is another of your inquirys) as you'll find in his own will, that famous & extraordinary piece (which I am sure cannot have escaped you), wherein he has omitted nothing concerning his owne simple birth, life, & wonderful progresse he made to arrive at so prodigious a fortune, as he has left his relations. Or if I could say more of it, I would not deprive you of the pleasure you must needes receive in reading it often.

The only particular I find he has taken no notice of, is the misadventure of his double-bottomed keel, which yet perishing in the tempestuous Bay of Biscay (where his other vessels were lost in the same storm) ought not at all reproach perhaps the best & most usefull mechanist in the world: for such was this *faber fortunæ*, Sr Wm Petty. I need not acquaint you with his recovering a certaine criminal young wench, who had ben hanged at Oxon; & being begg'd for a dissection he recovered to life, & (who) was afterward married, had children, & survived it 15 yeares. These among many other things very extraordinary, made him deservedly famous, & for several engines & inventions, not forgetting the expeditious method by which (getting to be the surveyor of the whole kingdom of Ireland) teaching ignorant soldiers to assist in the admeasurement, & reserving to himselfe the aikers assigned him for his reward: and the dispatch which gained him the favour of impatient soldiers, whose pay & arreres was to be out of the pretended forfeited estates, gave him opportunity to purchase their lots & debentures for little, which he got confirmed after ye Restoration. This was the foundation of the vast estate he since enjoyed. I need not tell you of his computations in what was published under the name of Mr. Graunt concerning the Bills of Mortality. And that with all this he was politely learned, a wit & a poet (see his Paraphase on Psalm 104, &c.); & was the most charming and instructing conversation in the world. But all these excellent talents of his, rather hindered than advanced his applications at Court, where the wretched favourites (some of whom for their virtue one "would not have set with the dogs of the flock," & some who yet sat at the helm) afraid of his abilities, stopt his progress there: nor indeed did he affect it, being to my observation and long acquaintance, a man of sincerity and infinitely industrious. Nothing was too hard for him. I mentioned his poetry, but sayd nothing of his preaching, which tho rarely and when he was in perfect humour to divert his friends he would hold forth in tone and action; passing from the Court pulpit to the Presbyterian, and then the Independent, Anabaptist,

Quaker, Fanatique, Frier, and Jesuit, as entertained the company to admiration, putting on the person of those sectarys with such variety and imitation, that it coming to be told the King, they prevail'd with him to shew his faculty one day at Court, where declaiming upon the vices of it, and miscarriages of the great ones, so verily as he needed not to name them, particularly the misgovernment of Ireland, as (tho' it diverted the King, who bare raillery the best in the world) so touched the Duke of Ormond there present & made him so unruly, as S^r W^m perceiving it, dextrously altered his style into a calmness and composure exceed^y admirable. One thing more (which possibly you may not have heard of) was his answering a challenge of Sr Allen Brodrick (in great favour with my Lord Chancellor); and it being the right of the apellant's antagonist to choose the place and name the weapon; he named the lists and field of battle to be in a dust cellar, and the weapon hatchets, himselfe being purblind, and not so skillful at the rapier; and so it concluded in a feast. But after all this, this poor, rich, and wonderfull man, and an excellent physician also, was suddenly taken away, by a gangrene in his leg, it seems too long neglected, a few days after we had dined together in cheerfull company. The coate armor which he chose and allways depicted on his coach, &c. was a mariner's compass, the style pointing to the polar star, the crest a beehive, if I remember well, the *lemma operosa et sedula*, than which nothing could be more apposite. And now I am extremely sensible of my detaining you so long, in giving you rather the history of Sr Wm Petty instead of satisfying your inquiry concerning his lady, and who married the widdow of Sr Maurice *Felton* (not Fenton), a Norfolk family, daughter of that arch rebel Sr Hardresse Waller, a great commander in Ireland, by whom he had 3 or 4 children, to whom he left vast fortunes. This wife is yet living, a very stately dame, in one of the stateliest palaces of that citty.

But now, asking you pardon againe for this (perhaps impertinent) aberration, I returne to Mr. Boyle, who had besides all we have enumerated, that were his acquaintance and admirers, the Lord Viscount Brouncker, first President of the Royal Society; that worthy person and honest Scot, Col. W. Murray; the famous Sr Kenelm Digby; Dr. Godard; and of later date, Dr. Burnet, now Bishop of Sarum, and generally all strangers and learned persons, pretending to chymistry, & other uncommon arts: nor did any Ambassador from abroad think he had seene England till he had visited Mr. Boyle.

As to the affinity and relation of my Wife's family to Mr. Boyle's, take the following account, she received from that most religious and excellent lady, his niece, the late Countess of Clancarty; who coming down one day to visit my Father-in-law, Sr R^d Browne, who lay incommoded with the goute, and sitting by his bed side, upon some casual discourse of her family, and how they allways esteemed him as of kindred, related this pretty passage of a kinsman of Sr Richard's mother's first husband, whose name was Geofrey Fenton, who neglecting his study, being designed for a lawyer, so exceedingly displeased his uncle, that he sent him into Ireland, as an abandoned young man, to seek his fortune there. The young student, considering his condition, soone recovered his uncle's favour by so diligently applying himself to that study, as in short time he became one of the most eminent of that profession. Now the first Earl of Cork being then but Mr. Boyle (a Kentish man, &, perhaps I may have told you, a school-master at Maidstone; but this particular being nothing of the Countess's narrative and a secret betwixt you and I only, and perhaps uncertaine) coming to advise with Sr Geof: Fenton, now knighted, & finding him engaged with another client, and seeing a pretty child in the nurse's armes, entertained himselfe with them, till Sr Geofrey came to him, making his excuse for making him waite so long. Mr. Boyle pleasantly told him, he had been courting a young lady for his wife. And so it fortuned, that sixteene years after it, Mr. Boyle made his addresse in good earnest to her, and married the young lady, from whom has sprung all this numerous family, of earls and lords branching now into the noblest families of England. How many sons and daughters he left I do not remember, only that Roger Boyle was the eldest son, whom his father sent young into England, to be educated under the care of his relation, my grandmother, at Deptford, where was then a famous schole. Thus, Sir, have you the original of the relation you inquire after, and of the kindness which always continued between them. This Roger Boyle is the young gentleman, who dying in Sr R. Brown's house at Says-Court in Deptford, was interred in that parish church.

I will now endeavour to commute for your patience with a pleasant passage, current with the Boyles: When King Charles II. newly come to his Crown, and using frequently to saile down the river in his yachts for diversion, and accompanied by all the greate men and courtiers waiting upon him, it was often observed, that when the vessel passed by a certain place opposite to the Church at Deptford, my Lord Burlington constantly pull'd off his hat, with some kind of reverence. This being remarked by some of the Lords standing by him, they desired he would tell them what he meant by it: to which he replied, " Do you see that steeple there? Have I not reason to pay a respect to the place where my elder brother lies buried, by which I

enjoy the Earldom of Cork?" Worthy Sir, I remain
Your most humble and obliged serv^t,

J. EVELYN.

P. S. Where I speak of this family perhaps it may not be amisse to see what Sr Wm Dugdale says of it in his Baronage; tho' what the Heralds write is often sorry and mercenary enough. I am able to bring my own Pedigree from one Evelyn, nephew to Androgius, who brought Julius Cæsar into Britain the second time: will you not smile at this? Whilst Onslow, Hatton, and Evelyn came, I suppose, much at the same time out of Shropshire into Surrey and adjacent counties (from places still retaining their names) some time during the Barons Wars.

Methinks you speake of your not being at London till next spring: a long day for *Octogenarius* to hope for that happiness, who have of late seene so few moments I can call so all this past year: I have been much impaired in my health, by a defluxion which fell into one of my legs, caused by a slight scraze on my shin-bone, falling on a stump as I was walking in Brompton Parke to take the fresh air; and might have been healed with a little Hungary-water in a day or two (for my flesh never rankles); but this neglected, a chirurgeon, my Godson, whom almost 40 years since was bound apprentice to that profession, persuading me to apply a miraculous plaster of his; it drew down a sharp humour, which kept me within three months, and that being at last diverted and perfectly cured, it has since tormented me with the hemorhoides, if I may so call tumours that do not bleed (or rather blind piles), which make me exceedingly uneasy. I have yet adventured to pay my duty to my Lord Guernsey, who did me the honour to visit me at Dover Street whilst I was not able to stir, and has lately called often since he came out of Kent.

My young Grandson improves laudably in his studye of both laws, history, chronology, and practical mathematics: 'tis pity he has not a correspondent that might provoke him to write Latin epistles, in which I am told by some able to judge, and that have seen some of them, he is master of an handsome style: he does not forget his Greek, having read Herodotus, Thucydides, and the rest of that class. I do not much encourage his poetry, in which he has yet a pretty veine; my desire being to make him an honest useful man, of which I have great hopes, being so grave, steady, and most virtuously inclyned. He is now gone to see Chichester and Portse-mouth, having already travelled most of the inland counties; and went the last summer before this, as far as the Land's-end in Cornwall. Thus you see I make you part of my concernes, hardly abstaining from the boasts of men of my dotage.*

---

* Doute-age.

I have payd the visit we lately received from Mr. Hare and his lady, very glad to find them both in so good state of health. He longs to see Mr. Wooton, as well as your humble servant,

J. E.

The Master of Trinity was often at St. James's without being so kind as to visite the *Clinic*.

W. Wotton to J. Evelyn.

Honored S^r,   Octr 30, 1703.

I am heartily ashamed that I deferred so long to answer your's wherein you sent me so large and so obliging an answer to all my queries. I could say my family has ben indisposed (my wife having been lately brought to bed of a daughter), and that has broke my thoughts. But even that excuse satisfies me not, and so I shall pass it. I onely beg I may not forfeit your favor, and entreate you to accept of my sincere promises of future amendment. Your hand in this last, wch I received last night, seems stronger and healthier than in your former. God grant your health, wch now I hope is perfectly recovered, may long continue to ye joy of your family and your friends, and to ye satisfaction of all the learned world, to w^{ch}, whilst you live, you can'ot but be doing good. Another edition of your Silva I should be glad to see. It is a noble work, and y^e

reception it has met with amongst ye competent judges, demonstrates it to have bin so esteemed. Another edition of your " Parallel of Architecture" I could rejoice to see done by yourself. I know you have noble materials for another impression by you, which ye public greedily longs for.

Before I shut up this paper, I must rejoice with you for ye prospect you have in young Mr. Evelyn. May that good Providence wch has preserved him to you and your admirable lady, thus far give you every day an encrease of satisfaction in him for ye future. This is ye unfeigned praier of,

Honored S^r,
Your most obedient and faithful servant,
W. Wotton.

I should be glad to know when you think of seeing London, and for how long.

For the Honored John Evelyn, Esq.
at Wotton Place, neare Dorkinge in Surrey.

From the MSS. at Wotton.

Sayes Court.

The hithermost Grove I planted about	1656
The other beyond it	1660
The lower Grove	1662
The holly hedge, even with the Mount hedge below	1670

I planted every hedge & tree not onely in the garden, groves, &c. but about all the fields & house since 1653, except those large, old, & hollow elms in the stable court & next the sewer; for it was before, all one pasture field to the very garden of the house, wch was but small; from which time also I repaired the ruined house, & built the whole of the kitchen, the chapel, buttry, my study, above & below, cellars & all the outhouses & walls, still-house, orangerie, & made the gardens, &c. to my great cost, & better had I don to have pulled all down at first, but it was don at several times.

Mr. Evelyn was acquainted with the use and value of Potatoes, which he calls Irish, tasting like an old bean or roasted chesnut, not very pleasant till use have accustomed, yet of good nourishm^t & excellent use for relief of poor, yea & of one's own household where there are many servants in a dear year.

Prince Rupert invented a Turfing-plough, but without any description of its use.

Dredge is barley & Oats mixed.

Hops cost 20^l an acre before any considerable profit.

	£	s.	d.
Digging	2	10	0
5000 roots	2	10	0
1st year, dressing	2	10	0
2d year, ditto	2	10	0
Poles	10	0	0

40 loads of dung on an acre, the produce not above 6^l an acre.*

An acre of Hemp may be worth 8^l, & after this the land will be proper for barley, wheat, and pease successively.

Orchards improve land f^m 10^s an acre, wch is commonly the value of the best sort of tillage, & even of best pasture not above 2^l to 4^l.

An acre planted with cherries has been sett at 10^l, 100 miles f^m London.

About Sandwich & Deal they hedge & fence their corn fields with flax & hemp, but flax chiefly, wch they affirm keep out cattle, being bitter; they sow it about 20 f^t deep into the field—sow whole fields of canary-seed—great grounds of hyssop & thime in tufts, for seeds only—the soil light & sandy, but the hyssop in richer ground.

---

* The following account of expence and produce of Hop-ground at Farnham, in Surrey, about the year 1812, is given in Manning and Bray's History of that County, vol. III. p. 166.

The average rent of hop-ground about £9. 10s. an acre. The first expence of making and planting an acre, £26. The hops are not in perfection till the third year after planting. The ground is dressed every year with good stable-dung, rags, hair, wool-clippings, lime, &c. Average expence £35 an acre. Ash and withy poles are best, length from 16 to 20 feet, prices from 26 to 40s. per hundred delivered in. Produce very uncertain; but on good ground, the average of three years may be about seven hundred weight from an acre.

CHARACTER OF MRS. EVELYN,

BY DR. BOHUN.

FROM THE ORIGINAL IN HIS HAND-WRITING.

CHARACTER OF MRS. EVELYN,

BY DR. BOHUN.*

I HAD lately occasion to review severall letters to me from Mrs. Evelyn of Deptford. After reading y^m, I found they were much to be valued, because they contained not only a compleat description of the private events in the family, but publick transactions of ye times, where are many curious and memorable things described in an easy and eloquent style.

Many forgotten circumstances by this means are recalled afresh to my memorie; by so full and perfeet a narration of y^m, they are again present to my thoughts, and I see y^m re-acted as it were before my eyes. This made strong impressions on my mind, so y^t I could not rest till I had recollected ye substance of y^m, and from thence some generall

---

* The Rev. Dr. Ralph Bohun, D. C. L. was a scholar at Winchester College, and was elected probationary fellow of New College, Oxford, at the early age of 19. In 1671 he wrote a Discourse on the History and Nature of Wind; and in 1685, he completed his Doctor's degree.

reflexions thereon, and from thence drew a character of y^eir author, so farr only as by plain and natural inferences may be gathered from y^eir contents. This was not perform'd in a manner worthy of ye design, but hastily and uncorrectly, wch cost no more time y^n cou'd be employed at one sitting in an afternoon; but in this short model, Mrs. Evelyn will appeare to be ye best daughter and wife, ye most tender mother, and desirable neighbour and friend, in all parts of her life. The historicall account of matters of fact sufficiently set forth her prayses, wherein there cou'd be no error or self-conceit; and declare her to be an exact pattern of many excellent vertues; but they are concealed in such modest expressions, y^t ye most envious censurers can't fix upon her ye least suspicion of vanity or pride. Tho' she had many advantages of birth and beauty, and wit, yet you may perceive in her writings, an humble indifference to all worldly enjoyments, great charity, and compassion to those y^t had disobliged her, and no memory of past occurrenees, unlesse it were a gratefull acknowledgment of some friendly office; a vein of good-nature and resignation, and self denial runs through y^m all. There's nothing so despis'd in many of these letters as the fruitles & empty vanitys of ye town; and they seem to pity ye misfortune of those who are condemned by y^eir greater quality or stations to squander away y^eir precious time in unprofitable diversions, or bestow it in courtly visits & conversations. Where there happens to be any mention of children or friends, there's such an air of sincerity & benevolence for ye one, and religious concern for ye happines of ye other, as if she had no other design to live in ye world, yⁿ to perform her own duty, and promote ye welfare of her relations and acquaintance.

There's another observation to be collected, not less remarkable yⁿ ye rest, wch is her indefatigable industry in employing herself, and more for the sake of others yⁿ her own: This she wrote, not out of vain glory, or to procure commendation, but to entertain y^m with whom she had a familiar correspondence by letters, with ye relation of such accidents or bysnes wherein she was engag'd for the month, or the week past.

This was a peculiar felicity in her way of writing, y^t tho she often treated of vulgar and domestic subjects, she never suffer'd her style to languish or flag, but by some new remark or pleasant digression kept it up to its usual pitch.

The reproofs in any of these numerous letters were so softly insinuated, y^t ye greatest punishment to be inflicted upon any disobligation was only to have ye contrary vertue to ye fault they had ben guilty of, highly applauded in the next correspondence, wch was ever so manag'd as to pleas and improve.

Scarce an harsh expression, much less any evill surmise or suspicion cou'd be admitted where every line was devoted to charity and goodnes. This is no effect of partiality, but appears in ye particular instances, so y^t ye same judgment must be made by all unprejudiced persons who shall have a sight of y^m.

Any misfortune or disappointment was not mournfully lamented, but related in such a manner as became a mind y^t had laid in a sufficient provision of courage & patience before-hand to support it under afflictions. All unfortunate accidents are allaid by some consolatory argument taken from solid principles. No kind of trouble but one seems to interrupt ye constant intention to entertain & oblige, but that is dolorously represented in many of ye letters, wch is ye loss of children or friends. That being an irreparable separation in this world, is deplored with the most affectionat tenderness wch words can express. You may conclude y^t they who write in such a manner as this, must be suppos'd to have a just sens of religion, becaus there can scarce be assign'd one act of a beneficent and charitable temper but has many texts of ye Gospell to enforce it. So y^t all good Xtians must be very usefull and excellent neighbours and friends; wch made this lady ever esteemed so. Shee was ye delight of all ye conversations where she appear'd, she was lov'd and admir'd, yet never envy'd by any, not so much as by ye women, who seldom allow ye perfections of y^eir own sex, least they ecclips y^eir own; but as this very manifestly & upon all occasions was her temper, ye world was very gratefull to her upon y^t account. This happines was gain'd and preserv'd by one wise qualification, for tho' no person living had a closer insight into ye humors or characters of persons, or cou'd distinguish y^eir merits more nicely, yet she never made any despising or censorious reflexions: her great discernment and wit were never abus'd to sully ye reputation of others, nor affected any applaus y^t might be gain'd by satyrical jests. Tho' shee was extreamly valu'd, and her friendship priz'd and sought for by y^m of the highest condition, yet she ever treated those of ye lowest with great condescension and humanity. The memory of her vertues and benefits made such deep impression on her neighbors of Deptford & Greenwich, that if any one should bring in another report from this, or what was generally receiv'd among y^m, they'd condemn as fals, and ye effect of a slanderous calumny; either they wou'd never yield y^t any change shou'd happen to this excellent lady, or they'd impute it to sickness, or time, or chance, or ye unavoidable frailtys of human nature. But I have somewhat digress'd from my subject, wch was to describe her person or perfections no otherwise yⁿ they may be gathered from yᵉ letters I receiv'd;* they contain historical passages and accounts of any more or less considerable action or accident yᵗ came to her knowledge, with diverting or serious reflections as yᵉ subject requir'd, but generally in an equall and chaste style, supported by a constant gravity, never descending to affected sallys of ludicrous wit.

It's to be further observ'd, yᵗ tho she recites and speaks French exactly, & understands Italian, yet she confines herself with such strictnes to yᵉ purity of yᵉ English toung, yᵗ she never introduces foreign or adopted words: that ther's a great steadines & equality in her thoughts; and yᵗ her sens & expressions have a mutual dependance on each other may be infer'd from hence—you shall never perceive one perplext sentence, or blot, or recalling a word in more yⁿ twenty letters.

Many persons with whom she convers'd or were related to her, or had any publick part in yᵉ world, were honour'd by very lively characters confer'd on them, always just, and full of discernment, rather inclining to yᵉ charitable side, yet no otherwyse yⁿ as skillfull masters who paint like, yet know how to give some graces and advantages to yᵐ whose

---

* Copies of several letters to Dr. Bohun, have been found at Wotton, but not those here referred to. A few of them will follow, as specimens of her manner and great good sense.

pictures they draw. The expressions are clear and unaffected, ye sentences frequent & grave, ye remarks judicious, ye periods flowing & long, after the Ciceronian way, yet tho' they launch out so farr, they are strict to ye rules of grammar, and ever come safe home at last without any obscurity or incoherence attending y^m.

I'le only give one instance of a person who was caracteris'd by her in a more favorable manner y^n he durst presume y^t he deserved; however, to shew ye method of her writing, I shall set it down. "I believe (such an one) to be a person of much wit, great knowledge, judicious and discerning, charitable, well natur'd, obliging in conversation, apt to forget & forgive injuries, eloquent in ye pulpit, living according to known precepts, faithfull to his friend, generous to his enemie, and in every respect accomplisht; this in our vulgar way is a desirable character, but you'll excuse if I judge unrefinedly who have ye care of cakes & stilling, & sweetmeats & such usefull things."

Mrs. Evelyn has been often heard to say concerning ye death of her admirable & beloved Daughter, that tho' she had lost her for ever in this world yet she wou'd not but y^t she had been, becaus many pleasing ideas occurr to her thoughts y^t she had convers'd with her so long, and ben made happy by her for so many years.

Oxon, 1695, Sept. 20.

LETTERS FROM MRS. EVELYN.

For Mr. BOHUN.

21 May 1668.

If it be true that wee are generally enclined to covett what wee admire, I can assure you my ambition aspires not to the fame of Balzac, and therefore must not thank you for entitling me to that great name. I do not admire his style, nor emulate the spirit of discontent which runns through all his letters. There is a lucky hitt in reputation which some obtaine by the deffect in their judges, rather than from the greatnesse of their merit; the contrary may be instanced in Doctor Donne, who had he not ben really a learned man, a libertine in witt and a courtier, might have been allowed to write well, but I confess in my opinion, with these qualifications he falls short in his letters of the praises some give him.

Voiture seems to excell both in quicknesse of fancy, easinesse of expression, & in a facile way of insinuating that he was not ignorant of letters, an advantage the Court ayre gives persons who converse with the world as books.

I wonder at nothing more than at the ambition of printing letters; since, if the designe be to produce witt and learning, there is too little scope for the one, and the other may be reduced to a lesse compasse than a sheet of gilt paper, unlesse truth were more communicative. Buisinesse, love, accidents, secret displeasure, family intrigues, generally make up the body of letters, and can signifie very little to any besides the persons they are addressed to, and therefore must loose infinitely by being exposed to the unconcerned. Without this declaration I hope I am sufficiently secure never to runne the hazard of being censured that way, since I cannot suspect my friends of so much unkindnesse, nor myselfe of the vanity to wish fame on so doubtfull a foundation as the caprice of mankind. Do not impute my silence to neglect; had you seene me these tenne days continually entertaining persons of different humor, age, and sence, not only at meales, or afternoone, or the time of a civill visit, but from morning till night, you will be assured it was impossible for me to finish these few lines sooner; so often have I set pen to paper and ben taken off againe, that I almost despaired to lett you know my satisfaction that Jack* complies so well with your desires, and that I am your friend and servant,

M. Evelyn.

---

* Her son, then at College under Mr. Bohun's care.

To Mr. Bohun.

S^r, 1671.

I must believe you are very busy, hearing so seldome from you, and that you are much in the esteeme of Dr. Bathurst,* since he judges so favourably of y^r friends. It cannot be the effect of his discernment which makes him give sentence in my behalfe, being so great a master of reason as he is; but it is certainly a mark of his great kindnesse to you that he deffers to y^r jugment in opposition to his owne. I should not question y^{rs} in other things, but the wisest may be allow'd some grains, and I conclude you no lesse a courtier than a philosopher. Since my last to you I have seene " The Siege of Grenada," a play so full of ideas that the most refined romance I euer read is not to compare with it: love is made so pure, and valor so nice, that one would imagine it designed for an Vtopia rather then our stage. I do not quarrell with the poet, but admire one borne in the decline of morality should be able to feigne such exact virtue; and as poetick fiction has been instructive in former ages, I wish this the same event in ours. As to the strict

---

* Dr. Ralph Bathurst, Dean of Wells, and President of Trinity College, in Oxford, whose Life and Literary Remains have been published by Thomas Warton, Poetry Professor, and Fellow of the same College.

law of Comedy I dare not pretend to judge: some thinke the division of the story not so well as if it could all haue ben comprehended in the dayes actions: truth of history, exactness of time, possibilities of adventures, are niceties the antient cricks might require; but those who have outdone them in fine notions may be allowed the liberty to expresse them their owne way, and the present world is so enlightened that the old dramatique must bear no sway. This account perhaps is not enough to do Mr. Driden right, yet is as much as you can expect from the leisure of one who has the care of a nursery.

I am, Sir, &c.
M. Evelyn.

To Mr. Bohun at Oxford.

S^r,

Do not think my silence hitherto has proceeded from being taken up with the diversions of the towne, the eclat of the wedding, mascarades which trebled their number the second night of the wedding [so] that there was great disorder and confusion caused by it, and with which the solemnity ended; neither can I charge the houswifry of the country after my returne, or treating my neighbours this Christmas, since I never finde any buisinesse or recreation that makes me forget my friends.

Should I confesse the reall cause, it is y^r expectation of extraordinary notions of things wholy out of my way: Women were not borne to reade authors, and censure the learned, to compare lives and judge of virtues, to give rules of morality, and sacrifice to the Muses. We are willing to acknowledge all time borrowed from family duties is misspent; the care of children's education, observing a husband's comands, assisting the sick, relieving the poore, and being servicable to our friends, are of sufficient weight to employ the most improved capacities amongst us. If sometimes it happens by accident that one of a thousand aspires a little higher, her fate commonly exposes her to wonder, but adds little to esteeme. The distaff will defend our quarrells as well as the sword, and the needle is as instructive as the penne. A heroine is a kinde of prodigy; the influence of a blasing starre is not more dangerous, or more avoyded. Though I have lived under the roofe of the learned, and in the neighbourhood of science, it has had no other effect on such a temper as mine, but that of admiration, and that too but when it is reduced to practice. I confesse I am infinitely delighted to meet with in books the atchievements of the heroes, with the calmnesse of philosophers, and with the eloquence of orators; but what charms me irresistably is to see perfect resignation in the minds of men let what ever happens adverse to them in their fortune; that is being knowing and truly wise; it confirms my beleefe of antiquity, and engages my perswasion of future perfection, without which it were in vaine to live. Hope not for volumes or treatises; raillery may make me goe beyonde my bounds, but when serious, I esteeme myselfe capable of very little, yet I am, S^r,

Your friend and servant,

Jan. 4, 1672.　　　　　　　　　　　　　　M. E.

To my Lady TUKE, after the death of
S^r SAM. TUKE.

Madame,

I acknowledge these are trialls which make Christian philosophy usefull, not only by a resignation to the divine decree, but by that hope which encourages us to expect a more lasting happinesse then any this world can give. Without this wee were extreamly wretched, since no felicity here has any duration. Wee are solicitous to obtaine, wee feare whilst we possesse, and wee are inconsolable when wee loose. The greatest conquerors themselves are subject to this unsteady state of humane nature; lett us not murmure then, for wee offend, and though in compliance to y^r present sence of things I could joyne with you in greeving, having made as particular a losse as ever any did in a friend, I dare not indulge y^r sorrows, especially when I consider how prejudiciall it will prove to y^{r}selfe and those dear pledges that are left to your care; but I do rather beg of you cease greeving, and owe that to reason and prudence which time will overcome. Were I in so good health that I could quitt my chamber, I would be dayly with you and assure you how really I am concerned for you. You cannot doubt the affection of your, &c.

Jan. 28, 1672.

To Mr. Bohun.

S^r, Sayes-Court, 29 Jan. 1672.

If a friend be of infinite value living, hòw much cause have wee to lament him dead! Such a friend was Sr Sam. Tuke, who retired out of this life on St. Paul's day [25 Jan.] at midnight, and has changed the scene to him and us, and left occasion to all that knew him to bewayle the losse. You need not to be made sensible by a character of a person you knew so well, and you can enumerate virtues enough to lament and shed some teares justly; therefore spare me the sorrow of repeating what effect it has wrought on such a minde as mine, who think no missfortune worth regretting besides the losse of those I love. Do not blame me if I beleeve it allmost impossible to meet with a person so worthy in himselfe, and so disposed to esteeme me againe; and yet that is not the chiefest cause of my affliction. I might wave much of my owne interest, had I not so many partners that will suffer equally. These are the trialls which make Christian philosophy usefull, not only by a resignation to the Divine decree, but by that hope which encourages us to expect a more lasting happinesse then any this world can give, without which wee were extreamly wretched, since no felicity here has any duration. The greatest conquerors themselves are subject to this unsteady state of humane nature, therefore well may I submitt, whose concerns are triviall in respect of others. Yet this I conclude, that wee dye by degrees when our friends go before us. But whilst I discourse thus with you, I should consider what effeets melancholy reflections may have on a spleenetic person, one who needes not cherish that temper. I will only add that I am now able to quitt my chamber, which is more then I could do these 14 dayes, and that I am, Sir,

Your servant, M. Evelyn.

To Mr. Bohun, Fellow of New College, Oxford.
S^r,

When I have assured you that my usuall indisposition has treated me so severely this winter that I have had little leasure to think of any thing but the meanes of gaineing health and ease, I am perswaded you will excuse me if I have not decided in my thoughts which was the greatest captaine, Cæsar or Pompey; whether Mr. De Rosny were not a great polititian, a brave soldier, and the best servant that ever Prince had for capacity, fidelity and steadinesse, a man strangly disinterested, infinitely fortunate, and every way qualified to serve such a master as was Henry the Great, who notwithstanding humane frailties, was worthy to be faithfully dealt with, since he knew how to judge and to reward. But why do we allwayes look back into times past? wee may not reproch our owne, since heere is at this present a scene for galantrie and merit, and whilst wee may hope, wee must not condemne. Should I tell you how full of sorrow I have ben for the losse of Dr. Bretton,* you only would blame me; after death flattery ceases, therefore you may beleeve there was some cause to lament when thousands of weeping eyes witnessed the affliction their soules were in; one would have imagined every one in this parish had lost a father, brother, or husband, so great was the bewailing; and in earnest it dos appear there never was a better nor a more worthy man. Such was his temper, prudence, charity, and good conduct, that he gained the weake and preserved the wise. The sudenesse

---

* Minister of Deptford; he died in February 1671-2.

of his death was a surprise only to his friends; as for himselfe it might be looked upon as a deliverance from paine, the effect of sicknesse, and I am allmost perswaded God snatched him from us, least he might have ben prevailed with by the number of petitions to have left him still amongst us. If you suspect kindness in me makes me speake too much, Doctor Parr* is a person against whome you cannot object; it was he who preached the funerall sermon, and as an effect of truth as well as eloquence he himselfe could not forbeare weeping in the pulpit. It was his owne expression that there were 3 for whome he had infinitly greeved, the martyred King, my Lord Primate,† and Doctor Bretton; and as a confirmation of the right that was done him in that oration, there was not a drie eye nor a dissenting person. But of this no more.

M. Evelyn.

Sayes-Court, 2o March 1671-2.

---

* Richard Parr, D.D. Vicar of Reigate and Camberwell. He died Nov. 2, 1691. The funeral sermon alluded to, was printed in 1672. See Manning and Bray's History of Surrey, vol. I. p. 323.

† Archbishop Usher.

To Lady Tuke.

April 1685.

How to expresse the sorrow for parting with so deare a child is a difficult task. She was welcome to me from the first moment God gave her, acceptable through the whole course of her life by a thousand endearments, by the gifts of nature, by acquired parts, by the tender love she ever shew'd her father and me: a thred of piety accompanyed all her actions, and now proves our greatest consolation. The patience, resignation, humility of her carriage in so severe and fatall a disease, discover'd more than an ordinary assistance of the Divine goodnesse, never expressing feare of death, or a desire to live, but for her friends sake. The seaventh day of her illnesse she discoursed to me in particular as calmly as in health, desir'd to confesse and receive the blessed Sacrament, which she perform'd with great devotion, after which, tho' in her perfect senses to the last. she never signified the least concerne for the world, prayed often, and resigned her soule.— What shall I say! She was too great a blessing for me, who never deserved any thing, much lesse such a jewell. I am too well assured of y^r L^{ps} kindnesse to doubt the part you take in this losse; you have ever shewed y^{r}selfe a friend in so many instances, that I presume upon y^r compassion; nothing but this just occasion could have hindered me from well-coming you to towne, and rejoyceing with the best friend I have in the world—a friend by merit and inclination, one I must esteeme as the wife of so worthy a relation and so sincere a friend as Sr Sam: (Tuke) was to me and mine. What is this world, when we recall past things! what are the charms that keep our minds in suspence! without the conversation of those we love, what is life worth! How did I propose happinesse this sum'er in the returne of y^r L^p and my deare child—for she was absent almost all this winter!

She had much improved her selfe by the remarks she had made of the world and all its vanities— What shall I add! I could ever speake of her, and might I be just to her without suspition of partiality, could tell you many things. The papers which are found in her cabinet discover she profited by her readyng—such reflections, collections out of Scripture, confessions, meditations, and pious notions, evidence her time was not spent in the trifling way of most young women. I acknowledge, as a Christian, I ought not to murmur, and I should be infinitly sorry to incur God's further displeasure. There are those yet remaining that challenge my care, and for their sakes I endeavour to submitt all I can. I thank my poore Cousen a thousand times for her kind concerne, and wishe she may live to be the comfort you deserve in her, that God will con-

tinue the blessing to both, and make you happy—
which is the prayer of her who is

   Y^{rs} most affectionately,

         M. E.

Mrs. Evelyn to her Son.

I haue received y^r letter, and request for a supply of mony; but none of those you mention which were bare effects of y^r duty. If you were so desirous to answer our expectations as you pretend to be, you would give those tutors and overseers you think so exact over you lesse trouble then I feare they have with you. Much is to be wished in yor behalfe: that y^r temper were humble and tractable, y^r inclinations virtuous, and that from choice not compulsion you make an honnest man. Whateuer object of vice comes before you, should haue the same effect in y^r mind of dislike and aversion that drunkenesse had in the youth of Sparta when their slaves were presented to them in that brutish condition, not only from the deformity of such a sight, but from a motive beyond theirs, the hope of a future happinesse, which those rigorous heathens in morall virtue had little prospect of, finding no reward for virtue but in virtue itselfe. You are not too young to know that lying, defrauding, swearing, disobedience to parents and persons in authority, are offences to God and man: that debauchery is injurious to growth, health, life, and indeed to the pleasures of life: therefore now that you are turning from child to man endeavour to follow the best precepts, and chuse such wayes as may render you worthy of praise and love. You are assured of y^r Fathers care and my tendernesse: no mark of it shall be wanting at any time to confirme it to you, with this reserve only, that you strive to deserve kindnesse by a sincere honest proceeding, and not flatter y^r selfe that you are good whilst you only appear to be so. Fallacies will only passe in schools. When you throughly weigh these considerations, I hope you will apply them to your owne advantage, as well as to our infinite satisfaction. I pray dayly God would inspire you with his grace, and blesse you.

   I am,
    Y^r louing mother,
     M. EVELYN.

Mrs. Evelyn (who outlived Mr. Evelyn) by her will, dated 9 Feb. 1708, desired to be buried in a stone coffin near that of " my dear husband, whose love & friendship I was happy in 58 years 9 months, but by Gods Providence left a disconsolate widow the 27 day of February, 1705, in the 71st year of my age. His care of my education was such as might become a father, a lover, a friend, and husband, for instruction, tenderness, affection & fidelity to the last moment of his life; which obligation I mention with a gratitude to his memory, ever dear to me; & I must not omit to own the sense I have of my Parents care & goodnesse in placing me in such worthy hands."

INDEX

TO THE

DIARY AND LETTERS

CONTAINED IN THE

FIRST FOUR VOLUMES.

Where the letter n *is attached to a figure, the passage will be found in a note on the page referred to.*

ABBEVILLE, notice of, i 58.
Abbot, Dr. George, Archbishop of Canterbury, his Hospital, ii. 65. family of, iv. 347. portrait of, 307.
―――― Mr. an eminent Scrivener, ii. 435 n. condemned as a loyalist, iii. 17, 18.
Abdy, Mr. i. 348.
Abell, John, his counter-tenor voice, iii. 61.
Abingdon, Montague Bertie, Earl of, Lieutenant of the Tower, displaced, iii. 408.
Academies at Richelieu, i. 111. at Paris, ii. 19.
Acetaria, 1699, by Mr. Evelyn, iii. 374, 432, 435, 440.
Acoustics, &c. letter on, iv. 203, 204.
Act at Oxford, 1654, ii. 72, 73. 1664, 224. 1669, 312—315.
Acts, of the Apostles, MS. of, i. 219. of the Council of Basil, ii. 74.
Addresses to the King, origin of, iii. 362.
Adriatic Gulph, notice of the, i. 309.
ADSCOMB, Surrey, Mr. Draper's house at, iii. 378, 379, 395, 400.
Adventures of Five Hours, a Play, 1662, ii 205, 206, 207.
Æmiliana, Margaret, i. 337.
Ætna, Mount, eruption of, 1669, ii. 150 n. 318.
Agates, &c. curious, i. 61, 130, 339. ii. 98, 100.
Agrippina, Julia, mother of Nero, her Sepulchre, i. 251.
Ague, cure for the, iii. 62.
Aid, Royal, distribution of, 1665, iv. 162, 163.
Air, excellence of the Italian, i. 127. experiment on, ii. 189.
Aitzema, Leo D', his *History of the United Provinces*, 1657, i 21 n.
Aix, in Provence, account of, i. 120, 121.
Albano, tombs of the Horatii and Curiatii at, i. 255.
Albemarle, George Monk, Duke of, various references to, ii. 184' 208, 213, 226, 231, 235, 239, 240, 241, 244, 246, 247, 248, 251, 252, 280, 287, 289 and n, 369 *bis*. iii. 51, 72, 96. stays in London during the plague, 1665, ii. 255. appointed General at Sea, &c. 248. his victory over the Dutch fleet, 255, 256, 257. share of a Spanish Galleon, 1687, iii. 231. trials respecting an estate left by, 328, 354, 392. portrait of, iv. 306.
―――――― *See* Keppel, iii. 368 n.
―――――― Street, notice of, ii. 280 and n.
Albert Eremitano, bust of, i. 333.
Alberti, Cherubino, paintings by, i. 218.

INDEX.

ALBURY, Surrey, villa of Mr. Howard, referred to, i. 393. ii. 6, 102, 193. the grounds improved by Mr. Evelyn, ii. 296, 331 bought by Mr. Solicitor Finch, 1687, iii. 233. Mr. Evelyn desirous of possessing, 1657, iv. 5 & n.
Alchemist, a pretended one at Paris, 1650, ii. 28, 33 n. stories of an, 45.
Aldobrandini, Cardinal Pietro, i. 282, 283.
Alessandro, Signor, musician, i. 209, ii. 16.
Alexander III., Pope, (Roland, Bishop of Sienna), i. 317. painting respecting, 214.
——————— VII., Pope, Fabio Chigbi, his intrigues with the Queen of Sweden, iii. 38.
Algardi, Alessandro, architect, i. 228.
Al Koraun, written on a sheet of calico, ii. 75.
Allegri, Antonio da Corregio, paintings by, i. 81, 142, 207, 256, ii. 200, iii. 351. sum paid for a Venus by iii. 326.
Allen, Capt. Sir Thomas, ii. 236, 237 n, 239, 344.
Allestree, Dr. Richard, Dean of Westminster, ii. 160, 173, 314, 315. sermons of, 405. iii. 19.
Alleyn, Edward, College at Dulwich founded by, ii. 412.
Allington, William, Lord, ii 342. his house at Horseheath, 325, & n.
——————, Rev. John, preaches against regicides, ii. 93.
Allix, Dr. Peter, account of, iii. 192 & n. 212.
All Souls' College, Oxford, painting in the chapel of, ii. 224.
Allybone, Sir Richard, Justice of the King's Bench, a Papist, iii. 245.
Alois, Planta, its peculiarities, iv. 196.
Alps, journey over the, 1646, i. 366—374.
Alstedius, John Henry, referred to, ii. 34, 220. iii. 333.
Alston, Dr., President of the College of Physicians, 1664, ii. 220.
Althorp, Northamptonshire, seat of Lord Sunderland, ii. 409. iii. 247, 250, 346. earthquake at, iii. 300.
Amazons in Persia, iii. 33.
Ambassadors, *see* Embassies, encounter for precedency between the French and Spanish, 1661, ii. 177, 178. iii. 438. narrative by Mr. Evelyn, vindicating the King and his servants, 179 n. reprint of, 457—464.
Amber, spider, &c. enclosed in, iii. 65.
Amboise, Castle of, i. 105, 106.——Cardinal George D', his tomb, 88, 120
Ambrose, St., quoted, iv. 43.
Ambrosian library at Milan, i. 359, 360.
Ammanati, Vincenzo, architecture of, i. 267.
Amphitheatre at Venice, i. 118. at Perigueux, 123. of Vespasian, 179, at Verona, 351.
AMSTERDAM, account of, 1641, i. 27—32.
Anabaptists, their objection to oaths, ii. 125. increase of, 126.
Anatomy, school of, at Leyden, i. 34. at Padua, 334, 343. at Oxford, ii. 75.
Anchor, method of casting in Acts, xxvii. 29, illustrated, iii. 116.
Anchorite of Mount Calvary at Paris, ii. 13.
Anderson, Sir Richard, iii. 40, 80.
Andoyne, Abbot of, i. 50.
Andrews, Dr. Launcelot, Bishop of Winchester, ii. 96. iii. 5, 8, 90.
Angelico, an apothecary at Vincenza, i. 350.
Angeloni, Signor, his medals, &c. i. 171, 256.
Anglesea, Arthur Annesley, Earl of, Viscount Valentia, ii. 165, 304.
Anio, cascade of the, i. 286.
Anjou, Gasto Jean-Baptiste, Duke of, performs in an Opera, 1651, ii. 32. his embassy to Charles II., 154.

INDEX. 447

Anne, of Denmark, Princess, afterwards Queen, iii. 178 n. 158, 240, 265, 270, 284, 343. her marriage, 92 bis. refuses to dismiss Lady Marlborough, 314. William III. reconciled to, 338. entertained, when Queen, at Oxford, &c. 395. goes in procession to St. Paul's Cathedral, 397, 403, 404.

Annunciada——Annunciata, churches of, i. 132, 145, 295.
Antenor, founder of Padua, inscriptions to, i. 326.
Antibes, i. 124.
Antichrist, final destruction of, iii. 280.
Antoninus, Marcus Aurelinus, Emperor of Rome, his Baths, i. 259. column of, 265. his palace, 266.
Antonio, Marco, singer, i. 288.——an enameller, &c. at Paris, ii. 45.
ANTWERP, account of, 1641, i. 41—45.
Apennines, passage over the, 1645, i. 302.
Apiaries, transparent, notice of, ii. 76.
Apollo, Temples of, i. 249, 250.
Apology for the Royal Party, 1659, by Mr. Evelyn, ii. 142. iii. 431, 438.
Aponius, Peter, bust of, at Padua, i. 333.
Appian Way, its extent, &c. i. 230, 232.
Appii Forum, etched by Mr. Evelyn, iii. 431.
Aqua Claudia, i. 275.
Aqua Paula, fountain of, i. 228.
Aquapendente, town of, i. 153.
Arabian horses, account of some, iii. 123, 124.
Ara, Cœli, church of at Rome, i. 164, 212.
Arc, Joan of, her statue, i. 100.
Archæologia, cited, ii. 419 n. iii. 102.
Architects in Rome, 1645, i. 288.
Architecture, Parallel between Ancient and Modern, 1664, by Mr. Evelyn, ii. 221 & n, 225, 227. iii. 431. iv. 333. his directions for reprinting it, iv. 372, 373. M. D'Aviler's work on, 373—375.
Arconati, Cavaliero Galeazzo, his gift to the Ambrosian library, i. 360.
Aretino, Pietro, epigram on, i. 332 n.
Argyle, Archibald Campbell, Marquis of, ii. 112, 118. his son, 189. his rebellion, iii. 159. executed, 163.
ARLINGTON, Sir Henry Bennett, Earl of, Secretary of State, various references to, ii. 178, 180, bis, 188, 216, 226, 236, 238, 251, 260, 280, 289, 290, 292, 309, 310, 311, 322, 325, 329, 333, 338, 341, 342, 345, 347, 349, bis, 362, 371, 372, 378 n. 379, 381, 383, 386, 387, 394. iii. 102. iv. 218, 220. Lord Chamberlain, ii. 419, 421, 422, 426, 433. iii. 15, 16, 101, 140. disappointment of being Lord Treasurer, ii. 360, 361 n. mulberry garden granted to, 69 n. his daughter, 373, iii. 16. Goring House burned, ii. 397. his pictures, 424. rebuilt Euston church and parsonage, 427. his seat at Euston, 428—431. life and character, 431—433. died a Roman Catholic, iii. 181.

——————— Countess of, ii. 381. iii. 82, 99, 201, 219.

——————— House and Street, in London, historical notice of, ii. 236 n. iii. 30.

Armourer, Sir James and Sir Nicholas, ii. 290, 291.
Armoury at Genoa, i. 131. the Pope's in the Vatican, 220. at Florence, 297.
Armstrong, Sir Thomas, iii. 86. his execution, &c. 117, 118 & n, 350 and n.
Army, Rebel, 1648, i. 391, 393. expels the Parliament, ii. 142. Parliament's firmness in limiting the, iii. 367.
Arno, notice of the River, i. 137, 139.
Arnold, Michael, a brewer, against the seven bishops, 1688, iii. 245.

INDEX.

Arpino, *see* Cesari.
Arran, James Hamilton, Earl of, iii. 72, 175, 176. his marriage, 236, 250.
———— Lady Anne Spencer, Countess of, her death, iv. 328.
Arsenal at Florence, i. 300. at Venice, 328. at Geneva, 386.
Arundel and Surrey, Thomas Howard, Earl of, Earl Marshal, i. 19, 37, 48, 50, 51, 52, 260, 325, 346, 353, 360. his last sickness, &c. 346 and n. medals, &c. of, iv. 304.
———————— Henry Frederick Howard, Earl of, and Eliz. Stuart, his Countess, 1649, i. 393. ii. 8.
Arundel and Surrey, Henry Howard, Lord, married to Lady Mary Mordaunt, 1677, ii. 426. alluded to, 1680, iii. 46.
———————— Earl of, Manor of Worksop belonging to, ii. 88.
———— of Wardour, Lord, 1660, ii. 144. 1664—85, ii. 216, 341, 347. iii. 127, 143, 161. 1687, Privy Seal, iii. 223.
———— House, various references to, ii. 120, 181, 183, 185, 193, 208, 281, 286, 299, 391 and n, 444. *See also* Howard *and* Norfolk.
———— Street, notice of, ii. 392 n.
Arundelian Library, procured for the Royal Society by Mr. Evelyn, ii. 281, 445, 446.
——————— Marbles, procured by Mr. Evelyn for the University of Oxford, ii. 295, 296, 315.
Ascension-day, ceremony on at Venice, i. 311. sports of Ascension-week, 321.
Ashburnham, Mr. ii. 294.
Ashley, Sir Anthony Ashley Cooper, Lord, 1671—72, ii. 342, 361.
Ashmole, Elias, Windsor Herald, ii. 105, 124, 135. iii. 57 n, 166. his library, museum, portrait, and collection of coins, ii. 124 and n, 135, 441 and n, iv. 304.
ASHTED, Surrey, seat of Sir Robert Howard at, iii. 114, 115.
Ashton, John, executed, 1691, iii. 302.
Ashurst, Sir Henry, iii. 352.
———— Sir William, a subscriber, &c. to Greenwich Hospital, iii. 355 n, 357 n.
Ash-Wednesday, observance of neglected in England, ii. 67, 68.
Atkins, Sir Jonathan, ii. 391.
———— Sir Robert, Puisne Justice of the Common Pleas, ii. 12 n. iii. 235 n.
Atterbury, Dr. Francis, Bishop of Rochester, iii. 390 and n.
Attornies, number of reduced, iii. 378.
Atwood, Mr. iii. 235 n.
Aubigny, Lord, Almoner to the Queen, ii. 43, 185, 186, 216. his character, 185.
Aubrey, John, his *History of Surrey* referred to, 290, 291 n.
AUDLEY-END, Essex, Palace of the Earl of Suffolk, ii. 97, 327, 433. iii. 97 n.
Avernus, Lake, at Naples, i. 249.
Auger, Sir Anthony, ii. 291.
Augustine, St. D. Aurelius, citation from iv. 42, 43.
Augustus Octavianus Cæsar, Emperor of Rome, his aqueduct, i. 228. Temple of, at Puteoli, 247. Obelisk of, 269. his Mausoleum at Rome, *ib.*
Aviaries and Menageries, notices of various, i. 43, 47, 48, 85, 131, 172, 181, 275, 280, 285, 336. ii. 69, 112, 233, 234.
AVIGNON, account of, i. 119.
Aungier, Lord, ii. 98, 440.
Aurelius, Marcus, equestrian statue of, i. 161.
Aurum Potabile, prepared by M. Roupel, ii. 65.
Austen, Col. a subscriber to Greenwich Hospital, iii. 356 n.

INDEX. 449

Axtell, Daniel, Regicide, executed, ii. 156.
Aylesbury, Robert Bruce, Earl of, iii. 72, 263.
Ayliffe, Capt. ii. 237 n.
Ayscue, Sir George, captured by the Dutch, ii. 256.

Backhouse, Sir William, iii. 187 n. iv. 154 n.
Bacon, Sir Edward, ii. 427.
——— Sir Francis, Viscount St. Alban, various references to, i. 131. ii. 217, 222. iv. 300, 306.
——— Dr. at Rome, i. 156.
Bacula, Treatises concerning, iii. 432 n. iv. 213—216, 247.
Baden, Louis-Guillaume, Prince of, in London 1694, iii. 328.
Baglione, Cavaliere Giovanni, paintings by, i. 159, 262.
Bagni di Tritoli, i. 250.
Bagnios at Venice, i. 310.
Baiæ of the Romans, i. 242, 248, 251—253.
Baker, Mr. his house, on Epping Forest, ii. 318. iii. 77.
——— Capt. attempted the North-West Passage, ii. 421.
——— George, his *History of Northamptonshire* cited, ii. 413 n.
——— Sir Richard, his *Chronicle* referred to, iii. 416, 417.
Baldarius, Andrea, i. 332.
Baldassare. *See* Peruzzi.
Baldero, Dr. Sermon of, ii. 162.
Ball, Sir Peter, ii. 186.
Ballard, George, his *Memoirs of Learned Ladies* referred to, ii. 308 n.
Balle, Dr. Peter, his gift to the Royal Society, ii. 214.
Balls Park, Hertfordshire, i. 54 n
Banbury, Nicholas Knollys, Earl of, 1645, robbed in Italy, i. 229.
Bancroft, Dr. Richard, Archbishop of Canterbury, his library, ii. 96.
Bandinelli, Baccio, productions of, i. 141, 145, 146, 296.
Banditti in Italy, i. 229, 354. in France, ii. 32.
Bank, for the poor in Padua, i. 334. of England established, 1694, iii. 332, 335, 358.
Banks, Sir John, an opulent merchant, ii. 421.
Banquetting-house, touching for the Evil at the, ii. 151. creation of Peers there, 165. lottery held there, 219. auction of pictures at the, iii. 324.
Bansted, Surrey, Roman medals, &c. found near, ii. 137.
Baptism of a Turk and a Jew, i. 270. private, censured, iii. 278.
Baptist, Signor Giovanni, musician, iii. 118, 127.
Baptistery of San Giovanni, i. 136. of St. John Baptist, 193.
Bar, defects in educating for the, iv. 391, 292.
Baratarius, Nicholas, architect, i. 320.
Barbadoes, ii. 193, 242. conspiracy of Negroes at, 1693, iii. 321. trees, plants, &c. there, iv. 254, 354, 365.
Barberini, Cardinal Francesco, his courtesy to the English, i. 193, 281.
———Palazzo, i. 165, 263.
Barclay, John, his *Icon Animarum*, 1614, ii. 60, & n. 307 n.
———- Lord George, mechanical occupations of, iv. 158.
Bargrave, Dr. Isaac, Dean of Canterbury, ii. 366.
Barill, Mr. i. 391.
Barillon, Mons. French Ambassador, 1685, iii. 197.
Barlæus, Gaspar, *Historia Rerum in Brasilia*, 1647, iv. 254.
Barlow, Dr. Thomas, Bishop of Lincoln, ii. 74, 223, 233, 297 *bis*, 299, 315, 407. iv. 121.

VOL. IV.   2 G

Barlow, Francis, painter, notices of, ii. 109. iii. 53. iv. 30 n. letter to Mr. Evelyn on dedicating a plate to him, iv. 30. answer to do. 31.
—————, Mrs. alias Walters, various notices of, ii. 11. iii. 168, 169 n.
Barnaby, Mr. iv. 395.
Baron, Bernard, engraving from Titian by, ii. 134 n.
Baronius, Cæsar, his sepulchre, i. 168.
Barrow, Dr. Isaac, Bishop of Chester, sermon by, ii. 405 & n.
Bartholomew Fair, 1648, i. 392.
Bartolomeo. See Porta.
—————, Signor, musician, iii. 18, 62, 143.
Barton, Mr. John, his death, ii. 64. referred to, iv. 5.
Basil, Council of, original acts of the, ii. 74.
Basilisco at Ghent, i. 49.
Basire, Dr. Isaac, ii. 181, 200.
Bassano. See Ponte.
—————. Domenico, and his daughter, musicians, i. 341.
—————. Veronese, paintings of, i. 207.
Bassompiére, Francois de, his palace, i. 62.
Bastille at Paris, i. 71.
Bath, visit to, 1654, ii. 71.
——— John Grenville, Earl of, various references to, ii 165, 420, 437. iii. 73, 82, 131 and n, 140, 160, 234. trial with, concerning an estate left by the Duke of Albemarle, iii. 328, 354, 392. his death, 392.
Bath, Knights of the, ceremonies of their creation, 1661, ii. 164, 165.
Bathurst, Dr. Ralph, Dean of Wells, ii. 253, 281, 296, 401 n, 418. iv. 190, 432 and n. his death, iii. 403.
——————— Mr. a merchant, ii. 406.
Bauli, notice of, i. 251.
Bayley, Dr. Vice-Chancellor of Oxford, 1636, iii. 413.
BAYNARDS, at Ewhurst, Surrey, i. 391. described, ii. 121 and n.
Baynton, Sir Edward, his house at Spy Park, ii. 78.
Baxter, Lieutenant of the Tower, 1657, iv. 38 n.
Beach, Sir R. iii. 180.
Beale, Dr. letters of Mr. Evelyn to, on his *Acetaria*, and Hortulan collections, iii. 432—434. On philosophical subjects, and the means used for preserving his health, iv. 198—205.
Bear-garden, sports at the, 1670, ii. 322.
Beauchamp, Lady, ii. 105.
Beaufort, Henry Somerset, first Duke of, his house at Chelsea, iii. 3 n, 93. death of, 377 and n. his family, 77, 190.
Beaugensier, notices of, iv. 34 and n.
Beaumont, Francis, iv. 307.
Beauvais, town of, i. 58.
Becher, Mr. ii. 302, 293.
Beckford, Lady, iii. 23, 48.
Bede, Venerable, MS. of in the Bodleian Library, ii. 74.
BEDDINGTON, seat of the Carews, i. 9. ii. 136. iii 384 and n.
Bedford, William Russell, Earl of, ii. 165, 303. iii. 85, 127.
——————— House, Bloomsbury, ii. 233 n.
Bedloe, William, a witness against Sir George Wakeman, iii. 10.
Bedsteads, splendid ones noticed, i. 130, 170, 340. ii. 192.
Belin, Mr. ii. 221.
Bella, Stephano della, engraver, ii. 17.
Bellarmin, Cardinal Robert, his sepulchre, i. 166.
Bellasis, Henry Lord, ii. 207, 225, 303. iii. 221.

Bellcar, pictures possessed by, ii. 4.
Belle Cour at Lyons, i. 117.
Bellini, Giovanni, master of Titian, his portrait, ii. 158.
Bells, various notices of, i. 31, 32, 88. ii. 91.
Bellsize House, Hampstead, notice of, ii. 218 n.
Belluccio, Dr. of Sienna, i. 292.
Belvidere Gardens, i. 221.
Belvoir Castle, Lincolnshire, ii. 86.
Bembo, Cardinal Pietro, i. 271.
Benbow, John, Admiral, iii. 353, 360 n. his gallantry and death, 397.
Benedict VII. Pope, i. 273.
Benetti, an artist in *Pietra Comessa*, i. 143, 300.
Benevento, statue by, i. 145.
Benlowes, Edward, references to, and notice of, ii. 94 and n.
Bennett, Mrs. sister to Lord Arlington, ii. 216.
Bentivoglio, Cardinal Guido, his gardens, &c. i. 272. Castle Bentivoglio, 308.
Bentley, Dr. Richard, various references to, iii. 7 n, 329, 338, 360 n, 363. iv. 350, 375, 385, 400. delivers the Boyle lectures, iii. 315, 320, 327, 328, 329. letters of Mr. Evelyn to, concerning a new edition of the *Sylva*, iv. 379. on the library in St. James's Park, 380.
——— Mr. a bookseller, 1697, iv. 379.
Bergamo, Damiano di, inlaying by, i. 303.
Bergen-op-zoom, i. 40.
Berkeley, George first Earl of, various references to, ii. 136, 140, 141, 147, 198, 214, 260 bis, 385, 398 iii. 67, 90. ambassador to France for the treaty of Nimeguen, ii. 413, 418. seized with apoplexy, *ibid.* sets out for France, 415, 416. commits his affairs to Mr. Evelyn, 414, 415, 417, 421, 425.
——— of Stratton, John, Lord, his house in London, ii. 373, 374.
——— Lord, bombards Dieppe and Havre, 1694, iii. 335.
——— Lady, property of, from Berkeley Gardens, iii. 117.
——— Sir Robert, Puisne Justice of the King's Bench, his portrait, iv. 306. grandson of, ii. 102.
——— Sir Charles, ii. 177, 178, 207.
——— Mr. (son of Lord Berkeley) ii. 109, 110. iv. 16 n.
——— House, described, ii. 255, 374, 375 and n. gardens of, built over, iii. 117. residence of Princess Anne, 1696, 338.
Berkeley Castle East Indiaman sunk, iii. 330.
Berkenshaw, Mr. musician, ii. 219.
Berkshire, Charles Howard, Earl of, i. 311, 411. iii. 139.
Berkshire, or Cleveland House, ii. 280 and n.
Bernini, Giovanni Lorenzo, sculptor and architect, i. 288. works of, 165, 170, 189, 192, 260, 296. ii. 14. instance of his various talents, 189.
Bertie, Mr. ii. 256.
Berwick, James Fitz-James, Duke of, engaged in the conspiracy, 1696, iii. 348.
Bestland, Cantlo, engraving by, iii. 323 n.
Betchworth Castle, ii. 98.
Betterton, Thomas, his theatre in Dorset Gardens, ii. 334 n.
Beveridge, Dr. William, anecdote of, iii. 304.
Beverley, notice of the town of, ii. 290.
Bianchi, a singer in Rome, i. 288.
Bible, English MS. in the Bodleian Library, Oxford, ii. 74. various versions of the, 103.

Biblia Polyglotta, by Bishop Walton, ii. 62.
Bickerstaff, Sir Charles, purchases Pilton, iii. 116.
Bickerton, Mrs. Jane, daughter of Sir Robert, notices of, ii. 352 and n, 438 n, 442 n.
Biddulph, Sir Theophilus, ii. 205.
Bie, Jacques de, and Sieur de Bizot, their *Histoire Metallique*, iv. 366.
Billiards, Portuguese manner of playing, iii. 21.
Bills, Parliamentary, tacked to Money Bill, contested, iii. 380.
Bindley, Mr. James, ii. 179 n.
Biographia Britannica, referred to, i. *Introd.* ii. 40 n, 230 n. iii. 114 n, 293 n, 405 n, 435 n.
Biographia Dramatica, referred to, ii. 140 n.
Birch, Dr. ———, sermon by against Papists, iii. 219.
Birds, Royal Collection of in St. James's Park, ii. 233.
Birkenhead, John, his reply to the Jesuits, iv. 15.
Biron, Sir John, first Lord, ii. 45. family seat at Newstead Abbey, 88.
Bishops, inattentive to the Church at the Restoration, ii. 362. the six Bishops petition James II. against his declaration for liberty of conscience, iii. 242, 243. sent to the Tower, 243, 244. trial of, 244, 245. called upon to reconcile matters on the expected invasion, 1688, 253. the Bishops and Convocation at variance, 1701, 390.
Blackheath, camp at, 1673, ii. 382, 383. 1685, iii. 170. 1690, 298. fair on, 1683, iii. 79.
Blacksmiths, ingenious works of, ii 78.
Blackwall, Dr. Boyle Lecturer, iii. 375.
Blaew, William Jansen, i. 32.
Blague, or Blagg, Mrs. ii. 311, 372, 400, *bis*. marriage of, 406, 446, 447, 448. *See* Godolphin.
Blandford, Dr. Walter, Bishop of Worcester, ii. 375.
Blathwaite, Mr. Secretary at War, &c. iii. 233.
Blechingly, Surrey, house of Henry VIII. at ii. 103. sale of the manor of, 425.
Blenheim, thanksgiving for the victory of, iii. 403 and n.
Blois, notice of the town, &c. of, i. 102, 103.
Blood, Colonel, account of, ii. 340.
Bloomsbury-square, building of, ii. 233. Montague House erected in, 419. iii. 16, 201.
Blount, Sir Henry, ii. 141.
——— Col. ii. 57, 105, 110, 122, 141.
Bohart, acob, a botanist, and a descendant of, ii. 224 and n.
Bodleian Library, Oxford, curiosities of the, ii. 74.
Boet, Dr. ii. 28.
Boggi, a sculptor, i. 190.
Bohemia, Elizabeth, Queen of, i. 22. her funeral, ii. 188 and n.
Bohun, Dr. Ralph, tutor to Mr. Evelyn's son, ii. 244, 281, 333. letter to by Mr. Evelyn, iii. 359 n. living presented to him, iii. 388. Dr. Bathurst's legacy to, 403. character of Mrs. Evelyn by, i. *Introd.* iv. 423—429. notice of, 423 n. sermon by, ii. 425. letters of Mrs. Evelyn to, iv. 430, 432, 433, 436, 437.
——— Mr. his house and garden at Lea in Surrey, iii. 14, 69, 70, 94.
Bois-de-Boulogne, muster of gens d'armes in the, i. 98. referred to, ii. 17.
Bois-de-Vinciennes, Palace of, i. 71, 72. ii. 16.
Bois-le-Duc, Fortifications, &c. of, i. 37.
BOLOGNA, descriptive account of, i. 303—307. Torre d'Assinello and

INDEX. 453

Churches, 303. Palace of the Legate, 304. Dr. Montalbano, St. Michel in Bosco, 305. religious houses, &c. 306. observations on, 307.
Bologna Baldassa di, painting by, i. 173.
—————— Giovanni di, sculptures of, i. 63, 144, 145, 146.
Bolognesi, Giovanni Francesco, Grimaldi, called Il Bolognesi, painting by, i. 263.
Bolsena, Lake of, i. 153.
Bolton, Dr. his Consecration Sermon, ii. 203.
Bombardment, a cruel species of warfare, iii. 344, 345.
Bombs, experiments made upon, iii. 226.
Bommell, Town of, i. 25.
Bond, Sir Thomas, his house at Peckham, ii. 420. iii. 54.
Bonifacio, Father, at Venice, i. 345.
Bonnes Hommes, Convent of at Paris, i. 80. ii. 28.
Books, various particulars concerning, i. 14 and n, 60, 219 n, 386. ii. 74, 75, 76, 90, 94, 218, 445.
Booksellers, at Geneva, i. 382. loss of, by the Fire of London, iv. 178; their editions of the classics censured, 181.
Boord, Mad. de, censures the carving of Gibbon, ii. 338, 339.
Booth, Sir George, created Lord Delamere, ii 166.
—————— Mr. ii. 23.
Borell, Peter, work of referred to, iv. 34.
Boreman, Sir William, Clerk of Green Cloth, iii. 197.
Borghese, Cardinal Scipio, houses of, i. 207, 283.
Borghesi, Villa, i. 181—183, 280.
Borromean Islands, i. 367 n.
Borromeo, Cardinals St. Charles and Frederick, ii. 395. burial-place, i. 356. munificence of, 358, 359.
Boscawen, Mr. iii. 171. his daughter, 358, 391.
—————— Mrs. ii. 446.
Bosio, Antonio, his *Roma Sotterranea*, 1632, i. 278.
Boucharvant, Abbess of, ii. 33.
Bouillon, Duke and Duchess of, i. 274.
Boulogne, account of, i. 57.
Bourbon, L'Archambaut, i. 115.
Bourdon, Sebastian, his portrait of Mrs. Evelyn, ii. 6, 48, 51.
BOURGES, account of, i. 113.
Bowles, Sir John, iii. 104.
Bowyer, Sir Edward, ii 291. his seat at Camberwell, 123.
Boyle, Richard, First Earl of Cork, ii. 221. iv. 358. anecdotes of, 412, 413.
BOYLE, HON. ROBERT, various references to, ii. 110, 141, 163, 189, 193, 223, 417, iii. 256, 296, 313, 320. iv. 16 n, 404, 405, 434. experiment by, ii. 189. elected President of the Royal Society, iii. 40. letters of Mr. Evelyn to, on his *History of Trades*, and Ray's work on Flowers, iii. 434, 435. enclosing certain Treatises of Arts, iv. 47—49. on Essences of Roses, 74—76. on his works on Gardening, 80—82. on a plan for a Mathematical College, 82—90. on Mr. Boyle's *Seraphic Love*, 90—98. on a varnish and books of Mr. Boyle's, 107. on several new publications, 119. his death, and Bishop Burnet's funeral sermon, iii. 311. particulars of him, communicated from Mr. Evelyn to Mr. Wotton, iv. 352—362, 363, 385, 386, 397, 399, 401—408, 411.
—————— Mr. killed in a sea-fight, iv. 240.
Boyle Lecture, various notices of the, iii. 315, 320, 327, 328, 338, 347, 352, 375.

Boyne, battle of the, iii. 297, 299.
Bracciano, Duke di, his house, i. 210.
Bradshaw, George, of Balliol College Oxford, i. 13.
—— ——, John, (Regicide) i. 13, ii. 3, 9, 24 n, 58.
Bramante. *See* Lazzori.
Bramhall, Dr. John, Archbishop of Armagh, ii. 153, iii. 206.
Bramstone, Francis, Baron of the Exchequer, iv. 306. his son, i. 338, 341. ii. 303.
Brandenburgh, Duke of, his present to the Royal Society, 1682, iii. 65. to the Queen, 1693, 325, 326.
Brandon, Lord, Charles Gerard, trial and pardon of, iii. 195.
—————— Charles, Duke of Suffolk, painting of, ii. 442.
Bray, Sir Edward, ii. 121.
—————— William, F. S. A. *History of Surrey* referred to, ii. 5 n, 222 n, 279 n, 291 n. iii. 54 n, 126 n, 153 n, 207 n, 235 n, 285 n, 321 n, 377 n. iv. 419 n, 439 n. great age of, iv. 200 n.
Brazen Tables at Lyons, i. 117.
Breakwater at Plymouth, i. 132 n.
Breames, Sir Richard, ii. 279.
Breda, ship of war, blown up, iii. 300.
Brederode, family of, i. 37. ii. 431.
Brenta, fine country on its banks, i. 335.
Brentford, battle of, i 53.
—————, Lord, ii. 290.
Brereton, Mr. —————— son of Lord Brereton, ii. 141.
Brescia, account of, i. 349, 354.
Bret, Colonel, iii. 55.
Bretagne language, its great resemblance to the Welsh, ii. 407.
—————— Dr. John, sermon by, ii. 319.
Breton, Mr. Vicar of Wotton, sermons by ii. 181. his death, funeral sermon, and Mr. Evelyn's regret for, 358, 359. iv. 438.
Brett, Sir Edward, ii. 247.
Brevell, Mons. ii. 357.
Brevent, Dr. —————— Dean of Durham, ii. 20.
Breughel, Peter, (called the Old) painting by, i. 47. ii. 318.
—————— John, (called Velvet Breughel) i. 47, 359, 391. ii. 4.
Brick-Close, Deptford, granted to Mr. Evelyn, ii. 303.
Brideoak, Dr. Ralph, Bishop of Chichester, ii. 405, 417.
Bridgeman, Sir Orlando, ii. 342, 376, 421. iii. 161. iv. 306.
—————— Mr. Clerk of the Council, his death, iii. 370.
—————— Mrs. iii. 108.
Bridges, various particulars concerning, i. 63, 64, 83, 87, 88, 91, 113, 116, 119, 137, 139, 150, 153, 239, 248, 275, 284, 351, 369, 385, 387, ii. 22, 89.
Bridgewater, Francis Egerton, Duke of, his improvements, ii. 301 n.
Brightman, Thomas, an expounder of the Revelation, iii. 297.
Brill, Paul, paintings of, i. 81, 200, 218.
Briloft, curious mechanism at the, i. 30.
Brindley, James, Engineer, notice of ii. 301 n.
Brisbane, Mr. —————— Secretary to the Admiralty, 1681, iii. 49, 102.
Bristol, ii. 71. St. Vincent's Rock at, 72.
—————— George Digby, Earl of, ii. 180, 186, 191. iv. 306. his house and library at Wimbledon, 188, 437, 439. house of, in Queen-street, 342.
—————— Countess of, iii. 93, 249. her house at Chelsea, iii. 3, 6, 17, 93.
Brochi, Vincentio, Sculptor, i. 300.

INDEX. 455

Brodrick, Sir Alan, ii. 403. iv. 410.
Broghill, Richard Lord, Plays by, ii. 236, 276 and n.
Bromley, Mr. John, his house at Horseheath, ii. 325 n.
Brompton Park, rare plants in, iii. 331.
Bronzine, Agnolo, paintings by, i. 143, 299.
Brooke, Francis Greville, Lord, his house at Warwick, ii. 83.
——— Lady, her garden at Hackney, ii. 68.
——— Seat of Lady Camden, ii. 86.
Brooks, W. architect of the London Institution, ii. 375 n.
Broomfield and Deptford, Kentish loyalists meet in, i. 392.
Brounker, William, Viscount, First President of the Royal Society, ii. 172, 197 bis. 215, 426, 437. iii. 239. iv. 355.
———Mr. Henry, ii. 342. iii. 37. his house at Sheen, 444.
Brown, ———, detained in Holland, iv. 272.
——— Sir Adam, of Betchworth, iii. 5, 153 bis. 398 n.
——— Sir Ambrose, of Betchworth, ii. 98, 135.
——— Sir Richard, temp. Elizabeth and James I. iii. 75.
BROWNE, SIR RI^CHARD, Ambassador to France, father-in-law of Mr. Evelyn, various references to, i. 62, 389 bis. ii. 6, 14, 17, 18, 19, 20, 21 n, 31, 38, 42 and n, 47, 49, 60, 61, 149 bis. 158 n, 159, 302, 338, 341, 390, 406, 407. his support of the church while abroad, 20, 40 n, 149. iii. 75. disappointed of the wardenship of Merton College, Oxford, ii. 163. resigns the clerkship of Council, 357. master of the Trinity House, 379. his death and funeral, iii. 74. eulogium on, 74—76. debts owing to, from the Crown, 230. dispatches of, iv. 261. letter of Mr. Evelyn to, on the death of his son, 59—61.
——— Lady, ii. 55. her death, 61.
——— Sir Thomas, ii. 352. his curiosities, 353, 354.
Brownrigg, Dr. iv. 307.
Bruce, Robert, Lord, i. 324, ii. 109. iii. 108.
Bruges, notice of, i. 50.
BRUSSELS, account of, i 45, 46—48. ii. 428.
——— The late news from Brussels unmasked, 1660, ii. 146 and n. iii. 438.
Buat, Mons. brother to Admiral Van Tromp, ii. 280.
Bucentaur, the Doge's vessel at Venice, i. 329.
Buchanan, George, portrait referred to, ii. 307 n.
Buckhurst, Thomas Sackville, Lord High Treasurer, iv. 306.
Buckingham, George, Villiers, First Duke of, ii 106 and n, 115. iv. 306.
——— ——— Second Duke, ii. 11, 86 and n, 226, 305, 342, 355, 438. iii. 18. his *Rehearsal* performed, ii. 356 and n. his glass-work, 423. seat of, at Clifden, iii. 13. his estate at Helmsley, iii. 354 and n.
——— ——— Duchess of, 1686, iii. 212.
——— ——— house erected, ii. 69 n.
Buckle, Sir Christopher, ii. 137.
Buda, thanksgiving on the capture of, 1686, iii. 215. iv. 284.
Buffaloes at Pisa, i. 137.
Bulkeley, Sir Richard, chariot invented by, ii. 190,
Bull, Mr. ——— F.R.S. ii. 172.
Buonarroti, Michel Angelo, architecture of, i. 157, 164, 172, 173, 176. paintings by, 81, 82 bis. 142, 199, 216, 225, 297. iii. 353. sculpture, &c. of i. 141, 145, 192, 199, 201, 271, 296, 299, 302. iii. 235, 236.
Burghers, Michael, engraving by, ii. 224 n.
Burial in Churches censured, iii. 76, 77, 278.

456

Burleigh, Rober
  letters of, refe
Burleigh on the
Burlington, Earl
BURNET, DR. G
  History of the
  mons by, iii. 6
  311. *Pastor*
  ences to, ii. 25
  206 n, 209 n.
Burton, Mr. She
———— Mr. of H
Burrow Green,
Bury St. Edmun
Busby, Dr. Rich
Bushell's Wells
Butler, Mrs. ii. 4

Cabinets, of inla
Cade, Dr. a Cor
Cadiz, bombard
Caen, Town and
Cæsar, C. Julius
———— Augustus
Cagliari, Paolo,
  ii. 200.
Cajetan, Cardin
Calais, notices
Calcography, H
  193, and n. ii
Caldwell, Mrs.
Caligula, C. Er
Calista, a come
  400 note.
CAMBRIDGE, de
Camden, Willi
  Britannia, ed
  iii. 340.
———— Lady,
Camomile-flow
Campania, noti
Campanile, at
Campion, Edm
Campo di Fiori
Campo Martio
Campo Martius
Campo Santa a
Campo Scelera
Campo Vaccin
Can, Dr. sermo
Canary Mercha
Cannes, notice
Cannon, of lea
  90. at Venic
Canterbury Cat

Printed by BoD™in Norderstedt, Germany